George Field, Ellis A. Davidson

A grammar of colouring

applied to decorative painting and the arts

George Field, Ellis A. Davidson

A grammar of colouring
applied to decorative painting and the arts

ISBN/EAN: 9783742895189

Manufactured in Europe, USA, Canada, Australia, Japa

Cover: Foto ©ninafisch / pixelio.de

Manufactured and distributed by brebook publishing software (www.brebook.com)

George Field, Ellis A. Davidson

A grammar of colouring

CONTENTS.

PART I.
OF COLOUR GENERALLY.

CHAPTER I.

Colour, as an element of beauty, not utility, how produced . . PAGE 1

CHAPTER II.

The Three Orders of Colours: Primary, Secondary, and Tertiary—How the Secondary colours are compounded from the Primary, and the Tertiary from the Secondary . . .

CHAPTER III.

The contrasts and accordances of colours—The complementary colours—The scale of equivalents 4

CHAPTER IV.

Illustrations of colouring—Suggestions for studies—The harmony of Blue with Orange, Red with Green, Yellow with Purple—The harmony of succession and contrast; of colour with neutrality—The blue background to sculptures amongst the Greeks—Application of principles necessary in addition to literary knowledge—Colour no less a science than musical sounds 9

PART II.
PRACTICAL COLOURING.

CHAPTER V.

Material Colours: Colours distinguished as inherent and transient . . **13**

CHAPTER VI.

Qualities of Pigments: 1, beauty of colour, including purity, brightness, and depth; 2, body; 3, transparency, or opacity; 4, working well; 5, keeping their place; 6, drying well; 7, durability—In mixing colours, the artist should avoid using a greater number of pigments than necessary—The improvements in the modern manufacture of colours . . **14**

CHAPTER VII.

Of White and its Pigments: The term colours as distinguished from pigments—White and its qualities—White lead—London and Nottingham whites—Flake white—Blanc d'argent—Roman white—Sulphate of zinc—Zinc white—Tin white—Pearl white—Constant white—White chalk—Chinese white **16**

CHAPTER VIII.

Tints: White the basis of all tints—Paris white—French grey—Silver grey—Carnation—Coquilicot—Blush of flowers—Primrose—Straw-colour—Isabella—Lilac—Lavender—Peach-blossom—Pea-green—Tea-green—Methods of compounding Lavender tints, Grey tints, Brown tints, Green tints, Yellow tints **24**

CHAPTER IX.

the Primary Colours: Yellow, nearest in relation to white; is the ruling colour in citrine; enters largely into buff, bay, tawny, tan, dun, drab, chestnut, roan, sorrel, hazel, auburn, isabella, fawn, feuille-morte; in combination with red produces orange, with blue constitutes green; the powers of colours upon the vision; the eye should be refreshed by the clear light of day; Yellow contrasts most powerfully with black, excepting white; the sensible effects of Yellow—Chrome yellow—Patent yellow—Naples yellow—Massicot—Yellow ochre—Roman ochre—Brown ochre—Terra di Sienna—Argillaceous, meaning of the term—Iron yellow—Yellow orpiment—King's yellow—Chinese yellow—Arsenic yellow—Cadmium yellow—Gamboge—Gall-stone—Indian yellow—Dutch pink, English and Italian pinks—Stil de Grain **26**

CHAPTER X.

Red, the second and intermediate colour, stands between yellow and blue; most positive of all colours; mixed with blue produces purple; with yellow forms orange; gives warmth to all colours; is the principal colour in the tertiary russet; enters into the composition of marrone, chocolate, puce, murrey, morello, mordore, pompadour, and more or less into browns, some greys, &c.; Nature uses Red sparingly as compared with green—Vermilion—Chinese vermilion; origin of the name—Iodine scarlet—Red lead—Minium red ochre—Indian red—Persian red—Light red—Venetian red—Dragon's Blood—Lake—Rubric, or Madder lakes—Scarlet lake—Lac lake—Carmine—Madder carmine—Rose pink . 39

CHAPTER XI.

Blue, the third and last of the primary colours, bears the same relation to shade that yellow does to light; is the most retiring of all colours, excepting purple and black; is the coldest colour; with yellow forms green, and with red, purple; characterizes the tertiary blue; is the prime colour in neutral black, the semi-neutral greys, slate, and lead colours, &c.; is discordant in juxtaposition with green; the paucity of Blue pigments in comparison with the yellow and red ones—Ultramarine—Factitious ultramarine—Cobalt—Smalt—Royal blue—Prussian blue—Antwerp blue—Indigo—Blue verditer—Saunders blue—Bice 52

CHAPTER XII.

The Secondary Colours: Orange; how composed; enters into composition of citrine; with purple forms russet; is an advancing colour; Orange is pre-eminently a warm colour; list of Orange pigments very deficient; method of mixing—Chrome orange—Orange ochre—Mars orange—Burnt Sienna earth—Orange lead—Antimony orange—Anotta . 63

CHAPTER XIII.

Of Green, the second of the secondary colours; most perfect in hue when constituted in the proportion of three of yellow to eight of blue; it is the most effective of all compound colours; the general garb of the vegetable creation; whilst it is universally effective in contrasting other colours, it is the least useful in compounding them; principal discord of Green is blue; its less powerful discord, yellow—Mixed greens: Varley's green, Hooker's green—Terre-Verte—Chrome green—Cobalt green—Copper green—Verdigris—Green verditer—Emerald green—Mineral green—Mountain green—Scheele's green—Prussian green—Sap green—Invisible green 68

CHAPTER XIV.

Of Purple, the third and last of the secondary colours; composed of red and blue in proportions of five red to eight blue; the proportions in which it contrasts with other colours; mixed with green produces olive; mixed with orange forms russet; is the coolest of the secondary colours, and nearest to black, or shade; next to green is the most pleasing of the consonant colours; when inclining to red is a regal or magisterial colour—Mixed purples—Gold purple, or Cassius's Purple Precipitate—Madder purple (Purple Rubiate, or Field's purple)—Burnt carmine—Purple lake—Purple ocre ... 76

CHAPTER XV.

Of the Tertiary Colours: Citrine; its composition and properties; original Citrine-coloured pigments not numerous—Mixed citrine—Brown pink—Raw umber ... 80

CHAPTER XVI.

Of Russet; its composition and properties—Mixed russet—Field's russet, or Madder brown—Prussiate of copper—Russet ochre, &c. ... 84

CHAPTER XVII.

Of Olive; its composition and properties—Mixed olive—Olve green—Burnt verdigris ... 87

CHAPTER XVIII.

Of Semi-neutral Colours: May be divided into Brown, Marrone, and Grey—The general qualities of brown—Vandyke brown—Manganese brown—Cappagh brown or Euchrone—Burnt umber—Cassel earth—Cologne earth—Rubens' brown—Brown ochre—Bone brown—Asphaltum—Mummy—Antwerp brown—Bistre—Sepia—Madder brown—Prussian brown ... 89

CHAPTER XIX.

Of Gray; composition and qualities of Gray—Mixed gray—Neutral tint—Ultramarine ashes—Phosphate of Iron ... 98

CHAPTER XX.

Of the Neutral: Black; of the nature and applications of Black; great number of Black pigments—Ivory black—Frankfort black—Blue black—Spanish black—Mineral black—Manganese black—Black ochre—Black chalk—Indian ink—Black lead ... 102

CHAPTER XXI.

Table I.: Of Pigments, the colours of which suffer different degrees of change by the action of light, oxygen, and pure air—Table II.: Of Pigments, the colours of which are little, or not at all, changed by light, oxygen, and pure air—Table III.: Of Pigments, the colours of which are subject to change by the action both of light and oxygen, &c.—Table IV.: Of Pigments which are not at all, or little, liable to change by the action of light, oxygen, and pure air, &c.—Table V.: Of Pigments subject to change variously by the action of white lead and other preparations of that metal—Table VI.: Of Pigments, the colours of which are subject to change by iron and other ferruginous substances—Table VII.: Of Pigments, the colours of which are more or less transparent, and are generally fit to be employed in graining and finishing—Table VIII.: Of Pigments, the colours of which are little or not at all affected by heat or the action of fire—Table IX.: Of Pigments which are little or not at all affected by lime, and in various degrees eligible for fresco, distemper, and crayon painting—Table X.: Of Heraldic Colours 110

CHAPTER XXII.

Table XI.: Of the Colours used in water-colour painting, assorted into various sized boxes, whether in cakes or moist in tubes or pans—Table XII.: Of the Powder Colours used in tempera painting—Table XIII.: Of Colours used in oil-painting—Remarks 122

PART III.
ON VEHICLES, OILS, AND VARNISHES.

CHAPTER XXIII.

The necessity for vehicles; their various classes—Water vehicles—Mucilages—Gum Senegal, Gum Arabic, Ammonia, Tragacanth—Size—Milk of Lime—Borax—Mediums—Dryers, the various kinds of, and how and when to use them . . 127

CHAPTER XXIV.

On Oils: Distinguished into Fat, Drying, and Volatile: the two first are called fixed and expressed, and the latter essential oils; the properties of each—Linseed oil—Pale Drying oil—Poppy oil—Megilp—Copaiba—Volatile oils—Oil of turpentine—Oil of lavender—Naphtha—Spirit of wine . . 135

CHAPTER XXV.

On Varnishes: Resinous varnishes—Mastic varnish—Copal varnish—White lac varnish—Lac—Cowdie—General remarks . **143**

PART IV.

THE MODES AND OPERATIONS OF PAINTING.

CHAPTER XXVI.

The pencil as distinguished from the brush—The simplest method: that in which water alone is added to the colours with which a mucilage has been previously mixed—The different qualities of drawing-papers and their sizes—Drawing-boards; the various kinds; suggestions in relation to—Method of stretching paper for water-colour painting—Sketching-blocks—Method of commencing to work with cake or moist water-colours—To compound tints—Method of mixing colour for a flat wash—Large brushes preferable to small ones—Instructions as to laying flat washes and painting in monochrome—Systematic practice—Method of graduating tints—To colour and shade cylindrical and spherical surfaces—Excellent lessons to be derived from a bunch of grapes, an orange, a group of apples, &c.—Decorative artist advised to study and paint flowers from nature, and make careful studies from nature, adapting the forms subsequently to ornamental purposes—General method of painting flowers—Figure-painting **151**

CHAPTER XXVII.

Painting in Tempera, why so called—The various media used by the Italians, &c.—Scene-painting—Tempera may be considered as opaque water-colour painting, the lights being added with body-colour instead of being caused by the white paper. In this, Tempera agrees with oil-painting, the difference being only in the vehicle—Tempera a very important style to the decorative artist—The same facilities for blending which exist in water-colour and oil-painting do not belong to Tempera—How the colours are blended and graduated; hatching; stippling—Painting in flat tints—Set of copies of flowers in this style published under the auspices of the Science and Art Department **160**

CHAPTER XXVIII.

Painting in Oil: The various oils—Megilp—Varnishes used in oil-painting—The ease with which the colours may now be obtained compared with the difficulties under which the artists of former days laboured—The various brushes generally used in oil-painting, and others which may be obtained for special purposes; how to select brushes for work; the qualities of hog-hair brushes; of sable loose hairs; badger softeners described; should be avoided as much as possible; how to clean brushes; "brush washers"—Of canvas: plain cloth, Roman, and ticken; the various sizes generally employed; origin of the term "Kit-cat"—Panels—Academy boards—Prepared mill-boards—Oil sketching-paper—Of the processes of painting in oil—Dead colouring—Glazing, the colours adapted for—Scumbling contrasted with glazing—Dry touching—Dragging—Impasting, its advantages and disadvantages—The easel—The palette; how new palettes should be prepared for use; how to clean palettes; how colours from the palette may be preserved for future use . 164

CHAPTER XXIX.

Of Fresco-painting: The art naturally adapted for decorative painting—Colours prepared with water and applied to the surface of wet plaster—As to durability, the compo and cements now so generally used would afford a new and advantageous ground for painting in fresco—Fresco, being executed in wet plaster, must be worked in portions—The cartoon, and how the outline is transferred to the plaster—The colours used are principally mineral ones—The preparation of the wall—The rough casting—The method of laying the "intonaco," or painting-ground—How the different portions of plaster should be conveniently arranged for painting—If the result is not satisfactory the portion must be cut away 173

CHAPTER XXX.

Useful Receipts: Cleaning and restoring—Removing varnish—Removing paint 176

PART V.

THE CHARACTERISTIC FEATURES OF THE VARIOUS STYLES OF ORNAMENT.

CHAPTER XXXI.

PAGE

The decorative artist should understand the systematic application of ornament; should be acquainted with the styles of architecture, and the corresponding systems of ornamentation—Ornament divided into symbolic and æsthetic; characteristics of each—Style in ornament—Flat ornament compared with the relieved—The three great periods of ornament: ancient, middle age, and modern. The ancient: Egyptian, Assyrian, Grecian, Roman; the middle age: Byzantine, Saracenic, and Gothic; the modern: the Renaissance, Cinquecento, and Louis Quatorze 179

CHAPTER XXXII.

The elements of Egyptian ornament have each a particular meaning, thus contrasting with modern styles, which aim only at effect; the simple symmetrical arrangement of Egyptian ornaments; adaptation of natural elements, and conventional mode of treating them: the lotus or water-lily, the fret or labyrinth, the zigzag, the winged globe, the zigzag, the wave scroll; gaudy diapers and gaiety of colour in the Egyptian style—The Assyrian style; chief characteristics; sculptured records of leading events; human-headed colossi—The feeling of the ancients which gave origin to sphinxes, and composite animals generally; the relievos of gods; the sacred tree and open flower; the chain ornament 181

CHAPTER XXXIII.

The Grecian style: Ornamental features now adopted for their beauty only; the sculpture in the pediments, the frieze, the metopes, the triglyphs; the Parthenon frieze, lesson as to the adaptation of ornamentation to the position in which it is to be placed, to be derived from it; the zigzag, and wave scroll, and labyrinth; the echinus, or egg and tongue, moulding; the anthemion or honeysuckle; the Doric, Corinthian, and Ionic; the flatness of Greek curves—The Roman style cannot be considered as an original one; chief characteristic; great magnificence; the acanthus scroll fully developed; the Roman acanthus distinct from that used by the Greeks; the Tuscan capital simply an altered form of the Doric 187

CHAPTER XXXIV.

The Byzantine style: Its origin and sentiment of symbolism; the reason why the beautiful Classic forms were rejected; how scrolls and other pagan elements were gradually admitted—The chief varieties of the Romanesque: the Byzantine, Lombard, and Norman—The polychromatic decorations of the Byzantine period: the paintings; the three kinds of mosaics: the glass mosaics, the glass tesselation, and the marble tesselation: the methods of execution of each—The Saracenic: how originated, under the stringent conditions of the Mohammedan law; its characteristics; the late Mr. Owen Jones as an exponent of the style; important lessons to be derived from the system; the principles of design; ornamental lines flowing out of, or radiating from, a parent stem, based on natural growth, as in vine-leaf or horse-chestnut; ornaments specially adapted to the surface to be covered, however irregular its form; the scroll of this period contrasted with that of the ancients; in Saracenic ornament the curves are tangential to each other. . . 191

CHAPTER XXXV.

The Gothic style: How it developed out of the Byzantine; the divisions of the style: the Norman, Transition, Early English, Decorated, and Perpendicular—The chief ornaments of the Norman style: the ornamental bands on the recessed edges of the walls, the chevron or zigzag, the billet, the chain, &c.; the capitals—The characteristics of the transition: the "roll and fillet" moulding—The Early English: its lancet-headed windows; several lights gathered under one dripstone; the tympanum pierced; the origin of tracery; plate tracery; the capitals: the "stiff-leaved" foliage, the trefoil, the tooth ornament, wall-diapers, the crocket and finial—The Decorated period: the tracery, geometrical and flowing; the capitals: the foliage taken from nature: the oak, horse-chestnut, hazel, &c.; also the ball flower and square flower—The Perpendicular style: why so called; the character of the tracery and foliage; the flattened roofs and arches; the panel tracery; the fan tracery—The Tudor, the Debased or After-Gothic 198

CHAPTER XXXVI.

The general term Renaissance: The return to Classic elements; the different periods; the Trecento: its characteristic features—The Quattrocento: its rendering of natural elements; Lorenzo Ghiberti, his bronze gates of the Baptistry, at Florence; the panels representing scriptural subjects, the reliefs on the architrave emblematic of the fulness of the Creation—The Elizabethan style must be considered as an English rendering of the Renaissance: its characteristics —The Cinquecento the full development of the Renaissance; the perfection of its ornamentation; Raffaelle, Julio Romano, the Lombardi, Bramante, Michael Angelo; the arabesque scroll, animals, plants, vases, works of art; strap and shield work wholly excluded; the style has been considered the culmination of ornamental art—The Louis Quatorze: its leading characteristics; the high relief; the stucco work and gilding; dependent on play of light and shade more than on colour—The Louis Quinze: neglect of balancing of parts; decline in ornamental art; loss of symmetry—The Debased style, called the Rococo . . .

THE GRAMMAR OF COLOURING.

PART I.

OF COLOUR GENERALLY.

CHAPTER I.

THE ELEMENTS OF COLOURS.

If, in this utilitarian age, we are asked, "What is the use of colour?" we are constrained, however reluctantly, to answer: "Not any." True, it assists in distinguishing forms, but a few hard lines—though militating sadly against beauty—would accomplish this purpose, whilst distance could, as far as art is concerned, be indicated by lines of various degrees of depth; a fact which is proved by the exquisite effects thus obtained in engravings.

Nor do we find that even the colours of flowers serve any real purpose beyond charming the eye; and this same argument might be applied to sounds, for, if judged by the merely utilitarian standard, music must, as far as practical purposes are concerned, be pronounced useless.

Yet persons over whom music and colour have no influence are happily rarely met with. Can we fancy this glorious garden of the world peopled with dumb and colourless birds; our fields deprived of their grateful verdure; our hedges and our gardens robbed of their infinite variety of hues?

In the colours which pervade creation—as in the music which so gratefully affects our senses—our merciful Creator has superadded beauty to utility, and we feel that "man liveth not by bread alone," but that the works of the Almighty are designed so as to surround us with everything that shall make this work-day world one in which the higher faculties of the mind may be exercised, and in which the earth may yield to the man who cultivates it, not only the food for his children, but the flowers to beautify their home.

It is in this way that Decorative Art has arisen; for the history of the world has shown us that the moment the absolute necessities of shelter have been supplied, the next effort has been to beautify. In the ruder conditions of man, however, this desire has been satisfied by the use of bright and positive colours; it has been reserved for the cultivated taste of civilisation to define the relative proportions in which the colours should be used to each other, and the means by which they may be contrasted or harmonized with each other.

The elements or natural powers by which colours are produced are the positive and negative principles of Light and Darkness, and these in painting are represented by *white* and *black*, which are thence elementary colours; between the extremes of which exists an infinite gradation of shades or mixtures, which are called *greys*, affording a scale of neutral colours.

As by the deflection of a *point in space* may be generated all the elementary and complex figures and forms of geometrical and constructive science, so from a like

Fig. 1.

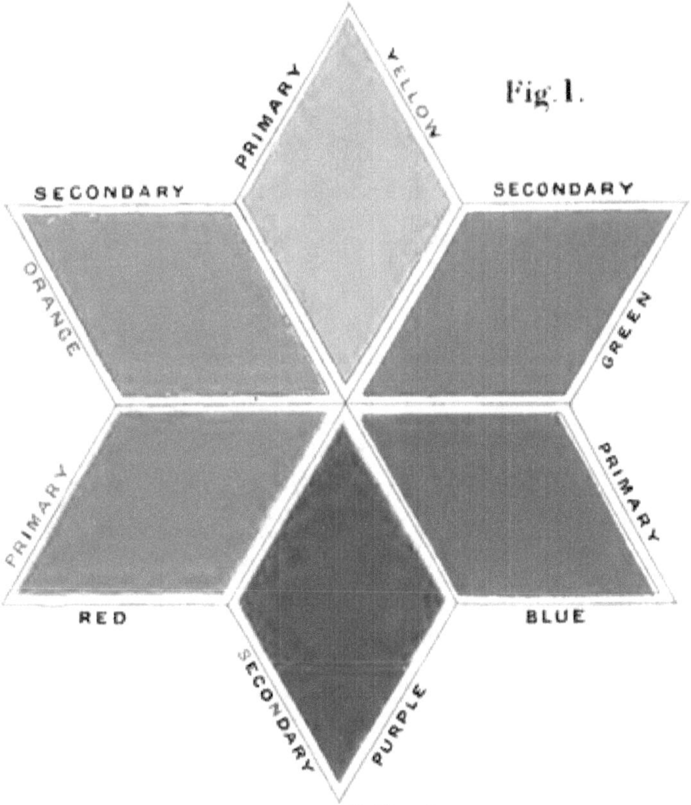

Fig 2.

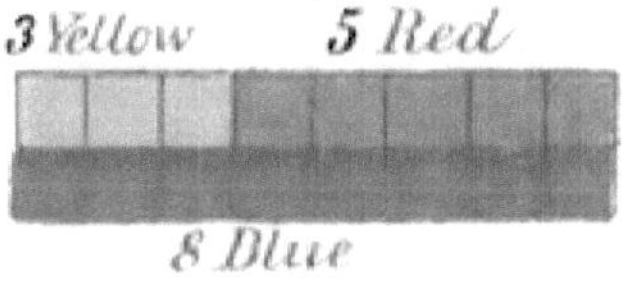

Fig. 3.

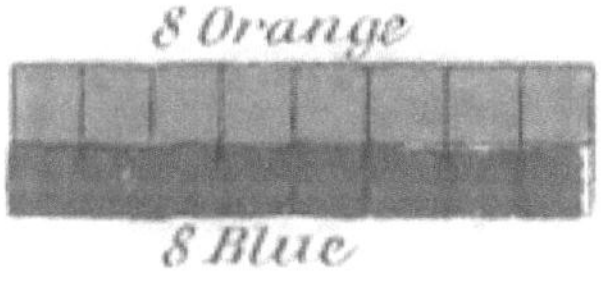

Fig. 4.

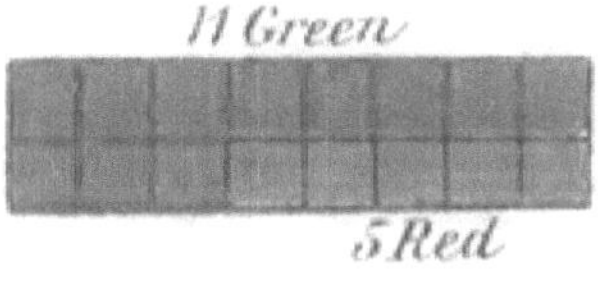

Fig. 5.

Ellis A Davidson fec^t

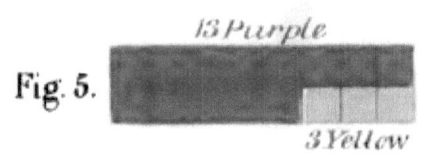

deflection of a *spot in place* may be generated all the elementary and compound hues and colours: the science of which is called Chromatics.

Thus a spot of any shade or colour on a ground or medium lighter or darker than itself, being viewed by a Lensic Prism, will be deflected by the ordinary refraction of light and shade into an orb of three colours. These three colours are the known *Blue*, *Red*, and *Yellow*, which as they are incapable of being produced by composition, and also of being resolved into other colours by analysis, are simple, original, and *primary colours*, elicited by the electrical excitement, or concurrence of the light and shade of the ground and spot.

Accordingly, if the ground and spot be varied from light to dark, or from black to white, the same process will afford the same three colours, differing only in the inversion of their arrangement, being the order of the colours in the celestial phenomenon of the rainbow—"the triple bow" of the poets—in which the sun supplies the central spot of light, which is deflected or refracted by the rain and atmosphere on the dark screen of the sky.

This evolution of colours from the positive and negative or polar principles of light and darkness is a simple fact of nature, however the colours may be produced by electrical influence, wherewith it accords that a due reunion of the three colours, or their compounds, will discharge the colours excited and restore the colourless spots and grounds; and in like manner the negative or *neutral* colours may be composed by mixture of the positive material colours, or pigments of the painter. And thus we have educed from nature the first order of colours in the sequence of their relation to black and white.

In these experimental evolutions of transient colours from light and darkness, a polar influence determines the blue colour, and its allies, towards black or darkness as the negative pole, and the yellow, followed by red and their allies, toward the positive pole of light, or white. And this is a constant law of chromatism, by which all the relations of colours are determined, as well in respect to vision and the requirements of taste and arrangement as to their physical properties and calorific powers. And it coincides also with the electrical affinities by which colours are determined chemically according to an undoubted universal law.

CHAPTER II.

THE THREE ORDERS OF COLOURS.

COLOURS may be classed under three heads—primary, secondary, and tertiary.

Any two of the primaries mixed in the proportions to be spoken of presently produce a perfect secondary colour, which harmonizes with the remaining primary. Thus Blue and Yellow form Green, which harmonizes with Red. Yellow and Red produce Orange, which harmonizes with Blue. Red and Blue form Purple, which harmonizes with Yellow.

Finally, in like manner, by the alternate compounding or mixing of these secondary colours in pairs, is produced a third order of colours, thence called *tertiary colours:* thus, if Green be mixed with Orange colour, they will form a *Citrine*, or citron-colour; if Orange be mixed with Purple, they form *Russet;* and if Purple be mixed with Green, they form *Olive* colour; and these new denominations of colours, *Citrine, Russet, and Olive, constitute the third order of colours*, each of which is variously compounded of the *three* original or primary colours, as the second order is of *two;* the primary order being *single* and uncompounded; and lastly by duly mixing or compounding either of the three orders of colours, *Black* will be produced, terminating the series in *neutrality of colour*.

By the varied and due admixture of these colours is produced the infinity of hues, shades, and tints with which the works of nature are decorated, and which abound in the works of art; and all those individual colours which every season of fashion brings forth under new denominations, but which have been regarded by vulgar, uncultivated sense as individually distinct, without order or dependence, the arbitrary inventions of fancy.

By an indefinite and disproportionate mixture, however, of the three colours of either order, or of the whole together, will be produced only the hues usually called dirty, or the anomalous colour *Brown*. The browns are nevertheless a valuable class of colours of predominantly warm hues; whence we have *Red and Yellow Browns*, and browns all hues except *Blue*, which is especially a cold colour affording in like manner the very useful but anomalous class of *Greys*, distinguished from the neutral *Grey*, being also the contrary and contrast of Brown.

The primary colours themselves may, however, be materially altered by admixture: thus, by mixing them in varied proportions, all *Hues* of colour are produced. These *hues* being diluted with white form *tints*, or by being toned with black give the different *shades* of colour.

Referring to the purity of colours, Mr. R. Redgrave says:—" It is necessary to remember that pigments, such as are used by the dyer or painter, are but representatives of colours, and that they but very imperfectly represent the primaries. There is no Yellow pigment, for instance, of which it can be safely averred that it is free from any mixture either of Red or Blue; no Red that is untainted by Yellow or Blue; nor any Blue so pure as to be without any mixture of Yellow or Red.

" If pigments could be obtained truly representing each primary, the laws of colour might be perfectly illustrated; but since this is not possible, either as respects purity of colour or power of mixing, explanations of the laws of harmony are beset with many difficulties. Even when pigments are obtained which nearly represent the respective primaries; from various causes, such as differences of transparency or opacity, chemical components, or other qualities, they do not perhaps mix to produce even an approach to a perfect secondary colour."

CHAPTER III.

CONTRASTS AND ACCORDANCES OF COLOURS.*

It has been shown that colours are primarily elicited analytically from the positive and negative principles

---

* Painting among the Hindoos, the Egyptians, and still in our days amongst the Chinese, imposes its regulations in the national worship and politic laws; the least alteration in the drawing or colouring or poles of light and shade, represented by White and Black, which are Neutral as colours, and that consequently by a due reunion or composition of the colours thus educed they are restored to the neutral state of *Black*, *White*, or *Grey*.

The production of the secondaries by mixture of the primaries will be understood from the illustration (Fig. 1), in which each primary is placed opposite to the secondary formed by the remaining two.

Such opposed colours, in adequate proportions, are called complementary, from the equivalence with which they neutralise each other; their powers in which respect we have demonstrated to be according to the following Scale of Chromatic Equivalents. (Fig. 2.)

In this *Scale of Equivalents* the fundamental powers of the primary colours in compensating and neutralising, contrasting and harmonizing, their opposed secondary colours are approximately as *three* Yellow, *five* Red, and *eight* Blue; consequently the secondary *Orange*, composed of three Yellow and five Red, is the equivalent of *Blue* the power of which is eight: they are accordingly equal powers in contrast, and compensating in mixture, and as such are properly in equal proportions for harmonizing effect. (Fig. 3.)

Again *Green* being composed of Blue the power of which is eight, and Yellow the power of which is three, is equivalent in contrast and mixture as eleven, to *Red* the power of which is five; being nearly as two to one. (Fig. 4.)

And finally *Purple* composed of Blue as eight, and Red the power of which is five, is equivalent in mixture or contrast as thirteen, to *Yellow* the power of which is

would incur a serious punishment. Among the Egyptians, writes Synesius, the prophets did not allow metal-founders or statuaries to represent the gods, for fear that they should deviate from the rules.— *Baron F. Portal on Symbolic Colours.*

three, or nearly as four to one. And such proportions of these opposed colours may be employed in forming agreeable and harmonious contrasts in colouring and decorative painting, either in pairs of contrasts, or several, or all together; and also for subduing each other in mixture. (Fig. 5.)

The tertiary colour *Citrine* harmonizes with the secondary colour *Purple* in the proportion of nineteen Citrine to thirteen Purple. The tertiary colour *Olive* harmonizes with the secondary *Orange* in the proportion of twenty-four Olive to eight Orange. The tertiary colour *Russet* harmonizes with the secondary *Green* in the proportion of twenty-one Russet to eleven Green. These proportions are illustrated in Figs. 6, 7, 8, 9.

And further it is apparent that all compound hues of these colours will partake of their compound numbers, and contrast each other according to a corresponding compound equivalence. Thus an intermediate Red-purple will contrast a like opposite Green-yellow with the power of eighteen to fourteen, and so on without limit all round the scale; and the triple compounds or tertiary colours are subject to like regulation.

There is no invariable necessity, nevertheless, that this regulation of contrasts should be followed strictly according to their numbers in harmonizing colours, although they denote their principal and most powerful effects; for every individual colour has its appropriate expression, for which it may be employed predominately as a key; thus affording an infinity of distinct harmonies to fertilise taste and invention, by brilliant and delicate or sober and sombre effects according to the purpose of the Artist or Decorator.*

* After the five colours come the compound hues: rose, purple, hyacinth, violet, grey, tan, &c. These hues receive their significations from the colours which compose them. That which predominates

CHAPTER IV.

ILLUSTRATIONS OF COLOURING.

The exercise of taste, and the demands of novelty and fashion, in decoration, and beautifying with colours, have a boundless field of exertion and production in the application of the foregoing principles, wherein the genius and taste of the Colourist has scope as ample for delighting the eye as that of the Musician in the art of harmonizing sounds; and to do justice by examples to these powers in either art would be a vast undertaking, if not a vain attempt.

As the object of these pages is not merely to enable the student to learn by rote a list of the numerical proportions of colours, but to assist him in the appreciation of the principles laid down, it is suggested that he should work out the system inculcated in a series of diagrams, for which the following hints will supply the data.

1. The harmonizing or contrasting of *Blue* with *Orange*, or of cold with warm colours, which are general equal powers or equivalents; and as such are instanced in nature by the warm sunshine and azure sky. It is in the same relation that Blue is employed effectively with Gold.

2. This study should be the accordance of *Red* with *Green;* the first of which is the extreme of colour, as the latter is the mean or middle colour, and they harmonize as one to two in power or equivalence, and

---

gives to the hue its general signification, and that which is subordinate, the modified. Thus purple, which is of a red azure, signifies the love of truth; and hyacinth, which is of a blue purple, represents the truth of love. These two significations would seem to confound themselves at their source, but the applications will show the difference which exists between them.—*Baron* ." *Portal on Symbolic Colours.*

are remarkable in the roseate blossom with the green foliage throughout nature.

3. This arrangement should be the general accordance of *Yellow with Purple*, which are complementary nearly as one to four; the first as an advancing or light, the second as a retiring or shade colour; and they are reciprocally employed by nature in giving effect to Purple and Yellow flowers. The above are leading examples only; but it would be easy, were it expedient, to multiply them to any amount.

It is a matter of necessary knowledge to the Artist, and of useful information to the Decorator of taste, that in nature *the colours of shadows and shadings are always true contrasts to their lights*, and affords a rule to harmonious art, the neglect of which is a common cause of failure, and dulness of effect. Hence it may merit attention that rooms, &c., lighted from a cold or northern aspect would be of best effect when having their ornamental designs shaded with warm colours; and that, on the contrary, cool shadows are required in rooms of a southern and sunny aspect. The artist, however, who is acquainted with the true relations of light and colours, will be at no loss in adapting his practice to the peculiarity of the case or situation.

Not only are there the foregoing harmonies of Succession and Contrast among positive colours, there also is a like contrast of Colour with Neutrality, or of positive Hues with negative Shades. It is hence that coloured backgrounds agreeably relieve sculptures, which are white or neutral; and that *Blue* does so more effectively than other colours, because sculptures having their own relief, and being powerfully reflective of light, are best contrasted and advanced by that colour which is of nearest affinity with shade, and such is blue. We find accordingly that the Greeks relieved the sculptures of their temples, &c., by Blue backgrounds, which at once harmonized with the sculpture and the sky.

So again, in contrasting Black objects with coloured grounds, such as engravings, neutral drawings or designs, &c., the colour nearest in relation to light, being a warm Yellow, is for the above reason theoretically and practically of best effect. And these will be sufficient to suggest the proper practice in the conduct of Colours and Neutrality in other cases.

It is to be observed that the simple principles we have adduced as a guide to the ordinary employment of colours are but the suggestive elements of a science as boundless as practical geometry, into the intricacy of which the decorator needs not enter, any more than into the subtilities of the latter science; and the mind delighting in such speculations, or emulating the higher accomplishments of art, will find the inquiry extended in our "Chromatics; or the Analogy, Harmony, and Philosophy of Colours," and other works.

So much then in briefness for the theoretic relations of colours, the knowledge of which is to be regarded as essential to their free and appropriate application in painting; and indispensable for elegance of design in all arts calling for an harmonious and original display of taste, for which some practical hints will appear in our subsequent notes on individual colours and pigments, further detailed also in our "Chromatography."

Fashion, it is true, governs Operatives and Decorators in their works and designs, but when these artists are well instructed and masters in principles, they will guide and influence fashion by nature and good taste,—advancing art by purifying it from those barbarous and gaudy obtrusions on chaste design which ever denote art in its infancy or decline. As to the aids of literature, it can do little more for the artist and artisan than present them with these principles and precepts, the application of which is an affair of their own skill and faculties, in which they have liberty of action but not equality of powers, for these are divine gifts from nature, or the rewards of acquired skill and industry.

In the choice, admiration, and display of colours we find crude, natural, and uncultivated taste, as in children and savages, delighting in, and employing, entire and primary colours, and harsh, unbroken, or whole notes in their music; but as taste and sober judgment advance, sense becomes more conciliated by broken colours and half-tones, till, in the end, they refine into the more broken and enharmonic. The same laws still govern them in practice, and the contrasts of which we have given the first crude examples may still be as strictly employed with colours extremely subdued, and with the utmost refinement of broken tints and delicacy of expression.

Thus colours are no less a science than musical sounds, to which they are every way analogous; and as the musician may be thoroughly acquainted with harmonic science, and able to detect all the errors of the composer and performer of music without himself being able either to compose or perform,—so also it is with the informed and critical colourist, whether decorative artist or man of taste; for the excellent works of both arts are the productions of science, conducting genius or natural taste, and a practised hand. To this end our rules are offered as a compass to unrestrained fancy, that, without a guide, would run into tasteless extravagance and absurdity.

PART II.
PRACTICAL COLOURING.

CHAPTER V.

MATERIAL COLOURS.

Having exhibited the sensible principles, relations, and effects of colours sufficiently for general understanding and use in a theoretic view, it is expedient to practice that we briefly advert to their material or physical nature and habits; because upon these depend the durability, fugacity, and changes to which colouring substances and pigments are subject and their works exposed; while it supplies useful experience to the painter and colourist in the practice of their arts.

Colours we have distinguished into *Inherent* and *Transient*. Of the first kind are all material colours, more properly called pigments and dyes; of the second or transient kind are the colours of light and the eye, such as the rainbow, halos, prismic and ocular spectra, &c.; all of which, as before shown, are formed by the concurrence of the elements of light and darkness, which elements, in the language of the chemists, are oxygen and hydrogen, both of which enter inherently into the matter of solid pigments, and constitute the transient light of our atmosphere and of day. Hence paintings, &c., excluded from light and air in many cases become dark, and in other cases, when exposed to light and air, they bleach and fade, or variously change colour according to their chemical constitutions, as will be further noted of individual pigments.

We have employed the terms Oxygen and Hydrogen to denote the more properly *Photogenic* and *Sciogenic* elements of light and shade, not for their fitness, but because they have been adopted in an analogous elementary signification in chemistry. It would, however, be beside our purpose here to discuss the elementary doctrine of the physical causes of light and colours, having spoken thereof more at large in other works.

We proceed, therefore, in the next place, to detail the powers, properties, and preparations of the materials employed in the various practices of painting, among which pigments, or paints, are principal, reminding the student that the variety of lightness and darkness in colours is called *Shade;* the varieties of gradations in the mixtures of colours are called *Hues*, and the various mixtures of hues and colours with white and shades are called *Tints.* We preface these and other distinctions as necessary to the painter for the better understanding and compounding of his materials, with which it is the object of this part of our work to make him acquainted.

CHAPTER VI.

QUALITIES OF PIGMENTS.

The general qualities of good *Pigments*, technically called *Colours*, are: 1, beauty of colour, which includes pureness, brightness, and depth; 2, body; 3, transparency or opacity; 4, working well; 5, keeping their place; 6, drying well; and 7, durability; but few pigments possess all these qualities in equal perfection.

Body, in opaque and white pigments, is the quality of efficiently covering and hiding ground, but in transparent pigments it signifies richness of colour, or tinting power; working well depends much on sufficient grinding, or fineness of quality; keeping their places and drying well depend in a great degree on the vehicle, or liquid, with which they are tempered, and chiefly on the oil with which they are employed.

All substances are positively or negatively coloured, whence the abundance of natural and artificial pigments and dyes with which the painter and colourist in every art are supplied, and the infinity of others that may be added to them. As, however, it is *durability* that gives value to the beauty and other qualities of colours or pigments, and those of nature being for the most part adapted to temporary or transient purposes, few only are suited to the more lasting intentions of art, and hence a judicious selection is essential to the practice and purposes of artists.

And as the present inquiry is concerning the employment of solid colours in painting, properly called Pigments, it is our express business to form such selections from those in use as are best adapted to the various requirements of painting in oil or water-colours, in distemper, fresco, &c., and to denote their habits, mixture, and best modes of manipulation of each, and this we purpose in the order of the colours as delivered in the preceding scales.

In *mixing colours* the painter should avoid using a greater number of pigments than necessary to afford the tints required, as such mixtures are usually fouler than the colours used, and their drying and other qualities are commonly injured thereby. We by no means counsel the painter to lose his time in the preparation of original pigments, the processes of manufacture having in recent years been carried to such perfection that any attempt to compete either in levigation or admixture with the colours sold at the first-rate houses would be futile. Old pigments are also more to be depended on than new ones for drying, standing, &c. We proceed to speak of colours and pigments individually.

CHAPTER VII.

OF WHITE AND ITS PIGMENTS.*

WHITE †

Is the basis of nearly all opaque painting designed for the laying and covering of grounds, whether they be

---

* "Colours" and "Pigments" are commonly confounded, but pigments, or, as they are popularly termed, *paints*, are those substances possessing colouring power in so eminent a degree that they are used on account of that property; pigments are, so to speak, material colours. "Colours" have a generic signification, including the phenomena of colour, whether considered in the abstract or the concrete.—GULLICK AND TIMBS, *Painting Popularly Explained*.

† *Of white colour.*—The Moors designate, by this emblem, purity, sincerity, innocence, indifference, simplicity, candour; applied to a woman, it implies chastity; to a young girl, virginity; to a judge, integrity; to a rich man, humility. Heraldry, borrowing this catalogue, ordained that, in coats of arms, argent should denote whiteness, purity, hope, truth, and innocence. Ermine, which was at first all white, was the emblem of purity and of immaculate chastity; and we hold, says Lamothe Le Vayer, the whiteness of our lily, of our scarfs, and royal pennant, a symbol of purity as well as of liberty. White represents immaculate chastity—it was consecrated to the Virgin; her altars are white, the ornaments of the officiating priest are white, and likewise, on her festival-day, the clergy are in white.—*Baron F. Portal on Symbolic Colours.*

of wood-work, metal, stone, plaster, or other substances, and should be as pure and neutral in colour as possible for the better mixing and compounding with other colours without changing their hues, while it renders them of lighter shades, and of the tints required; it also gives solid body to all colours.

It is the most advancing of colours; that is, it comes forward and catches the eye before all others, and it assists in giving this quality to other pigments, with which it may be mixed, by rendering their tints lighter and more vivid. Hence it appears to cause colours which are placed near it to recede, and it powerfully contrasts dark colours, and black most so of all. The term *colour* is however equivocal when attributed to the *neutrals*, White, Black, and Greys, yet the artist is bound to regard them as colours; and in philosophic strictness they are such latently, compounded and compensated; for a thing cannot but be that of which it is composed, and the neutrals are composed of and comprehend all colours.

White is the nearest among colours in relation to Yellow, and is in itself a pleasing and cheerful colour, which takes every hue, tint, and shade, and harmonizes with all other colours, and is the contrast of Black, added to which it gives solidity in mixture, and a small quantity of black added to white cools it, and preserves it from its tendency to turn yellow. White mixed with Black forms various Greys and Lead-colour so called.

From the above qualities of white it is of more extensive use in painting than any other colour, and it is hence of the first importance to the painter to have its pigments of the best quality. These are abundant, of which we shall here notice those only of practical importance to the painter and decorator.

Notwithstanding white pigments are an exceedingly

numerous class, an unexceptionable white is still a desideratum. The white earths are destitute of body in oil and varnish, and metallic whites of the best body are not permanent in water; yet when properly discriminated, we have eligible whites for most purposes, of which the following are the principal:—

WHITE LEAD,

Or ceruse, and other white oxides of lead, under the various denominations of London and Nottingham whites, &c., Flake white, Crems or Cremnitz, Roman and Venetian whites, Blanc d'argent or Silver white, Sulphate of lead, Antwerp white, &c. The heaviest and whitest of these are the best, and in point of colour and body are superior to all other whites. They are all, when pure and properly applied in oil and varnish, safe and durable, and dry well without addition; but excess of oil discolours them, and in water-painting they are changeable even to blackness. They have also a destructive effect upon all vegetable lakes, except the madder lakes and madder carmines; they are equally injurious to red and orange leads or minium, king's and patent yellow, massicot, gamboge, orpiments, &c.: but ultramarine, red and orange vermilions, yellow and orange chromes, madder colours, sienna earth, Indian red, and all the ochres, compound with these whites with little or no injury. In oil-painting white lead is essential in the ground, in dead colouring, in the formation of tints of all colours, and in scumbling, either alone or mixed with all other pigments. It is also the best local white when neutralized with black, but must not be employed in water-colour painting, distemper, crayon painting, or fresco, nor with any pigment having an inflammable basis, or liable to be destroyed by fire: for with all such they occasion change of colour, either by becoming dark themselves, or by fading the colours they are mixed with. Cleanliness in using these pigments is necessary for health; for though not virulently poisonous, they are pernicious when taken into or imbibed by the pores or otherwise, as are all other pigments of which lead is the basis. A fine natural white oxide, or carbonate of lead, would be a valuable acquisition, if found in abundance; and there occur in Cornwall specimens of a very beautiful carbonate of lead, of spicular form, brittle, soft, and purely white, which should be collected for the artist's use.

The following are the true characters of these whites according to our particular experience:—

LONDON AND NOTTINGHAM WHITES.

The best of these do not differ from each other in any essential particular, nor from the white leads of other localities. The latter, being prepared from flake white, is generally the greyer of the two. The inferior white leads are adulterated with whitening or sulphate of barytes and other earths, which injure them in body and brightness, dispose them to dry more slowly, to keep their places less firmly, and to discolour the oil with which they are applied. All the above are carbonates of lead, and liable to froth or bubble when used with aqueous, spirituous, or acid preparations. There are no better whites for architectural painting, and for all the purposes of common oil-painting; they are kept in the shops under the names of best and common white leads ready ground in oil, and require only to be duly diluted with linseed oil and more or less turpentine according to the work; and also for mixing with other colours and producing tints.

KREMS, CREMS, OR KREMNITZ WHITE,

Is a white carbonate of lead, which derives its names from Crems, or Krems, in Austria, or Kremnitz in Hungary, and is called also Vienna white, being brought from Vienna in cakes of a cubical form. Though highly reputed, it has no superiority over the best English white leads, and varies like them according to the degrees of care or success with which it has been prepared.

FLAKE WHITE

Is an English white lead in form of scales or plates, sometimes grey on the surface. It takes its name from its figure, is equal or sometimes superior to Krems white, and is an oxidized carbonate of lead, not essentially differing from the best of the above. Other white leads seldom equal it in body, and, when levigated, it is called body-white.

BLANC D'ARGENT,

Or Silver white. These are false appellations of a white lead, called also French white. It is brought from Paris in the form of drops, is exquisitely white, but of less body than flake white, and consequently does not cover so well. It has all the properties of the best white leads; but, being liable to the same changes, is unfit for general use as a water-colour, though good in oil or varnish.

ROMAN WHITE

Is of the purest white colour, but differs from the former only in the warm flesh-colour of the external surface of the large square masses in which it is usually prepared.

SULPHATE OF LEAD

Is an exceedingly white precipitate from any solution of lead by sulphuric acid, much resembling the blanc d'argent; and has, when well prepared, quite neutral, and, thoroughly edulcorated or washed, most of the properties of the best white leads, but is rather inferior in body and permanence.

The above are the principal whites of lead; but there are many other whites used in painting, of which the following are the most worthy of attention:—

ZINC WHITE

Is an oxide of zinc, which has been more celebrated as a pigment than used, being perfectly durable in water and oil, but wanting the body and brightness of fine white leads in oil; while, in water, constant or barytic white is superior to it in colour, and equal in durability. Nevertheless, zinc white is valuable, as far as its powers extend in painting, on account of its durability both in oil and water, and its innocence with regard to health. When duly and skilfully prepared, the colour and body of this pigment are sufficient to qualify it for a general use upon the palette, although the pure white of lead must merit a preference in oil.

TIN WHITE

Resembles zinc white in many respects, but dries badly, and has even less body and colour in oil, though superior to it in water. It is the basis of the best white in enamel painting.

There are various other metallic whites of great body and beauty,—such are those of bismuth, antimony, quicksilver, and arsenic; but none of them are of any value or reputation in painting, on account of their great disposition to change of colour, both by light and foul air, in water and in oil.

PEARL WHITE.

There are the two pigments of this denomination: one falsely so called, prepared from bismuth, which turns black in sulphuretted hydrogen gas or any impure air, and is used as a cosmetic; the other, prepared from the waste of pearls and mother-of-pearl, which is exquisitely white, and of good body in water, but of little force in oil or varnish: it combines, however, with all other colours without injuring the most delicate, and is itself perfectly permanent and innoxious.

CONSTANT WHITE,

Permanent white, or Barytic white, is a sulphate of barytes, and when well prepared and free from acid is one of our best whites for water-painting, being of a superior body in water, but destitute of this quality in oil.

As it is of a poisonous nature, it must be kept from the mouth;—in other respects and properties it resembles the true pearl white. Both these pigments should be employed with as little gum as possible, as it destroys their body, opacity, or whiteness; and solution of gum ammoniac answers better than gum arabic, which is commonly used: but the best way of preparing this pigment, and other terrene whites, so as to preserve their opacity, is to grind them in simple water, and to add toward the end of the grinding sufficient only of size, or clear cold jelly of gum tragacanth to attach them to the ground in painting. Barytic white is seldom well purified from free acid, and, therefore, apt to act injuriously on other pigments.

WHITE CHALK

Is a well-known native carbonate of lime, used by the artist only as a crayon, or for tracing his designs; for which purpose it is sawn into lengths suited to the porte-crayon. White crayons, and tracing-chalks, to be good, must work and cut free from grit. From this material, whitening and lime are prepared, and are the basis of many common pigments and colours used in distemper, paper-staining, &c.

There are many terrene whites under equivocal names, among them are Morat or Modan white, Spanish white or Troys, or Troy white, Rouen white, Bougeval white, Paris white, Blanc de Roi, China white, Satin white, the latter of which is a sulphate of lime and alumine, which dries with a glossy surface, is said to be prepared by mixing equal quantities of lime and alum, the first slacked and the latter dissolved in water. The common oyster-shell contains also a soft white in its thick part, which is good in water; and egg-shells have been prepared for the same purpose; white has likewise been obtained from an endless variety of native earths. From this unlimited variety of terrene whites we have selected above such only as merit the attention of the artist; the rest may be variously useful to the paperstainer, plasterer, and painter in distemper; but the whole of them are destitute of body in oil, and, owing to their alkaline nature, are injurious to many colours in water, as they are to all colours which cannot be employed in fresco.

CHINESE WHITE.

This exceedingly useful colour is a preparation of white oxide of zinc mixed with mucilage of gum tragacanth, gum arabic, and a small quantity of glycerine; it is generally used in water-colour painting, both in compounding tints and in high lights: it is sold in bottles and in compressible tubes; the former are to be preferred, though perhaps not so convenient in fitting into sketching-cases as the latter. The colour washes well, and, as now prepared, is a most valuable adjunct to the list of pigments. The use of body-white has in recent years become a fashion in water-colour painting; but the excessive use of this and other body-colours deteriorates much from the true character of water-colour painting, in which as a rule the lights should be obtained from the paper itself, otherwise the picture must be said to be executed in tempera. Besides this, the very best of whites are liable to discolour, and in that case the effect becomes diametrically the opposite to that intended.

CHAPTER VIII.

TINTS.

WHITE is in every way important in painting, not only as a ground, but as the basis of all tints, as necessary in compounding the endless variety of pale hues which taste and fashion require of the painter and decorator, which every season brings out under new denominations, to give way in turn to others and be forgotten. Thus white tinted with blue, &c., have afforded Paris white, &c., French greys, Silver greys, &c.; while among red tints we have pink, carnation, coquilicot, and all the blushes of flowers, &c.; and yellow with white has afforded Primrose, Straw-colour, Isabella, &c. To the colours compounded more or less with white, we are indebted for the innumerable tints of Lilac, Lavender, Peach-blossoms, Pea-green, Tea-green, &c.

In order to afford some instruction in compounding a few useful tints the following list is given. The student is advised to mix each of these tints in different hues, giving in each experiment a predominance to one or other of the component colours. The method of applying these colours will be given in another section. These tints are intended for water-colour painting, but most of them may be mixed for tempera or oil painting by the addition of white in varied proportions.

LAVENDER TINTS—which may be diluted until they give the palest French greys.

 Lake and Indigo.
 Lake and Cobalt.
 Indian Red and Cobalt.
 Vermilion and Cobalt.

GREY TINTS—of a brown hue--

 Madder Brown and Cobalt.
 Madder Lake, Cobalt, and Yellow Ochre.
 Indian Red and Indigo.
 Light Red and Cobalt.
 Gamboge, Lake, and Indigo.
 Burnt Sienna, Lake, and Indigo.

BROWN TINTS—

 Lake Cobalt, and Yellow Ochre.
 Lake, Indigo, and Yellow Ochre.
 Raw Sienna, Madder Lake, and Cobalt.
 Light Red and Indigo.

Vandyke Brown, Lake, and Indigo.
Burnt Sienna, Gamboge, and Indigo.
Vandyke Brown, Gamboge, and Indigo.
Vandyke Brown and Lake.
Burnt Sienna and Lake.

Green Tints—

Italian Pink and Antwerp Blue.
Italian Pink and Lamp Black.
Yellow Ochre and Indigo.
Burnt Sienna and Indigo.
Brown, Pink, and Indigo.
Raw Umber and Indigo.

Yellow Tints—

Yellow Ochre and Lake.
Yellow Ochre and Light Red.
Yellow Ochre and Vandyke Brown.

CHAPTER IX.

OF THE PRIMARY COLOURS.

YELLOW.*

Yellow is the first of the primary or simple colours, nearest in relation to, and partaking most of the nature of, the neutral white, mixed with which it affords the

* This celestial light revealed to men, finds its natural symbol in the light which shines on earth; the heat and the brightness of the sun designate the love of God which animates the heart, and the wisdom which enlightens the intellect. These two attributes of God, manifest in the creation of the world and the regeneration of men,

faint hues called Straw-colour, &c.; it is accordingly a most advancing colour, of great power in reflecting light. Compounded with the primary red, it constitutes the secondary orange, and its relatives, scarlet, &c., and other warm colours.

It is the ruling colour of the tertiary citrine;—it characterizes in like manner the endless variety of the semi-neutral colours called brown, and enters largely into the complex colours denominated buff, bay, tawny, tan, dun, drab, chestnut, roan, sorrel, hazel, auburn, Isabella, fawn, feuillemorte, &c. Yellow is naturally associated with red in transient and prismatic colours, and they comport themselves with similar affinity and glowing accordance in painting, as well in conjunction as composition. In combination with the primary *blue*, yellow constitutes all the variety of the secondary *green*, and, subordinately, the tertiaries *russet* and *olive*. It enters also in a very subdued degree into cool, semi-neutral, and broken colours, and assists in minor proportions with blue and red in the composition of *black*.

As a pigment, yellow is a tender, delicate colour, easily defiled, when pure, by other colours. In painting it diminishes the power of the eye by its action in a strong light, while itself becomes less distinct as a colour; and, on the contrary, it assists vision and becomes more distinct as a colour in a neutral somewhat declining light. These powers of colours upon vision require the particular attention of the colourist. To remedy the ill effect arising from the eyes having dwelt

appear inseparable in the signification of the sun, of gold, and yellow. Divine wisdom had white for a symbol, as divine love, red; golden yellow reunites these two significations and forms them into one; but with the character of manifestation and revelation. This explains an ancient tradition current in emblazonry; authors on the heraldic art pretend that the yellow colour is a mixture of red and white.—*Baron F. Portal on Symbolic Colours.*

upon a colour, they should be gradually passed to its opposite colour, and refreshed in the clear light of day.

In a warm light, yellow becomes totally lost, but is less diminished than all other colours, except white, by distance. The stronger tones of any colour subdue its fainter hues in the same proportion as opposite colours and contrasts exalt them. The contrasting colours of yellow are a purple inclining to blue when the yellow inclines to orange, and a purple inclining to red when the yellow inclines to green, in the mean proportions of thirteen purple to three of yellow, measured in surface or intensity; and yellow being nearest to the neutral white in the natural scale of colours, it accords with it in conjunction. Of all colours, except white, it contrasts black most powerfully.*

The sensible effects of yellow are gay, gaudy, glorious, full of lustre, enlivening, and irritating; and its impressions on the mind partake of these characters, and acknowledge also its discordances.

The substitution of gold, &c., for yellow by the poets may have arisen not less from the great value and splendour of the metal, than from the paucity of fine yellows among those ancients who celebrated the Tyrian purple or red, and the no less famed Armenian blue;— so in the beautiful illuminated MSS. of old, and in many ancient paintings, which glowed with vermilion and ultramarine, the place of yellow was supplied by gilding, and in most cases the artist trusts to the gilding of his frame for some portion of the effect of this colour in his picture: and in every case of decorating with gildings similar allowance should be made.

Yellow is a colour abundant throughout nature, and its class of pigments abounds in similar proportion. We have arranged them under the following heads, agree-

* Ruskin's "Elements of Drawing," second edition, 1857, p. 7.

ably to our plan, according to their definiteness and brilliancy of colour; first the opaque, and then the transparent, or finishing colours. It may be observed of yellow pigments, that they much resemble whites in their chemical relations in general, and that yellow, being a primary and, therefore, a simple colour, cannot be composed by any mixture of other colours.

CHROME YELLOW

Is a pigment of modern introduction into general use, and of which there are several varieties, mostly chromates of lead, in which the latter metal more or less abounds. They are distinguished by the pureness, beauty, and brilliancy of their colours, which qualities are great temptations to their use in the hands of the painter; they are notwithstanding far from unexceptionable pigments;—yet they have a good body, and go cordially into tint with white, both in water and oil; but used alone, or in tint, they after some time lose their pure colour, and may even become black in impure air; they nevertheless resist the sun's rays during a long time. Upon several colours they produce serious changes, ultimately destroying Prussian and Antwerp blues, when used therewith in the composition of greens, &c. Chromes may be in three degrees of depth —pale, medium, and deep.

JAUNE MINÉRALE.

This pigment is also a chromate of lead, prepared in Paris, differing in no essential particular from the above, except in the paleness of its colour. The chrome yellows have also obtained other names from places or persons from whence they have been brought, or by whom they have been prepared, such as Jaune de Cologne; we pass over, however, such as have not been generally received. The following pigment passes also under the name of Jaune Minérale :—

PATENT YELLOW,

Turner's yellow, or *Montpellier yellow*, is a submuriate or chloruret of lead, which metal is the basis of most opaque-yellow pigments; it is a hard, ponderous, sparkling substance, of a crystalline texture and bright yellow colour; hardly inferior, when ground, to chromic yellow. It has an excellent body, and works well either in oil or water, but is soon injured both by the sun's light and impure air; it is, therefore, little used, except for the commoner purposes of painting.

NAPLES YELLOW

Is a compound of the oxides of lead and antimony, anciently prepared at Naples under the name of *Giallolini;* it is supposed also to have been a native production of Vesuvius and other volcanoes, and is a pigment of deservedly considerable reputation. It is not so vivid a colour as either of the above, but is variously of a pleasing light, warm, yellow tint. Like all the preceding yellows, it is opaque, and in this sense is of good body, and covers well. It is not changed by the light of the sun, and may be used safely in oil or varnish under the same management as the whites of lead; but, like these latter pigments also, it is liable to change even to blackness by damp and impure air when used as a water-colour, or unprotected by oil or varnish.

Iron is also destructive of the colour of Naples yellow, on which account great care is requisite, in grinding and using it, not to touch it with the common steel palette-knife, but to compound its tints on the palette with a spatula of ivory or horn. For the same reason it may be liable to change in composition with the ochres, Prussian and Antwerp blues, and all other pigments of which iron is an ingredient or principle. Oils, varnishes, and in some measure strong mucilages, are preventive of chemical action, in the compounding of colours, by intervening and clothing the particles of pigments, and also preserve their colours: and hence, in some instances, heterogeneous and injudicious tints and mixtures have stood well, but are not to be relied on in practice. Used pure, or with white lead, its affinity with which gives permanency to their tints, Naples yellow is a valuable and proved colour in oil, in which also it works and dries well.

It may also be used in enamel painting, as it vitrifies without change, and in this state it was formerly employed under the name of *Giallolini di fornace*, and has been again introduced, under an erroneous conception that vitrification gives permanence to colours, when in truth it only increases the difficulty of levigation, and injures their texture for working. Naples yellow does not appear to have been generally employed by the early painters in oil. Antimony yellows are prepared of various depths.

MASSICOT,

Or *Masticot*, is a protoxide of lead, of a pale yellow colour, exceedingly varying in tint, from the purest and most tender yellow or straw-colour to pale ash-colour or grey. It has in painting all the properties of the white lead, from which it is prepared by gentle calcination in an open furnace, but in tint with which, nevertheless, it soon loses its colour and returns to white: if, however, it be used pure or unmixed, it is a useful delicate colour, permanent in oil under the same conditions as white lead, but ought not to be employed in water, on account of its changing in colour even to blackness by the action of damp and impure air. It appears to have been prepared with great care, and successfully employed, by the old masters, and is an admirable dryer, being in its chemical nature nearly the same as litharge, which is also sometimes ground and employed in its stead.

YELLOW OCHRE,

Called also *Mineral yellow*, is a native pigment, found in most countries, and abundantly in our own. It varies considerably in constitution and colour, in which latter particular it is found from a bright but not very vivid yellow to a brown yellow, called *spruce ochre*, and is always of a warm cast. Its natural variety is much increased by artificial dressing and compounding. The best yellow ochres are not powerful, but as far as they go are valuable pigments, particularly in fresco and distemper, being neither subject to change by ordinary light, nor much affected by impure air or the action of lime; by time, however, and the direct rays of the sun they are somewhat darkened, and by burning are converted into light reds. They are among the most ancient of pigments, may all be produced artificially in endless variety as they exist in nature, and iron is the principal colouring matter in them all. The following are the principal species, but they are often confounded:—

OXFORD OCHRE

Is a native pigment from the neighbourhood of Oxford, semi-opaque, of a warm yellow colour and soft argillaceous* texture, absorbent of water and oil, in both

---

* Argillaceous, of a clayey character.

which it may be used with safety according to the general character of yellow ochres, of which it is one of the best. Similar ochres are found in the Isle of Wight, in the neighbourhood of Bordeaux, and various other places.

STONE OCHRE

Has been confounded with the above, which it frequently resembles, as does also Roman ochre. True stone ochres are found in balls or globular masses of various sizes in the solid body of stones, lying near the surface of rocks among the quarries in Gloucestershire and elsewhere. These balls are of a smooth compact texture, in general free from grit, and of a powdery fracture. They vary exceedingly in colour, from yellow to brown, murrey, and grey, but do not differ in other respects from the preceding, and may be safely used in oil or water in the several modes of painting, and for browns and dull reds in enamel. Varieties of ochrous colours are produced by burning and compounding with lighter, brighter, and darker colours, but often very injuriously, and adversely to the certainty of operation, effect, and durability.

ROMAN OCHRE

Is rather deeper and more powerful in colour than the above, but in other respects differs not essentially from them;—a remark which applies equally to yellow ochres of other denominations. There are ochres of every country.

BROWN OCHRE,

Spruce Ochre, or *Ocre de Rue*, is a dark-coloured yellow ochre, in no other respects differing from the preceding: —it is much employed, and affords useful and permanent tints. This and all natural ochres require grinding and washing over to separate them from extraneous substances, and they acquire depth and redness by burning. They form with Prussian blue a variety of greens, and are of use in mixture of other colours.

TERRA DI SIENNA, OR RAW SIENNA,

Is also a ferruginous* native pigment, and appears to be an iron ore, which may be considered as a crude natural yellow lake, firm in substance, of a glossy fracture, and very absorbent. It is in many respects a valuable pigment, — of rather an impure yellow colour, but has more body and transparency than the ochres; and being little liable to change by the action of either light, time, or impure air, it may be safely used according to its powers, either in oil or water, and in all the modes of practice. By burning it becomes deeper, orange, and more transparent and drying. See *Burnt Sienna Earth* (page 66). It is a valuable colour in graining.

IRON YELLOW,

Jaune de Fer, or *Jaune de Mars*, &c., is a bright iron ochre, prepared artificially, of the nature of Sienna earth. In its general qualities it resembles the ochres, with the same eligibilities and exceptions, but is more transparent. The colours of iron exist in endless variety in nature, and are capable of the same variation by art, from sienna yellow, through orange and red, to purple, brown, and black, among which are useful and valuable distinctions, which are brighter and purer than native ochres. They were formerly introduced by the author, and have been lately received under the names of *orange de mars, rouge de mars, brun de mars*, names which have the merit at least of not misleading

---

* Ferruginous (Lat. *ferrum*, "iron"), impregnated with iron.

the judgment. When carefully prepared, these pigments dry well in proportion to their depth, and have the general habits of sienna earths and ochres

YELLOW ORPIMENT,

Or *Yellow Arsenic*, is a sulphuretted oxide of arsenic, of a beautiful, bright, and pure yellow colour, not extremely durable in water, and less so in oil: in tint with white lead it is soon destroyed. It is not subject to discoloration in impure air. This property is not, however, sufficient to redeem it with the artist, as it has a bad effect upon several valuable colours, such as Naples yellow; and upon the Chromates, Masticot, and Red lead, and most other oxides and metallic colours; but with colours dependent upon sulphur or other inflammables for their hues it may be employed with less danger, and was probably so employed by the old painters, with ultramarine in the composition of their greens; and is well suited to the factitious or French ultramarines. Although this pigment is not so poisonous as white arsenic, it is dangerous in its effect upon health. Yellow orpiment is of several tints, from bright cool yellow to warm orange, the first of which are most subject to change; and it has appeared under various forms and denominations :—these seem to have been used by several of the old masters, with especial care to avoid mixture; and as they dry badly, and the oxides of lead used in rendering oils drying destroy their colour, levigated glass was employed with them as a dryer, or perhaps they were sometimes used in simple varnish. They are found in a native state under the name of *zarnic* or *zarnich*, varying in colour from warm yellow to green. But orpiment, in all its varieties, powerfully deprives other substances of their oxygen, and therefore is subject to change, and to be changed by, every pigment whose colour depends on that element, and more especially all metallic colours; if employed, they must theref re be so in a pure and unmixed state. See *Orange Orpiment* (page 67).

KING'S YELLOW.

Yellow orpiment has been much celebrated under this name, as it has also under the denomination of—

CHINESE YELLOW,

Which is a very bright sulphuret of arsenic, brought from China.

ARSENIC YELLOW,

Called also *Mineral Yellow*, is prepared from arsenic fluxed with litharge, and reduced to powder. It is much like orpiment in colour, dries better, and, not being affected by lead, is less liable to change in tint. It must not be forgotten that it is poisonous, nor that all arsenic colours are destructive of every tint of colours mixed with white lead.

CADMIUM YELLOW,

Sulphuret of Cadmium. The new metal, cadmium, affords, by precipitation with solution of sulphuretted hydrogen, a bright warm yellow pigment, which passes readily into tints with white lead, appears to endure light, and remains unchanged in impure air; but the metal from which it is prepared being hitherto scarce, it has been little employed as a pigment, and its habits are, therefore, not ascertained.

GAMBOGE,

Or *Gumboge*, is brought principally from Cambaja in India, and is the produce of several kinds of trees. Is a concrete vegetal substance, of a gum-resinous nature, and beautiful yellow colour, bright and transparent, but not of great depth. When properly used, it is more durable than generally reputed both in water and oil; and conduces, when mixed with other colours, to their stability and durability, by means of its gum and resin. It is deepened in some degree by ammoniacal and impure air, and somewhat weakened, but not easily discoloured, by the action of light. Time effects less change on this colour than on other bright vegetal yellows; but white lead and other metalline pigments injure, and terrene and alkaline substances redden it. It works remarkably well in water, with which it forms an opaque solution, without grinding or preparation, by means of its natural gum; but is with difficulty used in oil, &c., in a dry state. In its natural state it however dries well, and lasts in glazing when deprived of its gum. Glazed over other colours in water, its resin acts as a varnish which protects them; and under other colours its gum acts as a preparation which admits varnishing. It is injured by a less degree of heat than other pigments.

GALL-STONE

Is an animal calculus formed in the gall-bladder, principally of oxen. This concretion varies a little in colour, but is in general of a beautiful golden yellow, more powerful than gamboge, and is highly reputed as a water-colour; nevertheless, its colour is soon changed and destroyed by strong light, though not subject to alteration by impure air.

It is rarely introduced in oil-painting, and is by no means eligible therein.

INDIAN YELLOW

Is a pigment long employed in India under the name *Puree*, but has not many years been introduced generally into painting in Europe. It is imported in the form of balls, and is of a fetid odour. However produced, it appears to be an urio-phosphate of lime, of a beautiful pure yellow colour, and light powdery texture; of greater body and depth than gamboge, but inferior in these respects to gall-stone. Indian yellow resists the sun's rays with singular power in water-painting; yet in ordinary light and air, or even in a book or portfolio, the beauty of its colour is not lasting. It is not injured by foul air, and in oil is exceedingly fugitive, both alone and in tint.

YELLOW LAKE.

There are several pigments of this denomination varying in colour and appearance according to the colouring substances used, and modes of preparation. They are usually in the form of drops, and their colours are in general bright yellow, very transparent, and not liable to change in an impure atmosphere,—qualities which would render them very valuable pigments, were they not soon discoloured, and even destroyed, by the opposite influence of oxygen and light, both in water and oil; in which latter vehicle, like other lakes in general, they are bad dryers, and do not stand the action of white lead or metallic colours. If used, therefore, it should be as simple as possible.

AUREOLIN.

This is a nitrate of Cobalt, and is a very pure and permanent colour. It is as nearly as possible a pure yellow, and is used in water or oil.

DUTCH PINK, ENGLISH AND ITALIAN PINKS,

Are sufficiently absurd names of yellow colours prepared by impregnating whitening, &c., with vegetal yellow tinctures, in the manner of rose pink, from which they borrow their name.

They are bright yellow colours, extensively used in distemper and for paper-staining and other ordinary purposes; but are little deserving attention in the higher walks of art, being in every respect inferior even to the yellow lakes, except the best kinds of English and Italian pinks, which are, in fact, yellow lakes, and richer in colour than the pigments generally called yellow lake.

The pigment called *Stil*, or *Stil de Grain*, is a similar preparation, and a very fugitive yellow, the darker kind of which is called brown-pink.

CHAPTER X.

RED.

RED is the second and intermediate of the primary colours, standing between *yellow* and *blue*; and in like intermediate relation also to *white* and *black*, or light and shade. Hence it is pre-eminent among colours, as well as the most positive of all, forming with yellow the secondary *orange* and its near relatives, scarlet, &c.; and with blue, the secondary *purple* and its allies, crimson, &c. It gives some degree of warmth to all colours, but most to those which partake of yellow.

It is the archeus, or principal colour, in the tertiary

russet; enters subordinately into the two other tertiaries, *citrine* and *olive;* goes largely into the composition of the various hues and shades of the semi-neutral *marrone,* or chocolate, and its relatives, puce, murrey, morello, mordore, pompadour, &c.; and more or less into *browns, greys,* and all broken colours. It is also the second power in harmonizing and contrasting other colours, and in compounding *black,* and all neutrals, into which it enters in the proportion of five,—to blue, eight, —and yellow, three.

Red is a colour of double power in this respect also; that in union or connection with yellow it becomes hot and *advancing;* but mixed or combined with blue, it becomes cool and *retiring.* It is, however, more congenial with *yellow* than with blue, and thence partakes more of the character of the former in its effects of warmth, of the influence of light and distance, and of action on the eye, by which the power of vision is diminished upon viewing this colour in a strong light; while, on the other hand, red itself appears to deepen in colour rapidly in a declining light as night comes on, or in shade. These qualities of red give it great importance, render it difficult of management, and require it to be kept in general subordinate in painting; hence it is rarely used unbroken, or as the predominating colour, on which account it will always appear detached or insulated, unless it be repeated and subordinate in a composition. Accordingly, Nature uses red sparingly, and with as great reserve in the decoration of her works as she is profuse in lavishing green upon them; which is of all colours the most soothing to the eye, and the true compensating colour, or contrasting or harmonizing equivalent of red, in the proportional quantity of eleven to five of red, according to surface or intensity; and is, when the red inclines to scarlet or orange, a *blue-*

green; and when it inclines to crimson or purple, is a *yellow-green.*

Red breaks and diffuses with white with peculiar loveliness and beauty; but it is discordant when standing with orange only, and requires to be joined or accompanied by their proper contrast, to resolve or harmonize their dissonance.

In landscapes, &c., abounding with hues allied to green, a red object, properly placed according to such hues in light, shade, or distance, conduces wonderfully to the life, beauty, harmony, and connection of the colouring; and this colouring is the chief element of beauty in floreal nature, the prime contrast and ornament of the green garb of the vegetal kingdom.

Red being the most *positive* of colours, and having the *middle* station of the primaries, while *black* and *white* are the *negative* powers or neutrals of colours, and the *extremes* of the scale,—red contrasts and harmonizes these neutrals; and, as it is more nearly allied to white or light than to black or shade, this harmony is most remarkable in the union or opposition of white and red, and this contrast most powerful in black and red.

As a colour, red is in itself pre-eminently beautiful, powerful, cheering, splendid and ostentatious, and communicates these qualities to its two secondaries, and their sentiments to the mind.

Red, being a primary and simple colour, cannot be composed by mixture of other colours; it is so much the instrument of beauty in nature and art in the colour of flesh, flowers, &c., that good pigments of this genus may of all colours be considered the most indispensable: we have happily, therefore, many of this denomination, of which the following are the principal :—*

---

* In China, red colour is consecrated to religion, and the mourning worn by children is hempen sackcloth of a bright red. Love always

VERMILION

Is a sulphuret of mercury, which, previous to its being levigated, is called *cinnabar*. It is an ancient pigment, the κιννάβαρι of the Greeks, and is both found in a native state and produced artificially. The Chinese possess a native cinnabar so pure as to require grinding only to become very perfect vermilion, not at all differing from that imported in large quantities from China.

Chinese vermilion is of a cooler or more crimson tone than that generally manufactured from factitious cinnabar in England, Holland, and different parts of Europe. The artificial, which was anciently called *minium*, a term now confined to red lead, does not differ from the natural in any quality essential to its value as a pigment; it varies in tint from dark red to scarlet, and both sorts are perfectly durable and unexceptionable pigments. It is true, nevertheless, that vermilions have obtained the double disrepute of fading in a strong light and of becoming black or dark by time and impure air; but colours, like characters, suffer contamination and disrepute from bad association: it has happened, accordingly, that vermilion which has been rendered lakey or crimson by mixture with lake or carmine has faded in the light, and that when it has been toned to the scarlet hue by red or orange lead it has afterwards become blackened in impure air, &c., both of which adulterations were formerly practised, and hence the ill-fame of vermilion both with authors and artists. We therefore repeat, that neither light,

had a red colour for the symbol of infancy. Cupid is a child; celestial love is represented in Christian symbolism by infant angels. A child was initiated into the great mysteries at Eleusis; he performed a character in the last initiation, which was an emblem of death; he was named the child of the sanctuary; and the boys of the choir are to this day clothed in red.—*Baron F. Portal.*

time, nor foul air effects sensible change in true vermilions. and that they may be used safely in either water, oil, or fresco,—being colours of great chemical permanence, unaffected by other pigments, and among the least soluble of chemical substances.

Good vermilion is a powerful vivid colour, of great body, weight, and opacity; when pure, it will be entirely decomposed and dissipated by fire in a red heat, and is, therefore, in respect to the above mixtures, easily tested.

The name vermilion—derived from *vermiculus* (*vermis*, a worm)—seems to have had its origin in very early days, and would appear to be the scarlet referred to in the Bible (Exod. xxviii. 5), where the colour rendered in the authorised version "scarlet" is in the original Hebrew called " *Tolāath Shani*," *shining worm*.

The term vermiculus, used by the Moors, referred to the insect they called Kermes, and hence it seems the name Kermesino or Cremèsino which has in our time become Crimson.

The following brilliant pigment from iodine has been improperly called vermilion, and, if it should be used to dress or give unnatural vividness to true vermilion, may again bring it into disrepute. When red or orange lead has been substituted for or used in adulterating vermilion, muriatic acid applied to such pigments will turn them more or less white or grey: but pure vermilions will not be affected by the acid, nor will they by pure or caustic alkalis, which change the colour of the reds of iodine. By burning more or less, vermilion may be brought to the colour of most of the red ochres.

IODINE SCARLET

Is a new pigment of a most vivid and beautiful scarlet colour, exceeding the brilliancy of vermilion. It has received several false appellations, but is truly an *Iodide or Bi-iodide of mercury,* varying in degrees of intense redness. It has the body and opacity of vermilion, but should be used with an ivory palette-knife, as iron and most metals change it to colours varying from yellow to black. Strong light rather deepens and cools it, and impure air soon utterly destroys its scarlet colour, and even metallizes it in substance. The charms of beauty and novelty have recommended it, particularly to amateurs; and dazzling brilliancy might render it valuable for high and fiery effects of colour, if any mode of securing it from change should be devised; at any rate it should be used pure or alone. By time alone these colours vanish in a thin wash or glaze without apparent cause, and they attack almost every metallic substance, and some of them even in a dry state. When used in water, gum ammoniac appears to secure it from change; and it has been observed that, when gamboge is glazed over it, it preserves its hue with constancy.

RED LEAD,

Minium,[*] or *Saturine red,* is an ancient pigment, by some old writers confounded with cinnabar, and called *Sinoper* or *Synoper,* is a deutoxide of lead, prepared by subjecting massicot to the heat of a furnace with an expanded surface and free accession of air. It is of a scarlet colour and fine hue, warmer than common vermilion; bright, but not so vivid as the bi-iodide of mercury; though it has the body and opacity of both these pigments, and has been confounded, even in name, with vermilion, with which it was formerly customary to mix it. When pure and alone, light does not affect its colour: but white lead, or any oxide or preparation

---

[*] The artificial vermilion used in early manuscripts was termed *Minium.* The name is now, however, used to designate red lead only.

of that metal mixed with it, soon deprives it of colour, as acids do also; and impure air will blacken and ultimately metallize it.

On account of its extreme fugitiveness when mixed with white lead, it cannot be used in tints; but employed, unmixed with other pigments, in simple varnish or oil not rendered drying by any metallic oxide, it may, under favourable circumstances, stand a long time; hence red lead has had a variable character for durability. It is in itself, however, an excellent dryer in oil, and has in this view been employed with other pigments; but, as regards colour, it cannot be mixed safely with any other pigments than the ochres, earths, and blacks in general. Used alone, it answers, however, as a good red paint for common purposes.

RED OCHRE

Is a name proper rather to a class than to an individual pigment, and comprehends *Indian red, light red, Venetian red, scarlet ochre, Indian ochre, redding, ruddle, bole,* &c., besides other absurd appellations, such as *English vermilion* and *Spanish brown*, or *majolica*.

The red ochres are, for the most part, rather hues and tints than definite colours, or more properly classed with the tertiary, semi-neutral, and broken colours; they are, nevertheless, often very valuable pigments for their tints in dead colouring, and for their permanence, &c., in water, oil, crayons, distempers, and fresco, and in a low tone of colouring have the value of primaries. The greater part of them are native pigments, found in most countries, and very abundantly and fine in our own; but some are productions of manufacture, and we have produced them in the variety of nature by art. The following are the most important of these pigments, most of which are available in enamel-painting:—

INDIAN RED,

According to its name, is brought from Bengal, and is a very rich iron ore, hematite, or peroxide of iron. It is an anomalous red, of a purple-russet hue, of a good body, and valued when fine for the pureness and lakey tone of its tints. In a crude state it is a coarse powder, full of extremely hard and brilliant particles of a dark appearance, sometimes magnetic, and is greatly improved by grinding and washing over. Its chemical tendency is to deepen, nevertheless it is very permanent; neither light, impure air, mixture with other pigments, time, nor fire, effecting in general any sensible change in it; and, being opaque, it covers well. This pigment varies considerably in its hues; that which is most rosy being esteemed the best, and affording the purest tints: inferior red ochres have been formerly substituted for it, and have procured it a variable character, but it is now obtained abundantly, and may be had pure of respectable colourmen. *Persian red* is another name for this pigment.

LIGHT RED

Is an ochre of a russet-orange hue, principally valued for its tints. The common light red is brown ochre burnt, but the principal yellow ochres afford this colour best; and the brighter and better the yellow ochre is from which this pigment is prepared, the brighter will this red be, and the better flesh tints will it afford with white. There are, however, native ochres brought from India and other countries which supply its place, some of which become darkened by time and impure air; but in other respects light red has the general good properties of other ochres, dries admirably, and is much used both in figure and landscape painting. It affords also an excellent crayon.

Terra puzzoli and carnagione of the Italians differ from the above only in their hue, in which respect other denominations are produced by dressing and compounding.

VENETIAN RED,

Or *Scarlet ochre*. True Venetian red is said to be a native ochre, but the colours sold under this name are prepared artificially from sulphate of iron, or its residuum in the manufacturing of acids. They are all of redder and deeper hues than light red, are very permanent, and have all the properties of good ochres.

Prussian red, English red, Rouge de Mars, are other names for the same pigment, and Spanish red is an ochre differing little from Venetian red.

DRAGON'S BLOOD

Is a resinous substance, brought principally from the East Indies. It is of a warm, semi-transparent, rather dull, red colour, which is deepened by impure air, and darkened by light. There are two or three sorts, but that in drops is the best. White lead soon destroys it, and it dries with extreme difficulty in oil. It is sometimes used to colour varnishes and lackers, being soluble in oils and alcohol; but, notwithstanding it has been recommended as a pigment, it does not merit the attention of the artist. It was anciently called Cinnabar.

LAKE,

A name derived from the *lac* or *lacca* of India, is the cognomen of a variety of transparent red and other coloured pigments of great beauty, prepared for the most part by precipitating coloured tinctures of dyeing drugs upon alumine and other earths, &c. The lakes are hence a numerous class of pigments, both with respect to the variety of their appellations and the substances from which they are prepared. The colouring matter of common lake is Brazil wood, which affords a very fugitive colour. Superior red lakes are prepared from cochineal, lac, and kermes; but the best of all are are those prepared from the root of the *Rubia tinctoria*, or madder plant. Of the various red lakes the following are the principal :—

All lakes ground in linseed oil are disposed to fatten, or become livery, but ground stiff in poppy oil they keep better for use.

RUBRIC, OR MADDER LAKES.

These pigments are of various colours, of which we shall speak at present of the red or rose colours only; which have obtained, from their material, their hues, or their inventor, the various names of rose rubiate, rose madder, pink madder, and Field's lakes.

The pigments formerly called madder lakes were brick-reds of dull ochrous hues; but for many years past these lakes have been prepared perfectly transparent, and literally as beautiful and pure in colour as the rose; qualities in which they are unrivalled by the lakes and carmine of cochineal. The rose colours of madder have justly been considered as supplying a desideratum, and as the most valuable acquisition of the palette in modern times, since perfectly permanent and transparent reds and rose colours were previously unknown to the art of painting.

These pigments are of hues warm or cool, from pure pink to the deepest rose colour ;—they afford the purest and truest carnation colours known; form permanent tints with white lead; and their transparency renders them perfect glazing or finishing colours. They are not liable to change by the action of either light or impure air, or by mixture with other pigments; but when not thoroughly edulcorated, they are, in common with all lakes, tardy driers in oil, the best remedy for which is the addition of a small portion of japanner's gold-size: or, as they are too beautiful and require saddening for the general uses of the painter, the addition of manganese brown, cappagh brown, or of burnt umber, as was the practice of the Venetian painters in the using of lake, adds to their powers and improves their drying in oils.

Though little known in ordinary painting, they have been established by experience on the palettes of our first masters during nearly half a century. Madder lake may be tested by liquid ammonia in which its colour is *not* soluble as those of other lakes and carmines are.

SCARLET LAKE

Is prepared in form of drops from cochineal, and is of a beautiful transparent red colour and excellent body, working well both in water and oil, though, like other lakes, it dries slowly. Strong light discolours and destroys it both in water and oil; and its tints with white lead, and its combinations with other pigments, are not permanent; yet when well prepared and judiciously used in sufficient body, and kept from strong light, it has been known to last many years; but it ought never to be employed in glazing, nor at all in performances that aim at high reputation and durability. It is commonly tinted with vermilion, which has probably been mixed with lakes at all times to give them a scarlet hue, and add to their body; *Florentine* lake, *Hamburg lake*, *Chinese lake*, *Roman* and *Venetian lakes*, are but varieties of the same pigment.

LAC LAKE,

Prepared from the *lac* or *lacca* of India, is perhaps the first of the family of lakes, and resembles the former from Cochineal in being the production of similar insects. Its colour is rich, transparent, and deep,—less brilliant and more durable than that of cochineal, but inferior in both these respects to the colours of madder. Used in body or strong glazing, as a shadow colour, it is of great power and much permanence; but in thin glazing it changes and flies, as it does also in tint with white lead.

A great variety of lakes, equally beautiful as those of cochineal, have been prepared from this substance in a recent state in India and China, many of which we have tried, and found uniformly less durable in proportion as they were more beautiful. In the properties of drying, &c., they resemble other lakes.

This appears to have been the lake which has stood best in old pictures, and was probably used by the Venetians, who had the trade of India when painting flourished at Venice. It is sometimes called *Indian lake*.

CARMINE,

A name originally given only to the fine feculences of the tinctures of kermes and cochineal, denotes generally at present any pigment which resembles them in beauty, richness of colour, and fineness of texture: hence we hear of blue and other coloured carmines, though the term is principally confined to the crimson and scarlet colours produced from cochineal, by the agency of tin. These carmines are the brightest and most beautiful colours prepared from cochineal,—of a fine powdery texture and velvety richness. They vary from a rose colour to a warm red; work admirably; and are in other respects, except the most essential— the want of durability—excellent pigments in water and oil: they have not, however, any permanence in tint with white lead, and in glazing are soon discoloured and destroyed by the action of light, but are little affected by impure air, and are in other respects like the lakes of cochineal; all the pigments prepared from which may be tested by their solubility in liquid ammonia, which purples lakes prepared from the wood's, but does not dissolve their colours.

MADDER CARMINE,

Or *Field's carmine*, is, as its name expresses, prepared from madder. It differs from the rose lakes of madder principally in texture, and in the greater richness, depth, and transparency of its colour, which is of various hues, from rose colour to crimson. These in other respects resemble the rubric or madder lakes, and are the only *durable carmines* for painting either in water or oil; for both which their texture qualifies them without previous grinding or preparation.

ROSE PINK

Is a coarse kind of lake, produced by dyeing chalk or whitening with decoction of Brazil wood, &c. It is a pigment much used by paper-stainers, and in the commonest distemper painting, &c., but is too perishable to merit the attention of the artist.

CHAPTER XI.

BLUE.

The third and last of the primary or simple colours is *blue*, which bears the same relation to shade that yellow does to light; hence it is the most retiring and diffusive of all colours, except purple and black; and all colours have the power of throwing it back in painting, in greater or less degree, in proportion to the intimacy of their relations to light; first white, then yellow, orange, red, &c.

Blue alone possesses entirely the quality technically called *coldness* in colouring, and it communicates this property variously to all other colours with which it happens to be compounded. It is most powerful in a strong light, and appears to become neutral and pale in a declining light, owing to its ruling affinity with black or shade, and its power of absorbing light; hence the eye of the artist is liable to be deceived when painting with blue in too low a light, or toward the close of day, to the endangering of the warmth and harmony of his work.

Blue mixed with yellow forms *green*, and mixed with red it forms *purple*; it characterizes the tertiary *olive*, and is also the prime colour of the neutral *black*, &c., and also of the semi-neutral *greys, slate, lead colours*, &c.; hence blue is changed in hue less than any colour by mixture with black, as it is also by distance. It enters also subordinately into all other tertiary and broken colours, and, as nearest in the scale to black, it breaks and contrasts powerfully and agreeably with white, as in watchet or pale blues, the sky, &c. It is less active than the other primaries in reflecting light, and therefore sooner disappears by distance.

It is an ancient doctrine that the azure of the sky is a compound of light and darkness, and some have argued hence that blue is not a primary colour, but a compound of black and white; but pure or *neutral* black and white compound in infinite shades, all of which are neutral also or *grey*. It is true that a mixture of black and white is of a *cool* hue, because black is not a primary colour, but a compound of the three primary colours in which blue predominates, and this predominance is rendered more sensible when black is diluted with white.

Blue is discordant in juxtaposition with green, and in a less degree so with purple, both which are cool colours, and therefore *blue* requires its contrast, *orange*, in equal proportion, either of service or intensity, to compensate or resolve its dissonances and correct its coldness. Botanists remark that blue flowers are much more rare than those of the other primary colours and their compounds, and hence advise the florist to cultivate blue flowers more sedulously. Artists, too, have sometimes acted upon this principle of the botanist in introducing blue flowers into pictures, preferring therein rareness and novelty to truth and harmony: the artist has, however, more command of his materials than the botanist in resolving a discord;—Nature nevertheless, left to herself, is not long in harmonizing the dissonances men put upon her. Florists may further remark, that *blue flowers* are readily changed by cultivation into red and white, but never into yellow; that *yellow flowers* are as readily converted into red and white, but never into blue; and that *red flowers* are changeable into orange or purple, but never into blue or yellow: the reasons of all which is apparent according to our principles. Nature also regulates the variegation of flowers by the same law of colouring.

Of all colours, except black, blue contrasts white most powerfully. In all harmonious combinations of colours, whether of mixture or neighbourhood, blue is the natural, ruling tone, universally agreeable to the eye when in due relation to the composition, and may be more frequently repeated therein, pure or unbroken, than either of the other primaries. These are, however, matters of taste, as in music, and subject to artificial rules founded on the laws of chromatic combination.

As blue cannot be composed by mixture of other colours, it is an original and primary colour. The paucity of blue pigments, in comparison with those of yellow and red, is amply compensated by their value and perfection; nor is the palette without novelty, nor deficient in pigments of this colour: of which the following comprise all that are in any respect of importance to the painter.*

ULTRAMARINE,

Or *Azure*, is prepared from the lapis lazuli, a precious stone found principally in Persia and Siberia. It is the most celebrated of all modern pigments, and, from its name and attributes, is probably the same as the no less celebrated *Armenian blue*, or *Cyanus*, of the ancients.

Ultramarine has not obtained its reputation upon slight pretensions, being, when skilfully prepared, of the most exquisitely beautiful blue, varying from the

---

* The Salisbury Breviary contains several miniatures, in which appear biers covered with a blue mortuary cloth. On some others, but more rarely, the pall is red; finally, on one only is the pall red, and the dais which covers the catafalque blue. These two colours, one over the other, indicate divine love raising the soul to immortality. The dais is the emblem of heaven; violet, composed of red and blue, was likewise a mortuary colour. In the same MS. appears a coffin, with a violet pall.—*Baron F. Portal.*

utmost depth of shadow to the highest brilliancy of light and colour,—transparent in all its shades, and pure in its tints. It is of a true medial blue, when perfect, partaking neither of purple, on the one hand, nor of green on the other; it is neither subject to injury by damp and impure air, nor by the intensest action of light; and it is so eminently permanent that it remains perfectly unchanged in the oldest paintings; and there can be little doubt that it is the same pigment which still continues with all its original force and beauty, in the temples of Upper Egypt, after an exposure of at least three thousand years. The ancient Egyptians had, however, other blues, of which we have already mentioned their counterfeit Armenian blue, and several vitreous blues, with which they decorated their figures and mummies.

Ultramarine dries well, works well in oil and fresco, and neither gives nor receives injury from other good pigments. It has so much of the quality of light in it, and of the tint of air,—is so purely a sky colour, and is hence so singularly adapted to the direct and reflex light of the sky, and to become the antagonist of sunshine,—that it is indispensable to the landscape-painter; and it is so pure, so true, and so unchangeable in its tints and glazings, as to be no less essential in imitating the exquisite colouring of nature in flesh and flowers.

To this may be added, that it enters so admirably into purples, blacks, greens, greys, and broken colours, that it has justly obtained the reputation of clearing or carrying light and air into all colours both in mixture and glazing, and a sort of claim to universality throughout a picture.

It is true, nevertheless, that ultramarine is not always entitled to the whole of this commendation, being, as a precious material, subjected to *adulteration;* and it has been dyed, damped, and oiled to enrich its appearance: but these attempts of fraud may be easily detected, and the genuine may easily be distinguished from the spurious by dropping a few particles of the pigment into lemon-juice or any other acid, which almost instantly destroys the colour of the true ultramarine totally, and without effervescence. Ultramarine has been used in the arts from a very early period, and in the middle ages special stipulations were made in regard to its use in pictures; and it was a punishable offence for painters to use colours of an inferior quality—which, owing to the expensiveness of ultramarine in particular, they were likely to do.

Though unexceptionable as an oil colour, both in solid painting and glazing, it does not work so well as some other blues in water; but when extremely fine in texture, or when a considerable portion of gum, which renders it transparent, can be used with it to give it connection or adhesion while flowing, it becomes a pigment no less valuable in water painting than in oil; very little gum can however be employed with it when its vivid azure is to be preserved, as in illuminated manuscripts and missals.

Pure ultramarine varies in shade from light to dark, and in hue from pale warm azure to the deepest cold blue; the former of which, when impure in colour, is called *ultramarine ashes.*

FACTITIOUS ULTRAMARINE.

French and *German Ultramarine,* a variety of these, English, French, and German, have been before the public under various names. They are in general of deep rich blue colours, darker and less azure than fine ultramarine of the same depths, and answer to the same acid test, but are variously affected by fire and other agents: none of them, however, possess the merits of genuine ultramarine. Fire generally darkens these colours, but the best way of distinguishing factitious ultramarine from the natural is by the violent effervescence of the former when dropped into nitrous acid. They may be regarded as a great improvement upon the factitious blues of the palette, rivalling in depth, although not equalling in colour, the pure azure of genuine ultramarine, for which in some uses they may be substituted, and are a valuable acquisition in decoration where brilliancy is required.

These manufactured colours become darker when mixed with oil, and when used with gum or size as a medium require great care in mixing, for if too much of the medium be used, the colour dries much darker than the original powder, and, if too little, the blue is not fixed, but rubs off. These colours are largely used in printing, but as their hue is much injured by the yellow tinge of the oil with which they are mixed to form printing ink, it is advisable in fine work, and where purity of colour is required, to print in varnish only, and to dust the powder-blue over the sheets. The work is printed on highly glazed paper, and the colour thus adheres to the varnish only, and when dry the superfluous blue is dusted off.

COBALT BLUE

Is the name now appropriated to the modern improved blue prepared with metallic cobalt, or its oxides, although it properly belongs to a class of pigments including *Saxon blue*, *Dutch ultramarine*, *Thenard's blue*, *Royal blue*, *Hungary blue*, *Smalt*, *Zaffre* or *Enamel blue*, and *Dumont's blue*. These differ principally in the degrees of purity, and the nature of the earths with which they are compounded.

The first is the finest Cobalt blue, and may not improperly be called a blue lake, the colour of which is brought up by fire, in the manner of enamel blues; and it is, when well prepared, of a pure blue colour, tending neither to green nor purple, and approaching in brilliancy to the finest ultramarine. It has not, however, the body, transparency, and depth, nor the natural and modest hue, of the latter; yet it is superior in beauty to all other blue pigments. Cobalt blue works better in water than ultramarine in general does; and is hence an acquisition to those who have not the management of the latter, and also on account of its cheapness. It resists the action of strong light and acids, but its beauty declines by time and impure air.

It dries well in oil, does not injure or suffer injury from pigments in general, and may be used with a proper flux in enamel painting, and perhaps also in fresco.

Various appellations have been given to this pigment from its preparers and venders, and it has been called *Vienna blue, Paris blue, azure,* and, very improperly, *ultramarine.*

SMALT,

Sometimes called *Azure*, is an impure vitreous cobalt blue, prepared upon a base of silex, and much used by the laundress for neutralising the tawny or Isabella colour of linen, &c., under the name of *Powder-blue*. It is in general of a coarse gritty texture, light blue colour, and little body. It does not work so well as the preceding, but dries quickly, and resembles it in other respects;—it varies, however, exceedingly in its qualities; and the finer sort, called *Dumont's blue,* which is employed in water-colour painting, is remarkably rich and beautiful.

ROYAL BLUE

Is a deeper coloured and very beautiful smalt, and is also a vitreous pigment, principally used in painting on glass and enamel, in which uses it is very permanent; but in water and oil its beauty soon decays, as is no uncommon case with other vitrified pigments; and it is not in other respects an eligible pigment, being, notwithstanding its beautiful appearance, very inferior to other cobalt blues.

PRUSSIAN BLUE,

Otherwise called *Berlin blue, Parisian blue, Prussiate of Iron,* or *Cyanide of Iron,* is rather a modern pigment, produced by the combination of the prussic or hydrocyanic acid, iron, and alumina. It is of a deep and powerful blue colour, of vast body and considerable transparency, and forms tints of much beauty with white lead, though they are by no means equal in purity and brilliancy to those of cobalt and ultramarine, nor have they the perfect durability of the latter.

Notwithstanding Prussian blue lasts a long time under favourable circumstances, its tints fade by the action of strong light, and it is purpled or darkened by damp or impure air. It becomes greenish also sometimes by a development of the yellow oxide of iron, and it is therefore desirable to add to it a very small quantity of crimson lake, which in a great degree counteracts this tendency. The colour of this pigment has also the singular property of fluctuating, or of going and coming, under some changes of circumstances; which property it owes to the action and reaction by which it acquires and relinquishes oxygen alternately: and time has a neutralising tendency upon its colour. It must be used carefully in mixing, as it is very powerful, and so much of the colour with which it is to be mixed is often required to produce the desired tint, that a greater quantity is compounded than is wanted at the time, and waste is thus caused. The most advisable plan, say in compounding green, is to place the yellow first on the slab or palette, and to add the blue, little by little, until the exact tint is obtained.

It dries and glazes well in oil, but its great and principal use is in painting deep blues; in which its body secures its permanence, and its transparency gives force to its depth. It is also valuable in compounding deep purples with lake, and is a powerful neutraliser and component of black, and adds considerably to its intensity. It is a pigment much used when mixed with white lead in the common offices of painting, also in preparing blues for the laundress, in dyeing, and in compounding colours of various denominations. *Lime* and *Alkalis* injure or destroy this colour.

ANTWERP BLUE

Is a lighter-coloured and somewhat brighter Prussian blue, or ferro-prussiate of alumine, having more of the terrene basis, but all the other qualities of that pigment, except its depth. *Haarlem blue* is a similar pigment.

INDIGO,

Or *Indian blue*, is a pigment manufactured in the East and West Indies from several plants, but principally from the Anil or Indigofera. It is of various qualities, and has been long known, and of great use in dyeing.

In painting it is not so bright as Prussian blue, but is extremely powerful and transparent; hence it may be substituted for some of the uses of Prussian blue as the latter now is for indigo. It is of great body, and glazes and works well both in water and oil. Its relative permanence as a dye has obtained it a false character of extreme durability in painting, a quality in which it is nevertheless very inferior even to Prussian blue.

It is injured by impure air, and, in glazing, some specimens are firmer than others, but not durable; in tint with white lead they are all fugitive: when used, however, in considerable body in shadow, it is more permanent, but in all respects inferior to Prussian blue in painting. *Intense blue* is indigo refined by solution and precipitation, in which state it is equal in colour to Antwerp blue. By this process indigo also becomes more durable, and much more powerful, transparent, and deep. It washes and works admirably in water: in other respects it has the common properties of indigo. We have been assured by an eminent architect, that these blues of indigo have the property of pushing or detaching Indian ink from paper. The same is supposed to belong to other blues; but as this effect is chemical, it can hardly be an attribute of mere colour.

BLUE VERDITER

Is a blue oxide of copper, or precipitate of the nitrate of copper by lime, and is of a beautiful light blue colour. It is little affected by light; but time, damp, and impure air turn it green, and ultimately blacken it,—changes which ensue even more rapidly in oil than water; it is therefore by no means an eligible pigment in oil, and is principally confined to distemper painting and the uses of the paper-stainer, though it has been found to stand well many years in water-colour drawings and in crayon paintings when preserved dry. It has been improperly substituted for *Bice*.

SAUNDERS BLUE,

A corrupt name, from *Cendres Blues*, the original denomination probably of *ultramarine ashes*, is of two kinds, the natural and the artificial; the artificial is a verditer prepared by lime or an alkali from nitrate or sulphate of copper; the natural is a blue mineral found near copper-mines, and is the same as *Mountain blue*. A very beautiful substance of this kind, a *carbonate of copper*, both blue and green, is found in Cumberland. None of these blues of copper are, however, durable: used in oil, they become green, and, as pigments, are precisely of the character of verditers. *Schweinfurt blue* is a similar pigment.

CÆRULEUM.

This is a preparation from cobalt; it is of a much cooler tone than any other permanent blue, and is useful as a water colour. It has a very dense body, and therefore requires some skill in using. It is not adapted for mixing with oils, as the delicacy of its tone is thus injured.

BICE,

Blue, *Bice*, *Iris*, or *Terre Blue*, is sometimes confounded with the above copper blues; but the true bice is said to be prepared from the *lapis Armenius* of Germany and the Tyrol, and is a light bright hue. The true Armenian stone of the ancients was probably the lapis lazuli of later times, and the blue prepared therefrom the same as our ultramarine. Pale ultramarine may well supply the place of this pigment, but copper blues substituted for it are not to be depended on.

Ground smalts, blue verditer, and other pigments have passed under the name of bice; which has, therefore, become a very equivocal pigment, and its name nearly obsolete: nor is it at present to be found in the shops, although much commended by old writers on the art.

CHAPTER XII.

OF THE SECONDARY COLOURS.

ORANGE.

ORANGE is the first of the secondary colours in relation to light, being in all the variety of its hues composed of *yellow* and *red*. A true or perfect orange is such a compound of red and yellow as will neutralise a perfect blue in equal quantity either of surface or intensity, and the proportions of such compound are five of perfect red to three of perfect yellow. When orange inclines to red, it takes the names of *scarlet*, *poppy*, *coquilicot*, &c. In *gold* colour, &c., it leans towards yellow. It enters into combination with green in forming the tertiary *citrine*, and with purple it constitutes the tertiary *russet:* it forms also a series of warm semi-neutral colours with *black*, and harmonizes in contact and variety of tints with *white*.

Orange is an advancing colour in painting:—in nature it is effective at a great distance, acting powerfully on the eye: diminishing its sensibility in proportion to the strength of the light in which it is viewed; and it is of the hue and partakes of the vividness of sunshine, as it does also of all the powers of its components, red and yellow.*

This secondary is pre-eminently a *warm* colour, being the equal contrast or antagonist in this respect, as it is also in colour, to blue, to which the attribute of *coolness* peculiarly belongs: hence it is discordant when standing alone with yellow or with red, unresolved by their proper contrasts.

In the well-known fruit of the Aurantium, called *orange* from its golden hue, from which fruit this colour borrows its well-adapted name, nature has associated two primary colours with two primary tastes which seem to be analogous; a red and yellow compound colour, with a sweet and acid compound flavour.

The poets confound orange with its ruling colour yellow, and, by a metonymy, use in its place the terms golden, gilding, &c., as gilding sometimes supplies the place of this colour in painting

The list of original orange pigments is so deficient, that in some treatises orange is not even named as a colour, most of them being called reds or yellows: and orange being a colour compounded of red and yellow, the place of original orange pigments may be supplied by mixture of the two latter colours; by glazing one over the other; by stippling, or other modes of breaking and intermixing them in working, according to the nature of the work and the effect required. For reasons before given, mixed pigments are inferior to the simple or homogeneous in colour, working, and other properties: yet some pigments mix and combine more cordially than others. In oil the compounding of colours is more easily effected.

* The Oriflamme was the banner of St. Denis, identical with the Grecian Bacchus or Dionysios in sanctifying the soul. Its colour was purple azured and gold; the two colours producing orange were separated in the Oriflamme, but reunited in its name.—*Baron F. Portal.*

In mixing orange for water-colour painting, care must be taken that the colour is well stirred as each brushful is taken, in order that the two colours may not separate. This is particularly liable to be the case where a mineral and a vegetable colour are thus temporarily combined, as, for instance, vermilion and gamboge; the former of which, being very much heavier than the latter, sinks to the bottom, and the colour on the slab consists as it were of two strata, the lower pure vermilion and the upper simply gamboge. It is better to mix an orange in from two colours having similar bases, as in water colour, from gamboge and lake, &c.; in every case, however, the tint must be constantly stirred.

CHROME ORANGE

Is a beautiful orange pigment, and is one of the most durable and least exceptionable chromates of lead, and not of iron, as it is commonly called, or *Mars Scarlet*— another misnomer of this pigment, which is truly a subchromate of lead.

It is, when well prepared, of a brighter colour than vermilion, but is inferior in durability and body to the latter pigment, being liable to the changes and affinities of the chrome yellows in a somewhat less degree, but less liable to change than the orange oxide of lead. *Laque Mineral* is a French pigment, a species of chromic orange, similar to the above. This name is also given to orange oxide of iron, and *Chromate of Mercury*, which is improperly classed as a red with vermilion; for though it is of a bright ochrous red colour in powder, it is, when ground, of a bright orange ochre colour, and affords, with white, very pure orange-coloured tints. Nevertheless it is a bad pigment, since light soon changes it to a deep russet colour, and foul air reduces it to extreme blackness.

ORANGE OCHRE,

Called also *Spanish ochre*, &c., is a very bright yellow ochre burnt, by which operation it acquires warmth, colour, transparency, and depth. In colour it is moderately bright, forms good flesh tints with white, dries and works well both in water and oil, and is a very durable and eligible pigment. It may be used in enamel-painting, and has all the properties of its original ochre in other respects.

MARS ORANGE

Is an artificial iron ochre, similar to the above, of which we formerly prepared a variety brighter, richer, and more transparent than the above, and in other respects of the same character; but requiring to be employed cautiously with colours affected by iron, being more chemically active than native ochres, several of which and their compounds become orange by burning.

BURNT SIENNA EARTH

Is, as its name expresses, the *Terra di Sienna* burnt, and is of an orange russet colour. What has been said of orange ochre may be repeated of burnt Sienna earth. It is richer in colour, deeper, and more transparent, and works and dries better than *raw Sienna earth;* but in other respects has all the properties of its parent colour, and is permanent and eligible wherever it may be useful, and valuable in graining. *Light red* and *Venetian red*, before treated of, are also to be considered as impure, but durable orange colours; and several preparations of iron afford excellent colours of this class. Burnt Sienna is the best colour for shading gold. It works well on gold-leaf, when mixed with a small quantity of prepared ox-gall.

ORANGE LEAD

Is an oxide of lead of a more vivid and warmer colour than *red lead*, but in other respects does not differ essentially from that pigment in its qualification for the palette.

ORANGE ORPIMENT,

Or *Realgar*, improperly called also *Red orpiment*, since it is of a brilliant orange colour, inclining to yellow. There are two kinds of this pigment; the one *native*, the other *factitious*; the first of which is the *sandarac* of the ancients, and is of rather a redder colour than the factitious. They are the same in qualities as pigments, and differ not otherwise than in colour from *Yellow orpiment*, to which the old painters gave the orange hue by heat, and then called it *Alchymy* and *Burnt orpiment.*

ANTIMONY ORANGE

Is a *hydro-sulphuret of antimony* of an orange colour, which is destroyed by the action of strong light. It is a bad dryer in oil, injurious to many colours, and in no respect an eligible pigment either in oil or water.

ANOTTA,

Arnotta, *Annotto*, *Caruera*, *Chica*, *Terra Orleana*, *Roucou*, &c., are names of several vegetable substances of an orange red colour, brought from the West Indies; they are soluble in water and spirits of wine, but very fugitive and changeable, and not fit for painting. Anotta is principally used in dyeing, and in colouring cheese. It is also an ingredient in some lackers.

CHAPTER XIII.

OF GREEN.

GREEN, which occupies the middle station in the natural scale of colours and in relation to light and shade, is the second of the secondary colours: it is composed of the extreme primaries, *yellow* and *blue*, and is most perfect in hue when constituted in the proportions of *three* of yellow to *eight* of blue of equal intensities; because such a green will perfectly neutralise and contrast a perfect red in the proportions of *eleven* to *five* either of space or power, as adduced on our scale of Chromatic Equivalents. Of all compound colours, green is the most effective, distinct, and striking, affecting the mind with surprise and delight, when first produced by the mixture of blue and yellow; so dissimilar in its constituents does it appear to the untutored eye. Green, mixed with orange, converts it into the one extreme tertiary, *citrine;* and, mixed with purple, it becomes the other extreme tertiary, *olive:* hence its relations and accordances are more general, and it contrasts more agreeably with all colours, than any other individual colour. It has, accordingly, been adopted with perfect wisdom in nature as the general garb of the vegetable creation. It is, indeed, in every respect a central or middle colour, being the contrast and compensatory of the middle primary, *red*, on the one hand, and of the middle tertiary, *russet*, on the other: and, unlike the other secondaries, all its hues, whether tending to blue or yellow, are of the same denomination.

These attributes of green,* which render it so universally effective in contrasting of colours, cause it also

---

* In heraldry, sinople (the green of blazonry) also signified love, joy, abundance. "Archbishops," says Anselm, "wear a hat of sinople to become the least useful in compounding them, and the most apt to defile other colours in mixture; nevertheless it forms valuable semi-neutrals of the *olive* class with *black*, for of such subdued tones are the greens, by which the more vivid hues of nature are contrasted; accordingly, the various greens of foliage are always more or less semi-neutral in colour, declining into *grey*. As *green* is the most general colour of vegetable nature, and principal in foliage, so *red*, its harmonizing colour, and compounds of red, are most general and principal in flowers. *Purple* flowers are commonly contrasted with centres or variegations of bright *yellow*, as *blue* flowers are with like relievings of *orange;* and there is a prevailing hue, or character, in the green colour of the foliage of almost every plant, by which it is harmonized with the colours of its flowers.

The principal discord of green is blue; and when they approximate or accompany each other, they require to be resolved by the apposition of warm colours; and it is in this way that the warmth of distance and the horizon reconcile the azure of the sky with the greenness of the landscape. Its less powerful discord is yellow, which requires to be similarly resolved by a purple red, or its principles. In its tones green is cool or warm, sedate or gay, either as it inclines to blue or to yellow; yet it is in its general effects cool, calm, temperate, and refreshing; and, having little power in reflecting light, is in a mean degree a retiring colour, and readily subdued by distance; for the same reasons it excites the retina less than most colours, and is cool and grateful to the eye. As a colour individually, green is eminently beautiful and agreeable, but it is more particularly so when contrasted with its com-

with interlaced cords of green silk. . . . . Bishops likewise wear a hat of sinople."— *Baron F. Portal.*

pensating colour, red, as it often is in nature, and even in the green leaves and the young shoots of plants and trees; and they are the most generally attractive of all colours in this respect. They are hence powerful and effective colours on the feelings and passions, and require, therefore, to be subdued or toned to prevent excitement and to preserve the balance of harmony in painting.

The number of pigments of any colour is in general proportioned to its importance; hence the variety of greens is very great, though their classes are not very numerous. The following are the principal:—

MIXED GREENS.

Green being a compound of *blue* and *yellow*, pigments of these colours may be used to supply the place of green pigments, by compounding them in the several ways of working; by mixing, glazing, hatching, or otherwise blending them in the proportions of the hues and tints required. In compounding colours, it is desirable not only that they should agree chemically, but that they should also have, as much as may be, the same degree of durability; and in these respects Prussian or Antwerp blue and gamboge form a judicious, though not extremely durable, compound, similar to *Varley's green*, *Hooker's green*, &c., used in water. In common oil painting greens are formed by mixture of the ordinary blue and yellow pigments with additions of white. But these are less durable than the original green pigments prepared from copper, of which there are a great variety. But the yellow ochres with Prussian blue afford more eligible pigments than the brighter mixtures of chrome yellow afford. *Cobalt greens*, *chrome greens*, and *Prussian green* are names for similar mixtures.

TERRE-VERTE.

True Terre-Verte is an ochre of a bluish green not very bright, in substance moderately hard, and smooth in texture. It is variously a bluish or grey, coaly clay, combined with yellow oxide of iron or yellow ochre. Although not a bright, it is a very durable pigment, being unaffected by strong light and impure air, and combining with other colours without injury. It has not much body, is semi-transparent, and dries well in oil. There are varieties of this pigment; but the green earths which have copper for their colouring matter are, although generally of brighter colours, inferior in their other qualities, and are not true terre-vertes.

It has been called *Green Bice*, and the greens called *Verona green*, and *Verdetto*, or *Holly green*, are similar native pigments of a warmer colour. These greens are found in the Mendip Hills, France, Italy, and the Island of Cyprus, and have been employed as pigments from the earliest times.

CHROME GREENS,

Commonly so called, are compound pigments, of which chrome yellow is the principal colouring substance. These are also called *Brunswick green*, &c., and are compounds of chromate of lead with Prussian and other blue colours, constituting fine greens to the eye, suitable to some of the ordinary purposes of mechanic art, but unfit for fine art.

There is, however, a true chrome green, or *Native green*, the colouring matter of which is the pure oxide of chrome, and, being free from lead, is durable both against the action of the sun's light and impure air. It is of various degrees of transparency or opacity, and of several hues more or less warm or cool, which are all rather fine than brilliant greens, and afford pure natural and durable tints. *True Chrome greens* neither give nor receive injury from other pigments, and are eligible for either water or oil painting, in the latter of which they usually dry well. They afford valuable colours also in enamel painting. To this substance it is that the emerald owes its green colour.

COBALT GREENS.

There are two pigments of this denomination—the one a compound of cobalt blue and chromic yellow, which partakes of the qualities of those pigments, and may be formed by mixture,—the other, an original pigment prepared immediately from cobalt, with addition of oxide of iron, or zinc, which is of a pure but not very powerful green colour, and durable both in water and oil, in the latter of which it dries well. *Rinmann's green* is of this kind. Its habits are nearly the same as those of cobalt blue.

COPPER GREEN

Is the appellation of a class rather than of an individual pigment, under which are comprehended *Verdigris, Verditer, Malachite, Mineral green, Green bice, Scheele's green, Schweinfurt* or *Vienna green, Hungary green, Emerald green,* true *Brunswick green, Green lake, Mountain green, African green, French green, Saxon green, Persian green, Patent green, Marine green, Olympian green,* &c. Old authors mention others under the names of individuals who prepare them, such are Verde de Barildo, &c.

The general characteristics of these greens are brightness of colour, well suited to the purposes of house-painting, but not in general adapted to the modesty of nature in fine art. They have considerable permanence, except from the action of damp and impure air, which ultimately blacken them: to which they have also a tendency by time. They have a good body, and dry well in oil, but, like the whites of lead, are all deleterious substances. We will particularise the principal sorts.

VERDIGRIS,

Or *Viride Æris*, is of two kinds, common or impure, and crystallized or *Distilled Verdigris*, or, more properly, refined verdigris. They are both acetates of copper, of a bright colour inclining to blue. They are the least permanent of the copper greens, soon fading as watercolours by the action of light, &c., and becoming first white, and ultimately black, by damp and foul air. In oil, verdigris is durable with respect to light and air, but moist and impure air changes its colour, and causes it to effloresce or rise to the surface through the oil. It dries rapidly, and might be useful as a siccific with other greens or very dark colours. Fresh ground in varnish it stands better; but is not upon the whole a safe or eligible pigment, either alone or compounded. Vinegar dissolves it, and the solution is used for tinting maps, &c. The addition of refined sugar, with gentle boiling, facilitates the solution and improves the colour.

GREEN VERDITER

Is the same in substance as blue verditer, which is converted into green verditer by boiling. This pigment has the common properties of the copper greens above mentioned, and is sometimes called *Green bice*.

EMERALD GREEN

Is the name of a copper green upon a terrene base. It is the most vivid of this tribe of colours, being rather opaque, and powerfully reflective of light, and appears to be the most durable pigment of its class. Its hue is not common in nature, but well suited for brilliant works. It works well in water, but with difficulty in oil, and dries badly therein. The only true emerald green is, however, that of chrome, with which metal nature gives the green colour to the emerald.

MINERAL GREEN

Is the commercial name of *Green lakes*, prepared from the sulphate of copper. These vary in hue and shade, have all the properties before ascribed to copper greens, and afford the best common greens; and, not being liable to change of colour by oxygen and light, stand the weather well, and are excellent for the use of the house-painter, &c.: but are less eligible in the nicer works of fine art, having a tendency to darken by time and foul air.

MOUNTAIN GREEN

Is a native carbonate of copper, combined with a white earth, and often striated with veins of mountain blue, to which it bears the same relation that green verditer does to blue verditer; nor does it differ from these and other copper greens in any property essential to the painter. The *Malachite*, a beautiful copper ore, employed by jewellers, is sometimes called *Mountain green*, and *Green bice* is also confounded therewith, being similar substances and of similar use as pigments. It is also called *Hungary green*, being found in the mountains of Kernhausen, as it is also in Cumberland.

SCHEELE'S GREEN

Is a compound oxide of copper and arsenic, or arsenite of copper, named after the justly celebrated chemist who discovered it. It is variously of a beautiful, light, warm, green colour, opaque, permanent in itself and in tint with white lead, but must be used cautiously with Naples yellow, by which it is soon destroyed. *Schwein-furt green* and *Vienna green* are also names of a fine preparation of the same kind as the above. These pigments are less affected by damp and impure air than the simple copper greens, and are therefore in these respects rather more eligible colours than the ordinary copper greens.

PRUSSIAN GREEN.

The pigment celebrated under this name is an imperfect prussiate of iron, or Prussian blue, in which the yellow oxide of iron superabounds, or to which yellow tincture of French berries has been added, and is not in any respect superior as a pigment to the compounds of Prussian blue and yellow ochre. A better sort of Prussian green is formed by precipitating the prussiate of potash with nitrate of cobalt.

SAP GREEN,

Or *Verde Vessie*, is a vegetable pigment prepared from the juice of the berries of the buckthorn, the green leaves of the woad, the blue flowers of the iris, &c. It is usually preserved in bladders, and is thence sometimes called *Bladder green;* when good, it is of a dark colour and glossy fracture, extremely transparent, and of a fine natural green colour. Though much employed as a water-colour without gum, which it contains naturally, it is a very imperfect pigment, disposed to attract the moisture of the atmosphere, and to mildew; and, having little durability in water-colour painting, and less in oil, it is not eligible in the one, and is totally useless in the other.

Similar pigments, prepared from coffee-berries, and called *Venetian* and *Emerald greens*, are of a colder colour, very fugitive, and equally defective as pigments.

INVISIBLE GREEN.

A good ordinary green of this denomination, for out-of-door painting and fresco, may be prepared by mixture of the yellow ochres with black in small quantities; or by adding black to any of the ordinary green pigments. See *Olive Pigments*.

CHAPTER XIV.

OF PURPLE.

PURPLE, the third and last of the secondary colours, is composed of *red* and *blue*, in the proportions of five of the former to eight of the latter, which constitute a perfect purple, or one of such a hue as will neutralise and best contrast a perfect yellow in the proportions of thirteen to three, either of surface or intensity. It forms, when mixed with its co-secondary colour, green, the tertiary colour, *olive;* and, when mixed with the remaining secondary orange, it constitutes in like manner the tertiary colour, *russet.* It is the coolest of the three secondary colours, and the nearest also in relation to *black* or shade; in which respect, and in never being a warm colour, it resembles blue. In other respects also purple partakes of the properties of blue, which is its ruling colour; hence it is to the eye a most retiring colour, which reflects light little, and declines rapidly in power in proportion to the distance at which it is viewed, and also in a declining light. It is the most retiring of positive colours.

Next to green, purple is the most generally pleasing of the consonant colours; and has been celebrated as a regal or imperial colour, as much perhaps from its rareness in a pure state, as from its individual beauty. When inclining to the rose, or red, this colour takes the names of *crimson*, &c., as it does those of *violet*, *lilac*, &c., when it inclines toward its other constituent, blue; which latter colour it serves to mellow, or follows well into shade.

The contrast, or harmonizing colour of purple, is yellow on the side of light and the primaries; and it is itself the harmonizing contrast of the tertiary *citrine* on the side of shade, and less perfectly so of the semineutral *brown*. Purple, when inclining towards redness, is a regal, magisterial, and pompous colour. In its effects on the mind it partakes principally, however, of the powers of its archeus or ruling colour, blue.

As the extreme primaries, blue and yellow, when either compounded or opposed, afford the most pleasing consonance of the primary colours, so the extremes, purple and orange, afford the most pleasing of the secondary consonances; and this analogy extends also to the extreme tertiary and semi-neutral colours, while the mean or middle colours afford the most agreeable contrasts or harmonies. Purple pigments are rare, and lie under a peculiar disadvantage as to apparent durability and beauty of colour, owing to the neutralising power of yellowness in the grounds upon which they are laid, as well as to the general warm colour of light, and the yellow tendency of almost all vehicles and varnishes, by which this colour is subdued; for the same reason this colour disappears by candle-light.

MIXED PURPLES.

Purple being a secondary colour, composed of *blue* and *red*, it follows of course that any blue and red pigments, which are not chemically at variance, may be used in producing mixed purple pigments of any required hue, either by compounding or grinding them together ready for use, or by combining them in the various modes of operation in painting. In such compounding, the more perfect the original colours are, the better in general will be the purple produced. In these ways, *ultramarine* and the *rose colours of madder* constitute excellent and beautiful purples, which are equally permanent in water and oil, in glazing or in tint, whether under the influence of the oxygenous or the hydrogenous principles of light and impure air, by which colours are subject to change. The blue and red of cobalt and madder afford also good purples. Some of the finest and most delicate purples in ancient paintings appear to have been similarly compounded of *ultramarine* and *vermilion*, which constitute tints equally permanent, but less transparent than the above. Facility of use, and other advantages, are obtained at too great a sacrifice by the employment of perishable mixtures, such as are the carmines and lakes of cochineal with *indigo and other blue colours;* but common purples may be composed of Prussian blue and vermilion with additions of white.

GOLD PURPLE,

Or *Cassius's Purple Precipitate*, is the compound oxide which is precipitated upon mixing the solutions of gold and tin. It is not a bright, but a rich and powerful colour, of great durability, varying in degrees of transparency, and in hue from deep crimson to a murrey or dark purple, and is principally used in miniature. It may be employed in enamel-painting, works well in water and is an excellent though expensive pigment, but not much used at present, as the madder purple is cheaper, and perfectly well supplies its place.

MADDER PURPLE,

Purple Rubiate, or *Field's Purple*, is a very rich and deep carmine, prepared from madder. Though not a brilliant purple, its richness, durability, transparency, and superiority of colour have given it the preference to the purple of gold preceding, and to burnt carmine. It is a pigment of great body and intensity; it works well, dries and glazes well in oil, and is pure and permanent in its tints, neither giving nor sustaining injury from other colours.

BURNT CARMINE

Is, according to its name, the carmine of cochineal partially charred till it resembles in colour the purple of gold, for the uses of which in miniature and water-painting it is substituted, and has the same properties except its durability; of which quality, like the carmine it is made from, it is deficient, and therefore in this important respect is an ineligible pigment. A durable colour of this kind may, however, be obtained by burning *madder carmine* in a cup over a spirit lamp or otherwise, stirring it till it becomes of the hue or hues required.

PURPLE LAKE.

The best purple lake so called is prepared from cochineal, and is of a rich and powerful colour, inclined to crimson. Its character as a pigment is that of the cochineal lakes already described. It is fugitive both in glazing and tint; but, used in considerable body, as in the shadows of draperies, &c., it will last under favourable circumstances a long time. Lac lake resembles it in colour, and may supply its place more durably, although not perfectly so.

PURPLE OCHRE,

Or *Mineral Purple*, is a dark ochre, native of the Forest of Dean in Gloucestershire. It is of a murrey or chocolate colour, and forms cool tints of a purple hue with white. It is of a similar body and opacity, and darker colour than *Indian red*, which has also been classed among purples, but in all other respects it resembles that pigment. It may be prepared artificially, and some natural red ochres burn to this colour, which has been employed under the denomination of *Violet de Mars*.

CHAPTER XV.

OF THE TERTIARY COLOURS.

CITRINE.

CITRINE is the first of the tertiary class of colours, or ultimate compounds of the primary triad, *yellow, red,* and *blue;* in which *yellow* is the predominating colour, and blue the extreme subordinate; for citrine being an immediate compound of the secondaries, *orange* and *green,* of both which *yellow* is a constituent, the latter colour is of double occurrence therein, while the other two primaries enter singly into the composition of citrine,—its mean or middle hue comprehending eight blue, five red, and six yellow, of equal intensities.

Hence citrine, according to its name, which is the name of a class of colours, and is used commonly for a dark yellow, partakes in a subdued degree of all the powers of its archeus, yellow; and, in estimating its properties and effects in painting, it is to be regarded as participating of all the relations of yellow. By some this colour is improperly called brown, as almost all broken colours are. The harmonizing contrast of citrine is a *deep purple;* and it is the most advancing of the tertiary colours, or nearest in its relation to light. It is variously of a tepid, tender, modest, cheering character, and expressive of these qualities alike in painting and poetic art. In nature, citrine begins to prevail in landscape before the other tertiaries, as the green of summer declines; and as autumn advances it tends towards its orange hues, including the colours called aurora, chamoise, and others before enumerated under the head of *Yellow.*

To understand and relish the harmonious relations and expressive powers of the tertiary colours, requires a cultivation of perception and a refinement of taste for which study and practice are requisite. They are at once less definite and less generally evident, but more delightful,—more frequent in nature, but rarer in common art, than the like relations of the secondaries and primaries; and hence the painter and the poet afford us fewer illustrations of effects less commonly appreciated or understood.

Original citrine-coloured pigments are not numerous, unless we include several imperfect yellows, which might not improperly be called citrines: the following are, however, the pigments best entitled to this appellation :—

MIXED CITRINE.

What has been before remarked of the mixed secondary colours is more particularly applicable to the tertiary, it being more difficult to select three homogeneous substances, of equal powers as pigments, than two, that may unite and work together cordially. Hence the mixed tertiaries are still less perfect and pure than the secondaries; and as their hues are of extensive use in painting, original pigments of these colours are proportionately estimable to the artist. Nevertheless, there are two evident principles of combination, of which the artist may avail himself in producing these colours in the various ways of working: the one being that of combining two original secondaries,—*e.g.*, *green and orange* in producing a *citrine;* the other, the uniting the three primaries in such a manner that *yellow* predominates in the case of citrine, and *blue and red* be subordinate in the compound.

These colours are, however, in many cases produced with best and most permanent effect, not by the intimate combination of pigments but by intermingling them, in the manner of nature, on the canvas, so as to produce the effect at a proper distance of a uniform colour. Such is the *citrine* colour of fruit and foliage; on inspecting the individuals of which we distinctly trace the stipplings of orange and green, or yellow, red, and green. Similar beautiful consonances are observable in the *russet* hues of foliage in the autumn, in which purple and orange have broken or superseded the uniform green of leaves: and also in the *olive* foliage of the rose-tree, produced in the individual leaf by the ramification of purple in green. Yet mixed citrines may be compounded safely and simply by slight additions, to an original brown pigment, of that primary or secondary tone which is requisite to give it the required hue, and red and yellow ochres mixed form good common paints of this colour.

BROWN PINK

Is a vegetable lake precipitated from the decoction of French berries and dyeing woods, and is sometimes the residuum of the dyer's vat. It is of a fine, rich transparent colour, rarely of a true brown; but being in general of an orange broken by green, it falls into the class of citrine colours, sometimes inclining to greenness, and sometimes toward the warmth of orange. It works well both in water and oil, in the latter of which it is of great depth and transparency, but dries badly. Its tints with white lead are very fugitive, and in thin glazing it does not stand. Upon the whole, it is more beautiful than eligible.

UMBER,

Commonly called *Raw Umber*, is a natural ochre, abounding with oxide of manganese, said to have been first obtained from ancient Ombria, now Spoleto, in Italy; —it is found also in England, and in most parts of the world; but that which is brought from Cyprus, under the name of Turkish umber, is the best. It is of a brown-citrine colour, semi-opaque, has all the properties of a good ochre, is perfectly durable both in water and oil, and one of the best drying colours we possess, and injures no other good pigment with which it may be mixed. (See *Cappagh Brown*, some specimens of which are of a citrine hue.) Although not so much employed as formerly, umber is perfectly eligible according to its colour and uses, in graining, &c.

Several browns, and other ochrous earths, approach also to the character of citrine; such are the Terre de Cassel, Bistre, &c. But in the confusion of names, infinity of tones and tints, and variations of individual pigments, it is impossible to attain an unexceptionable or universally satisfactory arrangement.

CHAPTER XVI.

OF RUSSET.

The second or middle tertiary colour, *Russet*, like citrine, is constituted ultimately of the three primaries, *red, yellow*, and *blue;* but with this difference, that instead of yellow as in citrine, *red* is the predominating colour in russet, to which yellow and blue are subordinates: for *orange* and *purple* being the immediate constituents of russet, and **red** being a component part of each of those colours, it enters doubly into their compound in russet, while yellow and blue enter it only singly; the proportions of its middle hue being eight blue, ten red, and three yellow, of equal intensities. It follows that the russet takes the relations and powers of a subdued red; and many pigments and dyes of the latter denomination are in strictness of the class of russet colours: in fact, nominal distinction of colours is properly only relative; the gradation from hue to hue, as from shade to shade, constituting an unlimited series, in which it is literally impossible to pronounce absolutely where any shade or colour ends and another begins.

The harmonizing, neutralising, or contrasting colour of russet is a *deep green;*—when the russet inclines to orange, it is a *grey*, or subdued blue. These are often beautifully opposed in nature, being medial accordances, or in equal relation to light, shade, and other colours, and among the most agreeable to sense.

Russet, we have said, partakes of the relations of red, but moderated in every respect, and qualified for greater breadth of display in the colouring of nature and art; less so, perhaps, than its fellow-tertiaries in proportion as it is individually more beautiful, the powers of beauty being ever most effective when least obtrusive; and its presence in colour should be principally evident to the eye that seeks it. This colour is warm, complacent, solid, frank, and soothing. Common acceptation substitutes the term brown for russet.

Of the tertiary colours, russet is the most important to the artist; and there are many pigments under the denominations of red purple, &c., which are of russet hues. But there are few true russets, and one only which bears the name: of these are the following:—

MIXED RUSSET.

What has been remarked in the preceding chapter upon the production of mixed citrine colours, is equally applicable in general to the mixed russets: we need not, therefore, repeat it. By the immediate method of producing it materially from its secondaries, orange and purple ochres afford a compound russet pigment of a good and durable colour. Chrome-orange and purple-lake yield a similar but less permanent mixture.

Many other less eligible duple and triple compounds of russet are obvious upon principle, and it may be produced by adding red in due predominance to some browns; thus red and brown ochre duly mixed afford a good ordinary russet paint.

FIELD'S RUSSET,

Or *Madder Brown*, is, as its name indicates, prepared from the *Rubia tinctoria*, or madder-root. It is of a pure, rich, transparent, and deep russet colour, introduced by the author, and is of a true middle hue between orange and purple; not subject to change by the action of light, impure air, time, or mixture of other pigments. It has supplied a great desideratum, and is indispensable in water-colour painting, both as a local and auxiliary colour, in compounding and producing with yellow the glowing hues of autumnal foliage, &c., and with blue the beautiful and endless variety of greys in skies, flesh, &c. There are three kinds of this pigment, distinguished by variety of hue—russet, or *madder brown*, *orange russet*, and dark russet, or *intense madder brown*; which differ not essentially in their qualities as pigments, but as warm or cool russets, and are all good glazing colours, thin washes of which afford pure flesh-tints in water. The last dries best in oil, the others but indifferently. It is a valuable pigment in the graining of mahogany.

PRUSSIATE OF COPPER

Differs chemically from Prussian blue only in having copper instead of iron for its basis. It varies in colour from russet to brown, is transparent and deep, but being very liable to change in colour by the action of light and by other pigments, has been very little employed by the artist.

There are several other pigments which enter imperfectly into, or verge upon, the class of russet, which, having obtained the names of other classes to which they are allied, will be found under other heads; such are some of the ochres and Indian red. Burnt carmine and Cassius's precipitate are often of the russet hue, or convertible to it by due additions of yellow or orange; as burnt Sienna earth and various browns are, by like additions of lake or other reds.

RUSSET OCHRE.

Although there is no pigment of this name in the shops, many of the native ochres are of this denomination of colour, and may be employed accordingly; and the red and yellow ochres of commerce ground together and burnt afford excellent russet colours in every mode of painting.

CHAPTER XVII.

OF OLIVE.

OLIVE is the third and last of the tertiary colours, and nearest in relation to shade. It is constituted, like its co-tertiaries, citrine and russet of the three primaries, *blue*, *red*, and *yellow*, so subordinated, that blue prevails therein; but it is formed more immediately of the secondaries, *purple* and *green:* and, since blue enters as a component principle into each of these secondaries, it occurs twice in the latter mode of forming olive, while red and yellow occur therein singly and subordinately. *Blue* is, therefore, in every instance, the archeus, or predominating colour of olive; its perfect or middle hue comprehending SIXTEEN of blue to FIVE of red, and THREE of yellow; and it participates in a proportionate measure of the powers, properties, and relations of blue: accordingly, the antagonist, or harmonizing contrast of olive, is a *deep orange;* and, like blue also, it is a retiring colour, the most so of all the colours, being nearest of all in relation to *black*, and last of the regular distinctions of colours. Hence its importance in nature and painting is almost as great as that of black: it divides the office of clothing and decorating the general face of nature with green and blue; with both which, as with black and grey, it enters into innumerable compounds and accordances, changing its name, as either hue predominates, into *green*, *grey*, *ashen*, *slate*, &c.:

thus the olive hues of foliage are called *green*, and the purple hues of clouds are called *grey*, &c., for language is general only, and inadequate to the infinite particularity of nature and colours.

As olive is usually a compound colour both with the artist and mechanic, and as there is no natural pigment in use under this name, or of this colour, in commerce there are few olive pigments. *Terre-vert*, already mentioned, is sometimes of this class, and several of the copper greens acquire this hue by burning. The following need only to be noticed :—

MIXED OLIVE

May be compounded in several ways; directly, by uniting *green* and *purple*, or by adding to *blue* a smaller proportion of *yellow* and *red*, or by breaking much blue with little orange. Cool black pigments mixed with yellow ochre afford good olives. These hues are called *green* in landscape, and *invisible green* in mechanic painting.

OLIVE GREEN.

The fine pigment sold under this name, principally as a water-colour, is an arbitrary compound, or mixed green, eligible for its uses. Any ordinary green mixed with black forms this colour for exterior painting in oil, &c. And an olive-green paint may be economically prepared by the mixing of yellow or brown ochre with black, which may be varied by additions of blue or green.

BURNT VERDIGRIS

Is what its name expresses, and is an olive-coloured oxide of copper deprived of acid. It dries remarkably well in oil, and is more durable; and, in other respects, an improved and more eligible pigment than the original verdigris. Scheele's green affords by burning also a series of similar olive colours, which are as durable as their original pigment, and most of the copper greens may be subjected to the same process with the same results; indeed, we have remarked in many instances that the action of fire anticipates the effects of long-continued time, and that many of the primary and secondary colours may, by different degrees of burning, be converted into their analogous secondary and tertiary, or semi-neutral colours, that come usefully into the graining of rosewood, &c.

CHAPTER XVIII.

OF SEMI-NEUTRAL COLOURS.

BROWN.

As colour, according to the regular scale descending from *white*, properly ceases with the class of *olive*, the neutral *black* would here naturally terminate the series; but as, in a practical view, every coloured pigment, of every class or tribe, combines with black as it exists in pigments, a new series or scale of coloured compounds arises, having black for their basis, which, though they differ not theoretically from the preceding order inverted, are nevertheless practically imperfect or impure; in which view, and as compounds of black, we have distinguished them by the term *semi-neutral*, and divided them into three classes, Brown, Marrone, and Grey. Inferior as the semi-neutral are in point of colour, they comprehend, nevertheless, a great proportion of our most permanent pigments; and are, with respect to black, what *tints* are with respect to white, *i.e.*, they are, so to call them, black tints, or shades.

The first of the semi-neutral, and the subject of the present chapter, is BROWN, which, in its widest acceptation, has been used to comprehend vulgarly every denomination of dark broken colour, and, in a more limited sense, is the rather indefinite appellation of a very extensive class of colours of warm or tawny hues. Accordingly we have browns of every denomination of colours except blue; thus we have yellow-brown, red-brown, orange-brown, purple-brown, &c., but it is remarkable that we have, in this sense, no blue-brown nor any other coloured-brown, in any but a forced sense, in which blue predominates; such predominance of a cold colour immediately carrying the compound into the class of grey, ashen, or slate-colour. Hence brown comprehends the hues called feuillemort, mort d'ore, dun, hazel, auburn, &c.; several of which we have already enumerated as allied to the tertiary colours.

The term *brown*, therefore, properly denotes a warm, broken colour, of which *yellow* is a principal constituent: hence brown is in some measure to shade what yellow is to light, and warm or ruddy browns follow yellows naturally as shading or deepening colours. It is hence also that *equal quantities* of either of the three primaries, the three secondaries, or the three tertiaries, produce variously a brown mixture, and not the neutral black, &c.; because no colour is essentially single, and warmth belongs to two of the primaries, but coldness to blue alone. Browns contribute to coolness and clearness by contrast when opposed to pure colours: hence their vast importance in painting and the necessity of keeping them from other colours, to which they give foulness in mixture.

The tendency in the compounds of colours to run into brownness and warmth is one of the general natural properties of colours, which occasions them to deteriorate or dirt each other in mixture: hence *brown* is synonymous with foul or defiled, in a sense opposed to *fair* and pure; and it is hence, also, that brown, which is the nearest of the semi-neutrals in relation to light, is to be avoided in mixture with light colours.

This tendency will account also for the use of brown in harmonizing and toning, and for the great number of natural and artificial pigments and colours we possess under this denomination: in fact, the failure to produce other colours chemically or by mixture is commonly productive of a brown; yet are fine transparent browns obviously very valuable colours. If red or blue be added to brown predominantly, it falls into the other semi-neutral classes, marrone or grey.

The wide acceptation of the term brown has occasioned much confusion in the naming of colours, since broken colours in which red, &c., predominate, have been improperly called brown; and a tendency to red or hotness in browns obtains for them the reproachful appellation of *foxiness*. This term, brown, should therefore, be confined to the class of semi-neutral colours compounded of, or of the hues of, either the *primary yellow, the secondary orange, or the tertiary citrine, with a black pigment;* the general contrast or harmonizing colour of which will consequently be more or less purple or grey; and with reference to black and white, or light and shade, it is of the semi-neutrals the nearest in accordance with white and light.

Brown is a sober and sedate colour, grave and solemn, but not dismal, and contributes to the expression of strength, stability, and solidity, vigour, and warmth, and in minor degree to the serious, the sombre, and the sad.

The list of brown pigments is very long, and that of MIXED BROWNS literally endless, it being obvious that every warm colour mixed with black will afford a brown, and that equal portions of the primaries, secondaries, or tertiaries will do the same: hence there can be no difficulty in producing them by mixture when required, which is seldom, as there are many browns which are good and permanent pigments; among these are the following:—

VANDYKE BROWN.

This pigment, hardly less celebrated than the great painter whose name it bears, is a species of peat or bog earth of a fine, deep, semi-transparent brown colour. The pigment so much esteemed and used by Vandyke is said to have been brought from Cassel; and this seems to be justified by a comparison of *Cassel-earth* with the browns of his pictures. The Vandyke browns in use at present appear to be terrene pigments of a similar kind, purified by grinding and washing over: they vary sometimes in hue and in degrees of drying in oil, which they in general do tardily, owing to their bituminous nature, but are good browns of powerful body, and are durable both in water and oil. The *Campania brown* of the old Italian painters was a similar earth.

MANGANESE BROWN

Is an oxide of manganese, of a fine, deep, semi-opaque brown of good body, which dries admirably well in oil. It is deficient in transparency, but may be a useful colour for glazing or lowering the tone of white without tinging it, and as a local colour in draperies, dead colouring, &c. It is a perfectly durable colour both in water and oil.

CAPPAGH BROWN,

Or *Euchrome*, is a *Native Manganese Brown*, found on the estate of Lord Audley, at Cappagh, near Cork. It is a bog-earth or peat, mixed or mineralized by manganese in various proportions. The specimens in which the peat earth most abounds are of light weight, friable texture, and dark colour; those which contain more of the metal are heavy and of a lighter colour.

As pigments, the peaty Cappagh brown is the most transparent, deep and rich in colour, and dries promptly in oil, during which its surface rivels where it lies thick. This may be regarded as a superior Vandyke brown and Asphaltum.

The other and metallic sort is a less transparent, lighter, and warmer brown pigment, which dries rapidly and smoothly in a body or thick layer, and is a superior Umber. They do not keep their place while drying in oil by fixing the oil, like the dryers of lead, but run. The two extreme sorts should be distinguished as *light* and *deep* Cappagh browns; the first excellent for dead colouring, and grounds, the latter for glazing and graining. These pigments are equally applicable to painting in water, oil, and varnish, working well in each of these vehicles. They have been introduced into commerce for civil and marine painting under the names of *Euchrome* and *Mineral brown*, and have been called Caledonian, but are more properly Hibernian, browns, and are fine colours and valuable acquisitions in all their uses, and especially so in the graining of oak, &c.

BURNT UMBER

Is the fossil pigment called Umber, burnt, by which it becomes of a deeper and more russet hue. It contains manganese and iron, and is very drying in oil, in which it is employed as a dryer. It may be substituted for Vandyke brown, is a perfectly durable and eligible pigment in water, oil, and fresco, and may be produced artificially. The old Italians called it *falsalo*.

CASSEL EARTH,

Or, corruptly, *Castle earth*. The true *terre de Cassel* is an ochrous pigment similar to the preceding, but of a brown colour, more inclined to the russet hue. In other respects it does not differ essentially from Rubens and Vandyke browns.

COLOGNE EARTH,

Incorrectly called *Cullen's earth*, is a native pigment, darker than the two last, and in no respect differing from Vandyke brown in its uses and properties as a colour. Similar earths abound in our own country. They are all bituminous ochres.

RUBENS' BROWN.

The pigment still in use in the Netherlands under this appellation is an earth of a lighter colour and more ochrous texture than the Vandyke brown of the London shops; it is also of a warmer or more tawny hue than the latter pigment, and is a beautiful and durable brown, which works well both in water and oil, and much resembles the brown used by Teniers.

BROWN OCHRE.

See *Yellow Ochre*. *Iron Brown*, *Brun de Mars*, and *Prussian Brown* may be regarded as various kinds of brown ochre, of which there is abundance in nature, and all imitable by art. See *Spanish Brown*, or *Tiver*, and *Red Ochre*.

BONE BROWN

And *Ivory Brown* are produced by torrefying, or roasting, bone and ivory till by partially charring they become of a brown colour throughout. They may be made to resemble the five first browns above by management in the burning; and though much esteemed by some artists, are not perfectly eligible pigments, being bad dryers in oil; and their lighter shades not durable either in oil or water when exposed to the action of strong light, or mixed in tint with white lead. The palest of these colours are also the most opaque: the deepest are more durable, and most so when approaching black.

ASPHALTUM,

Called also *Bitumen*, *Mineral Pitch*, *Jews' Pitch*, &c., is a resinous substance rendered brown by the action of fire, natural or artificial. The substances employed in painting under this name are residua of the distillation of various resinous and bituminous matters in preparing their essential oils, and are all black and glossy, like common pitch, which differs from them only in having been less acted upon by fire, and in thence being softer. Asphaltum is principally used in oil-painting; for which purpose it is first dissolved in oil of turpentine, by which it is fitted for glazing and shading. Its fine brown colour and perfect transparency are lures to its free use with many artists, notwithstanding the frequent destruction which awaits the work on which it is much employed, owing to its disposition to contract and crack by changes of temperature and the atmosphere; but for which it would be a most beautiful, durable, and eligible pigment. The solution of asphaltum in turpentine, united with drying oil, by heat, or the bitumen torrefied and ground in linseed or drying-oil, acquires a firmer texture, but becomes less transparent, and dries with difficulty. If also common asphaltum, as usually prepared with oil of turpentine, be used with some addition of Vandyke brown, umber, or Cappagh brown ground in drying-oil, it will acquire body and solidity which will render it much less disposed to crack, and give it the qualities of native asphaltum; nevertheless, asphaltum is to be regarded in practice rather as a dark varnish than as a solid pigment, and all the faults of a bad varnish are to be guarded against in employing it. This pigment is now prepared in excessive abundance, as a product of the distillation of coal at the gas manufactories.

The native bitumen, Asphaltum, brought from Persia by Lieutenant Ford, had a powerful scent of garlic when rubbed. In the fire it softened without flowing, and burnt with a lambent flame; did not dissolve by heat in oil of turpentine, but ground easily as a pigment in pale drying-oil, affording a fine, deep, transparent brown colour, resembling that of the asphaltum of the shops; dried firmly, nearly as soon as the drying-oil alone, and worked admirably both in water and oil. Asphaltum may be used as a permanent brown in water, and the native kind is also superior to the artificial for this purpose, and would be useful from its transparent richness in graining.

MUMMY,

Or *Egyptian brown*, is also a bituminous substance combined with animal remains, brought from the catacombs of Egypt, where liquid bitumen was employed three thousand years ago in embalming; in which office it has combined, by a slow chemical change, during so many ages, with substances which give it a more solid and lasting texture than simple asphaltum: but in this respect it varies exceedingly, even in the same subject. Its other properties and uses as a pigment are the same as those of asphaltum, for which it is employed as a valuable substitute, being less liable to crack or move on the canvas. This also may be used, when ground, as a water-colour.

ANTWERP BROWN

Is a preparation of asphaltum ground in strong drying-oil, by which it becomes less liable to crack. See the two last articles. Ochrous bitumens, bituminous coal, jet, and other bituminous substances, afford similar browns. See also *Cappagh Brown*.

BISTRE

Is a brown pigment extracted by watery solution from the soot of wood-fires, whence it retains a strong pyroligneous scent. It is of a wax-like texture, and of a citrine-brown colour, perfectly durable. It has been much used as a water-colour, particularly by the old masters in tinting drawings and shading sketches, previously to Indian ink coming into general use for such purposes. In oil it dries with the greatest difficulty.

A substance of this kind collects at the back of fire-places in cottages where peat is the constant fuel burnt; which, purified by solution and evaporation, affords a fine bistre. Scotch bistre is of this kind. All kinds of bistre attract moisture from the atmosphere.

SEPIA,

Seppia or *Animal Æthiops*. This pigment is named after the Sepia, or *cuttle-fish*, which is called also the *ink-fish*, from its affording a dark liquid, which was used as an ink and pigment by the ancients. From this liquid our pigment sepia, which is brought principally from the Adriatic, and may be obtained from the fish on our own coasts, is said to be extracted; and it is supposed that it enters into the composition of the *Indian ink* of the Chinese. Sepia is of a powerful dusky brown colour, of a fine texture, works admirably in water, combines cordially with other pigments, and is very permanent.

It is much used as a water-colour, and in making drawings in the manner of bistre and Indian ink; but is not used in oil, in which it dries very reluctantly.

MADDER BROWN.

See Field's *Russet* (page 85). Brown Pink (page 83).

PRUSSIAN BROWN

Is a preparation of Prussian blue, from which the blue colouring principle has been expelled by fire, or extracted by an alkaline ley; it is an orange-brown, of the nature and properties of Sienna earth, and dries well in oil.

CHAPTER XIX.

OF GRAY.

Of the tribe of semi-neutral colours, GRAY is the third and last, being nearest in relation of colour to black. In its common acceptation, and that in which we here use it, gray denotes a class of cool cinereous colours, faint of hue; whence we have blue grays, olive grays, green grays, purple grays, and grays of all hues, in which blue predominates; but no yellow or red grays, the predominance of such hues carrying the compounds into the classes of brown and marrone, of which gray is the natural opposite. In this sense the *semi-neutral* GRAY is distinguished from the *neutral* GREY, which springs in an infinite series from the mixture of the neutral *black* and *white* :—between *grays* and *grey*, however, there is no intermediate, since where *colour* ends in the one, *neutrality* commences in the other, and *vice versâ ;*—hence the natural alliance of the semi-neutral gray with black or shade; an alliance which is strengthened by the latent predominance of blue in black, so that in the tints resulting from the mixture of black and white, so much of that hue is developed as to give apparent colour to the tints. This affords the reason why the tints of black and dark pigments are colder than their originals, so much so as in some instances to answer the purposes of positive colours.

The *grays* are the natural cold correlatives, or contrasts, of the warm semi-neutral *browns;* and they are degradations of blue and its allies ;—hence *blue* added to brown throws it into or toward the class of grays, and hence grays are equally abundant in nature and necessary in art; for the grays comprehend in nature and painting a widely diffused and beautiful play of retiring colours in skies, distances, carnations, and the shadowings and reflections of pure light, &c.

According to the foregoing relations, grays favour the effects and force of warm colours, which in their turn also give value to grays, and by reconciling opposites give repose to the eye.

A misapplication of colouring, however true—such as looking at nature through a prism and painting its effects—in decorations, is but to produce a fool's paradise, and to excite wonder and false admiration, in place of true effect, sentiment, and repose.

As blue is the ruling power of all the colours which enter into the composition of grays, the latter partake of the relations and affections of blue. *Grave* sounds, like *grey* colours, are deep and dull; and there is a similarity of these terms in sound, signification, and sentiment, if even they are not of the same etymology: be this as it may, *gray* is almost as common with the poet, and in its colloquial use, as it is in nature and painting. The grays, like the other semi-neutrals, are sober, modest colours, contributing to the expression of cool, gloom, and sadness, bordering in these respects upon the powers of *black*, but aiding the livelier and more cheering expressions of other *colours* by connection and contrast.

MIXED GRAYS

Are formed not only by the compounding of black and white, which yields *neutral greys*, and of black and blue, black and purple, black and olive, &c., which yield the *semi-neutral grays* of clouds, &c., but these may be well imitated by the mixture of russet rubiate, or madder browns, with blues, which form transparent compounds, which are much employed; grays are, however, as above remarked, so easily produced, that the artist will in this respect vary and suit his practice to his purpose. The *lead colours* of common painting are formed by adding black to white lead in oil. They are very useful grounds and dead colourings for greens, &c.

NEUTRAL TINT.

Several mixed pigments of the class of gray colours sold for Neutral tint, variously composed of sepia and indigo or other blues, with madder or other lakes, are designed for water-colour painting only, in which they are found extremely useful. And here it may be proper to mention those other useful colours, sold under the name of tints, which belong to no particular denomination of pigments; but being compounds, the result of the experience of accredited masters in their peculiar modes of practice, serve to facilitate the progress of their pupils. Such are *Payne's grey, Harding's* and *Macpherson's tints*, usually sold ready prepared in cakes and boxes for miniature and water-painting. These are composed of pigments which associate cordially; nevertheless, the artist will in general prefer a dependence upon his own skill for the production of his tints in painting, both in water and oil.

ULTRAMARINE ASHES,

Or *Mineral Gray*, are the recrement of Lapis lazuli from which ultramarine has been extracted, varying in colour from dull gray to blue. Although not equal in beauty, and inferior in strength of colour, to ultramarine, they are extremely useful pigments, affording grays much more pure and tender than such as are composed of black and white, or other blues, and better suited to the pearly tints of flesh, foliage, the grays of skies, and the shadows of draperies, but are not necessary to the ordinary painter, who can form them of cheaper pigments.

PHOSPHATE OF IRON

Is a native ochre, which classes in colour with the deeper hues of ultramarine ashes, and is eligible for all their uses. It has received the appellation of *blue ochre*.

Slate clays and several native earths class with grays; but the colours of the latter are not durable, as they become brown by the oxidation of the iron they contain.

PLUMBAGO.

See *Black Lead*, which forms *grey* tints of greater permanence and purity than the blacks in general use, and it is now employed for this purpose with approved satisfaction by experienced artists.

For various grey tints, see page 25.

CHAPTER XX.

OF THE NEUTRAL.

BLACK.

BLACK is the last and lowest in the series or scale of colours descending—the opposite extreme from white—the maximum of colour. To be perfect it must be neutral with respect to colours individually, and absolutely transparent, or destitute of reflective power in regard to light; its use in painting being to represent shade or depths, of which it is the element in a picture and in colours, as white is of light.

As there is no perfectly pure and transparent black pigment, black deteriorates all colours in deepening them, as it does warm colours by partially neutralising them, but it combines less injuriously with cold colours. Though it is the antagonist or contrast of white, yet added to it in minute portion it in general renders white more neutral, solid, and local, with less of the character of light. Impure black is brown, but black in its purity is a cold colour, and communicates this property to all light colours; thus it *blues* white, *greens* yellow, *purples* red, and degrades blue and other colours; hence the artist errs who regards black as of nearest affinity to hot and brown colours.

It is the most retiring of all colours, which property it communicates to other colours in mixture. It heightens the effect of warm as well as of light colours by a double contrast when opposed to them, and in like manner subdues that of cold and deep colours; but in mixture or glazing these effects are reversed, by reason of the predominance of cold colour in the constitution of black: having, therefore, the double office of colour and of shade, black is perhaps the most important of all colours to the artist, both as to its use and avoidance.

Black is to be considered as a synthesis of the three primary colours, the three secondaries, or the three tertiaries, or of all these together; and, consequently, also of the three semi-neutrals, and may accordingly be composed of due proportions of either tribe or triad. All antagonist colours, or contrasts, also afford the neutral black by composition; but in all the modes of producing black by compounding colours, blue is to be regarded as its predominating colour, and yellow as subordinate to red, in the proportions, when their hues are true, of eight blue, five red, and three yellow. It is owing to this predominance of blue in the constitution of black, that it contributes by mixture to the pureness of hue in white colours, which in general incline to warmth, and it produces the cool effect of blueness in glazing and tints, or however otherwise diluted or dilated. It accords with the principle here inculcated that, in glass-founding, the oxide of manganese, which affords the *red* hue, and that of cobalt, which affords the *blue*, are added to brown or *yellow* frit to produce a velvety-black glass; and that the dyer proceeds to dye black upon a deep *blue* basis of indigo, with the *ruddy* colour of madder and the *yellow* of quercitron, galls, sumach, &c.; and experience coincides with principle in these practices, but if the principle be wanting the artist will often fail in his performances.

All colours are comprehended in the synthesis of black; consequently the whole sedative power of colour is comprised in black. It is the same in the synthesis of white; and, with like relative consequence, white comprehends all the stimulating powers of colour in painting. It follows that a little black or white is equivalent to much colour, and hence their use as colours requires judgment and caution in painting; and in engraving, black and white supply the place of colours, and hence a true knowledge of the active or sedative power of every colour is of great importance to the engraver.

By due attention to the synthesis of black it may be rendered a harmonizing medium to all colours, and it gives brilliancy to them all by its sedative effect on the eye, and its powers of contrast; nevertheless, we repeat, as a pigment it must be introduced with caution in painting when *hue* is of greater importance than *shade;* and black pigments produced by charring have a disposition to rise and predominate over other hues, and to subdue the more delicate tints by their chemical bleaching power upon other colours, and their own disposition to turn brown or dusky. And for these reasons deep and transparent colours, which have darkness in their constitution, are better adapted in general for producing true natural and permanent effects.

Black is to be regarded as a compound of all other colours, and the best blacks and neutrals of the painter are those formed with colours of sufficient power and transparency upon the palette; but most of the black pigments in use are produced by charring, and owe their colour to the carbon they contain: such are *Ivory* and *Bone blacks*, *Lamp black*, *Blue black*, *Frankfort black*, &c. The three first are most in use, and vary according to their modes of preparation or burning; yet fine *Frankfort black*, though principally confined to the use of the engraver and printer, is often preferable to the others.

Native or *mineral blacks* are heavy and opaque, but dry well.

Black pigments are innumerable: the following are, however, the principal, all of which are permanent colours:—

IVORY BLACK

And *Bone Black* are ivory and bone charred to blackness by strong heat in closed vessels. These pigments vary principally through want of care or skill in preparing them. When well made, they are fine neutral blacks, perfectly durable, and eligible both for oil and water-painting; but when insufficiently burnt they are brown, and dry badly; and when too much burnt, they are cineritious, opaque, and faint in colour. Of the two, ivory affords the best pigment; but bone black is used for general purposes.

LAMP BLACK,

Or *Lamblack*, is a smoke black, being the soot of resinous woods, obtained in the manufacturing of tar and turpentine. It is a pure carbonaceous substance, of a fine texture, intensely black, and perfectly durable, which works well, but dries badly in oil. This pigment may be prepared extemporaneously for water-painting by holding a plate over the flame of a lamp or candle, and adding gum-water to the colour: the nearer the plate is held to the wick of the lamp, the more abundant and warm will be the hue of the black obtained; at a greater distance it will be more effectually charred and blacker. This is a good substitute for Indian ink, the colouring basis of which appears to be lamp black. The *Nero di foglio* of the Italians is prepared from the smoke of burnt paper.

FRANKFORT BLACK

Is said to be made of the lees of wine from which the tartar has been washed, by burning, in the manner of ivory black. Similar blacks are prepared of *vine twigs and tendrils*, which contain tartar; also from *peach stones*, &c., whence *almond black* and *peach black;* and the Indians employ for the same purpose the *shell of the cocoa-nut:* and inferior Frankfort black is merely the levigated charcoal of woods, of which the hardest, such as box and ebony, afford the best. Fine Frankfort black, though almost confined to copper-plate printing, is one of the best black pigments we possess, being of a fine neutral colour, next in intensity to lamp black, and more powerful than that of ivory. Strong light has the effect of deepening its colour; yet the blacks employed in the printing of engravings have proved of very variable durability. It is probable that this black was used by some of the Flemish painters, and that the pureness of the grays formed therewith is attributable to the property of charred substances to prevent discolourment; although they have not the power of bleaching oils as they have of many other substances.

BLUE BLACK

Is also a well-burnt and levigated charcoal, of a cool, neutral colour, and not differing in other respects from the common Frankfort black above mentioned. Blue black was formerly much employed in painting, and, in common with all carbonaceous blacks, has, when duly mixed with white, a preserving influence upon that colour in two respects; which it owes, chemically, to the bleaching power of carbon, and, chromatically, to the neutralising and contrasting power of black with white. A superior blue black may be prepared by calcining Prussian blue in a close crucible, in the manner of ivory black; and it has the important property of drying well in oil; innumerable black pigments may be produced in this way by charring.

SPANISH BLACK

Is a soft black, prepared by burning *cork* in the manner of Frankfort and ivory blacks; and it differs not essentially from the former, except in being of a lighter and softer texture. It is subject to the variation of the above charred blacks, and eligible for the same uses. *Paper black*, the *Nero di foglio* of the Italians, often prepared in the same way, much resembles Spanish black, as does also Prussian black prepared by roasting Prussian blue.

MINERAL BLACK

Is a native impure oxide of carbon, of a soft texture, found in Devonshire and Wales. It is blacker than plumbago, and free from its metallic lustre,—is of a neutral colour, greyer and more opaque than ivory black,—forms pure neutral tints,—and being perfectly durable, and drying well in oil, it is valuable in dead-colouring on account of its solid body, as a preparation for black and deep colours before glazing. It would also be the most durable and best possible black for frescoes. *Russian black* is of this class.

MANGANESE BLACK.

The common black oxide of manganese answers to the character of the preceding pigment, and is the best of all blacks for drying in oil without addition, or preparation of the oil. It is also a colour of much body and tinging power.

BLACK OCHRE

Is a variety of the mineral black above, combined with iron and alluvial clay. It is found in most countries, and should be washed and exposed to the atmosphere before it is used. Sea-coal, and innumerable black mineral substances, have been, and may be, employed as succedanea for the more perfect blacks, when the latter are not procurable, which rarely happens.

BLACK CHALK

Is an indurated black clay, of the texture of white chalk, and is naturally allied to the preceding article. Its principal use is for cutting into crayons, which are employed in sketching and drawing.

Fine specimens have been found near Bantry in Ireland, and in Wales, but the Italian has the best reputation. Crayons for these uses are also prepared artificially, which are deeper in colour and free from grit. Charcoal of wood is also cut into crayons for the same purpose, and the charcoals of soft woods, such as lime, poplar, &c., are fittest for this use.

INDIAN INK.

The pigment well known under this name is principally brought to us from China in oblong cakes, of a musky scent, ready prepared for painting in water; in which use it is so well known, and so generally employed, as hardly to require naming. It varies, however, considerably in colour and quality, and is sometimes, properly, called *China ink*. Various accounts are given by authors of the mode of preparing this pigment, the principal substance or colouring matter of which is a smoke black, having all the properties of our lamp black; and the variety of its hues and texture seems wholly to depend upon the degree of burning and levigating it receives. The pigment known by the name Sepia is supposed to enter into the composition of the better sort. The colour of Indian Ink is improved by the addition of a small quantity of Indigo, and a still smaller portion of Lake, by which its tendency to turn brown is neutralised.

BLACK LEAD,

Plumbago, or *Graphite*, is a native carburet of iron or oxide of carbon, found in many countries, but nowhere more abundantly, or so fine in quality, as at Borrodale in Cumberland, where there are mines of it, from which the best is obtained, and consumed in large quantity in the formation of crayons and the black-lead pencils of the shops, which are in universal use in writing, sketching, designing, and drawing; for which the facility with which it may be rubbed out by Indian rubber or caoutchouc, gutta percha, and the crumb of bread admirably adapts it.

Although not acknowledged as a pigment, its powers in this respect claim a place for it, at least among water-colours; in which way, levigated in gum-water in the ordinary manner, it may be used effectually with rapidity and freedom in the shading and finishing of pencil-drawings, &c., and as a substitute therein for Indian ink. Even in oil it may be useful occasionally, as it possesses remarkably the property of covering.

forms very pure *grey* tints, dries quickly, injures no colour chemically, and endures for ever. These qualities render it the most eligible black for adding to white in minute quantity to preserve the neutrality of its tint.

Although plumbago has usurped the name of *Black Lead*, there is another substance more properly entitled to this appellation, and which may also be safely employed in the same manner, and with like effects as a pigment. This substance is the *Sulphuret of Lead*, either prepared artificially, or as found native in the beautiful lead ore, or *Galena*, of Derbyshire.

CHAPTER XXI.

TABLES OF PIGMENTS, ETC.

As there are circumstances under which some pigments may very properly and safely be used, which under others might prove injurious or destructive to the work, the following Lists or Tables are subjoined, in which they are classed according to various general properties, as guides to a judicious selection. These Tables are the results of direct experiments and observation, and are composed, without regard to the common reputation or variable character of pigments, according to the real merits of the various specimens tried.

As the properties and effects of pigments are much influenced by adventitious circumstances, and are sometimes varied or altogether changed by the grounds on which they are employed, by the vehicles in which they are used, by the siccatives and colours with which they are mixed, and by the varnishes by which they are covered, these Tables are offered only as approximations to the true characters of pigments and as general guides to right practice

TABLE I.

Of Pigments, the colours of which suffer different degrees of change by the action of light, oxygen, and pure air; but are little, or not at all, affected by shade, sulphuretted hydrogen, damp, and foul air:—

Yellow
- Yellow Lake
- Dutch ⎫
- English ⎬ Pink
- Italian ⎭
- Yellow Orpiment
- King's Yellow
- Chinese Yellow
- Gamboge
- Gallstone
- Indian Yellow

Red
- Rose Pink
- Carmine ⎫
- Common ⎬ Cochineal Lakes
- Florence ⎭
- Scarlet
- Hambro'

Blue
- Indigo
- Intense Blue
- Antwerp Blue
- Prussian Blue

Orange
- Orange Orpiment
- Golden Sulphur of Antimony

Green ...Sap Green

Purple
- Purple Lake
- Burnt Carmine
- Lac Lake

Brown
- Brown Pink
- Light Bone Brown, &c.

REMARKS.—None of the pigments in this Table are eminent for permanence. No white or black pigment whatever belongs to this class, nor does any tertiary, and a few only of the original semi-neutrals. Most of those included in the list fade or become lighter by time, and also, in general, less bright.

TABLE II.

Pigments, the colours of which are little, or not at all, changed by light, oxygen, and pure air; but are more or less injured by the action of shade, sulphuretted hydrogen, damp, and impure air :—

White	Common White Lead Flake White Crems White Roman White Venetian White Blanc d'Argent Sulphate of Lead		Blue ...	Blue Verditer Sanders Blue Mountain Blue Royal Blue Smalt and other Cobalt Blues
Yellow	Massicot Patent Yellow Jaune Minérale Chrome Yellow Naples Yellow		Orange	Orange Lead Orange Chrome Chromate of Mercury Laque Minérale
Red ...	Red Lead Chrome Red Dragon's Blood Iodine Scarlet		Green	Green Verditer Mountain Green Common Chrome Green Mineral Green Verdigris, and other Copper Greens

REMARKS.—Most of our best white pigments are comprehended in this Table, but no black, tertiary, or semi-neutral colour.

Many of these colours, when secured by oils, varnish, &c., may be long protected from change. The pigments of this Table may be considered as more durable than those of the preceding; they are nevertheless ineligible in a water-vehicle, and in fresco; and most of them become darker by time alone in every mode of use.

This list is the opposite of Table I.

TABLE III.

Pigments, the colours of which are subject to change by the action both of light and oxygen, and the opposite powers of sulphuretted hydrogen, damp, and impure air :—

White	Pearl or Bismuth White Antimony White	Yellow	Turbith Mineral Patent Yellow

Red ..	{ Iodine Scarlet Dragon's Blood	Orange	{ Sulphate of Antimony Anotta Carucru
Blue ..	{ Royal Blue Prussian Blue Antwerp Blue	Green	.. Verdigris
		Russet	.. Prussiate of Copper

REMARKS.—This Table comprehends our most imperfect pigments, and demonstrates how few absolutely bad have obtained currency. Indeed several of them are valuable for some uses, and not liable to sudden or extreme change by the agencies to which they are here subjected. Yet the greater part of them are destroyed by time.

These pigments unite the bad properties of those in the two preceding Tables.

TABLE IV.

Pigments not at all, or little, liable to change by the action of light, oxygen, and pure air; nor by the opposite influences of shade, sulphuretted hydrogen, damp and impure air; nor by the action of lead or iron:—

White	{ Zinc White Constant, or Barytic White Tin White The Pure Earths	Blue ..	{ Ultramarine Blue Ochre
Yellow	{ Yellow Ochre Oxford Ochre Roman Ochre Sienna Earth Stone Ochre Brown Ochre	Orange	{ Orange Ochre Jaune de Mars Burnt Sienna Earth Burnt Roman Ochre Light Red, &c.
		Green	{ Chrome Greens Terre-Verte Cobalt Green
Red ..	{ Vermilion Rubiates, or Madder Lakes Madder Carmines Red Ochre Light Red Venetian Red Indian Red	Purple	{ Gold Purple Madder Purple Purple Ochre
		Russet	{ Russet Rubiate, or Madder Brown Intense Russet

Brown and Semi-neutral	{ Vandyke Brown Bistre Raw Umber Burnt Umber Cassel Earth Cologne Earth Asphaltum Mummy, &c. Ultramarine Ashes Sepia Manganese Brown Cappagh Brown		Black	{ Ivory Black Lamp Black Frankfort Black Mineral Black Black Chalk Indian Ink Graphite

REMARKS.—This Table comprehends all the best and most permanent pigments, and such as are eligible for water and oil painting. It demonstrates that the best pigments are also the most numerous, and browns the most abundant, and in these respects stands opposed to the three Tables preceding.

TABLE V.

Pigments subject to change variously by the action of white lead and other pigments, and preparations of that metal:—

Yellow	{ Massicot Yellow Orpiment King's Yellow Chinese Yellow Gamboge Gall-stone Indian Yellow Yellow Lake Dutch } English } Pink Italian }		Blue .... Indigo	
			Orange	{ Orange Lead Orange Orpiment Golden Sulphur of Antimony Anotta, or Roucou Carucru, or Chica
Red ..	{ Iodine Scarlet Red Lead Dragon's Blood Common } Cochineal } Florence } Lakes Scarlet } Hambro' } Lac } Carmine Rose Pink		Green ... Sap Green	
			Purple	{ Purple Lake Burnt Carmine
			Citrine .. Brown Pink	

REMARKS.—Acetate or sugar of lead, litharge, and oils rendered drying by oxides of lead, are all in some measure destructive of these colours. Light, bright, and tender colours are principally susceptible of change by the action of lead.

The colours of this Table are very various in their modes of change, and thence do not harmonize well by time: it follows, too, that when any of these pigments are employed, they should be used pure or unmixed; and, by preference, in varnish: while their tints with white lead ought to be altogether rejected.

TABLE VI.

Pigments, the colours of which are subject to change by iron, its pigments, and other ferruginous substances:—

White { Sulphate of Lead / Blanc d'Argent

Yellow { King's Yellow / Patent Yellow / Naples Yellow / Chinese Yellow

Red .. { Iodine Scarlet / Carmine / Scarlet Lake

Blue .. { Blue Verditer / Mountain Blue / Intense Blue

Orange { Golden Sulphur of Antimony

Green { Verdigris / Green Verditer

Russet ...Prussiate of Copper

REMARKS.—Several other delicate pigments are slightly affected by iron and its preparations; and with all such, as also with those of the preceding Table, and with all pigments not well freed from acids or salts, the iron palette knife is to be avoided or used with caution, and one of ivory or horn substituted in its place. Nor can the pigments of this Table be in general safely combined with the ochres. Strictly speaking, that degree of friction which abrades the palette knife in rubbing of pigments therewith is injurious to every bright colour.

TABLE VII.

Pigments more or less transparent, and generally fit to be employed as graining and finishing colours, if not disqualified according to Tables I., II., and III. :—

Yellow
- Sienna Earth
- Gamboge
- Indian Yellow
- Gallstone
- Italian ⎫
- English ⎬ Pink
- Dutch ⎭
- Yellow Lake

Red
- Madder Carmine
- Madder Lakes
- Lac Lake
- Carmine
- Common ⎫
- Florence ⎬ Lakes
- Scarlet ⎮
- Hambro' ⎭
- Dragon's Blood
- Rose Pink

Blue
- Ultramarines
- Cobalt Blue
- Smalt
- Royal Blue
- Prussian Blue
- Antwerp Blue
- Intense Blue
- Indigo

Orange
- Madder Orange
- Anotta
- Burnt Sienna Earth
- Jaune de Mars

Green
- Chrome Green
- Sap Green
- Prussian Green
- Terre-Verte
- Verdigris

Purple
- Madder Purple
- Burnt Carmine
- Purple Lake
- Lac Lake

Citrine
- Brown Pink
- Citrine Lake

Russet
- Madder Brown
- Prussiate of Copper

Brown
- Vandyke Brown
- Cologne Earth
- Burnt Umber
- Bone Brown
- Asphaltum
- Mummy
- Brown Pink
- Antwerp Brown
- Bistre
- Sepia
- Prussian Brown

Gray.... Ultramarine Ashes

Black
- Ivory Black
- Bone Black
- Lamp Black
- Frankfort Black
- Blue Black
- Spanish Black

REMARKS.—This Table comprehends most of the best water-colours; and their most powerful effects in oil-painting are attainable by employing them with resinous varnishes. Pigments not inserted in this Table may of course be considered of an opposite class, or *opaque* colours; with which, nevertheless, transparent effects in painting are produced by the skill of the artist in breaking and mingling without mixing them, &c.

The great importance of transparent pigments is to unite, and give tone and atmosphere generally, with beauty and life, to solid or opaque colours of their own hues; to convert primary into secondary, and secondary into tertiary colours with brilliancy; to deepen and enrich dark colours and shadows, and to give force and tone to black itself.

TABLE VIII.

Pigments, the colours of which are little or not at all affected by heat or fire:—

White	Tin White, Barytic White, Zinc White, The Pure Earths		Orange	Orange Ochre, Jaune de Mars, Burnt Sienna Earth, Burnt Roman Ochre
Yellow	Naples Yellow, Patent Yellow, Antimony Yellow		Green	True Chrome Green, Cobalt Green
Red	Red Ochre, Light Red, Venetian Red, Indian Red		Purple	Gold Purple, Purple Ochre
Blue	Royal Blue, Smalt, Dumont's Blue and all Cobalt Blues, Ultramarine		Brown	Rubens' Brown, Burnt Umber, Cassel Earth, Cologne Earth, Antwerp Brown, Manganese Brown
			Black	Graphite, Mineral Black

REMARKS.—Many of the pigments of this Table are available in enamel painting, and most of them are durable in the other modes.

TABLE IX.

Pigments which are little or not at all affected by *lime*, and in various degrees eligible for fresco, distemper, and crayon painting:—

White	Barytic White Pearl White Gypsum, and all pure Earths	Green	Green Verditer Mountain Green Chrome Green Mineral Green Emerald Green Verdigris and other Copper Greens Terre-Verte Cobalt Green
Yellow	Yellow Ochre Oxford Ochre Roman Ochre Sienna Earth Stone Ochre Brown Ochre Indian Yellow Patent Yellow Naples Yellow Massicot	Purple	Gold Purple Madder Purple Purple Ochre
Red	Vermilion Red Lead Red Ochre Light Red Venetian Red Indian Red Madder Reds	Brown and Semineutral	Bone Brown Vandyke Brown Rubens' Brown Bistre Raw Umber Burnt Umber Cassel Earth Cologne Earth Antwerp Brown Chestnut Brown Asphaltum Mummy Ultramarine Ashes Manganese Brown
Blue	Ultramarine Smalt, and all Cobalt Blues		
Orange	Orange Lead Orange Chrome Laque Minérale Orange Ochre Jaune de Mars Burnt Sienna Earth Light Red, &c.	Black	Ivory Black Lamp Black Frankfort Black Mineral Black Black Chalk Indian Ink Graphite

REMARKS.—This Table shows the multitude of pigments from which the painters in fresco, scagliola, distemper, and crayons may select their colours; in doing which, however, it will be necessary they should consult the previous Tables respecting other qualities of pigments essential to their peculiar modes of painting, as these modes are exciting renewed interest in the world of art, tending to their extension in practice, particularly the latter of them.

TABLE X.
HERALDIC COLOURS.

Emblazoned.	Engraved.	Colours.	Gentlemen. Tincture.	Nobles. Jewels.	Sovereign Princes. Planets.	Signs.
(triangle)	Blank.	White.	Argent.	Pearl.	Luna.	☽
(dotted shield)	Dotted.	Yellow.	Or.	Topaz.	Sol.	☉
(vertically-lined shield)	Perpendicular lines.	Red.	Gules.	Ruby.	Mars.	♂
(horizontally-lined lozenge)	Horizontal lines.	Blue.	Azure.	Sapphire.	Jupiter.	♃

TABLE X. (continued).

Emblazoned.	Engraved.	Colours.	Gentlemen. Tincture.	Nobles. Jewels.	Sovereign Princes. Planets.	Signs.
	Diagonal Dexter.	Green.	Vert.	Emerald.	Venus.	♀
	Diagonal Crossed.	Orange.	Tenne.	Jacynth.	Dragon's Head.	☊
	Diagonal Sinister.	Purple.	Purpure.	Amethyst.	Mercury.	☿
	Horizontal Diagonal.	Murrey.	Sanguin.	Sardonyx.	Dragon's Tail.	☋
	Horizontal Perpendicular.	Black.	Sable.	Diamond.	Saturn.	♄

REMARKS.—Heraldry, the most arbitrary of the sciences, having no foundation whatever in nature, has nevertheless employed colours with more consistent classification than the more natural and legitimate arts, and being intimately connected with decorative painting in the emblazoning of arms and the illuminating of missals, books, deeds, and treaties; and being also of occasional reference to higher art, a brief notice of heraldic colouring and its symbols may be considered as a useful appendage to a work on painting. The present Table may also serve, by the comparison of colours, jewels, &c., to denote the colours themselves, and identify their names according to natural resemblances, and as a guide to the constructing of signals, &c.

The manner of denoting colours by the scoring and crossing of lines on escutcheons may be usefully employed by artists in sketching as memoranda for painting the accidental and local colours of objects.*

* The Cathedral of Chartres offers an example worthy the attention of archæologists: over the grand entrance door, under the rose window, to the right, a stained glass represents the Indian cosmogony, as it is described in the Bhagavadam. On the window of Chartres, Vischnu, draped in blue and red, reposes on a sea of milk, of a yellowish white; above him is the red rainbow: from the bosom of Vischnu issues the white lotus. The upper window represents Brahma with his quadruple face and the crown on his head. Brahma is nearly naked, his skin is bistre or dun; he wears saltirewise a green mantle, which envelopes the lower part of his body; he reposes on the lotus, and in each hand he holds a stem. The upper windows, separated by iron bars, represent corresponding subjects. Finally, on the last and most elevated, Jesus appears, clothed in a blue robe, and wearing a bistre-coloured mantle; above his head descends the Holy Ghost, in the form of a dove. The lotus issuing from the bosom of Vischnu rises up to Jesus Christ, where it appears in full blossom. This window, much anterior to the period of the Renaissance, proves the communication of the Oriental myths at the epoch of the crusades; it unites the symbols of Christian with those of Indian initiation.—*Baron F. Portal.*

CHAPTER XXII.

TABLE XI.

THE PRINCIPAL COLOURS USED IN WATER-COLOUR PAINTING.

These may be purchased as moist colours in pans or collapsible tubes, or in whole, half, or quarter cakes.

BLUES.

Prussian Blue	Azure Blue
Indigo	Cobalt
Antwerp Blue	Intense Blue
French Ultramarine	Blue Verditer
Permanent Blue	Cæruleum
Smalt	

REDS.

Carmine	Light Red
Vermilion	Venetian Red
Pure Scarlet	Indian Red
Scarlet Lake	Red Lead
Crimson Lake	Madder Lake
Deep Rose	Pink Madder
Magenta	Rose Madder

YELLOWS.

King's Yellow	Gamboge
Lemon Chrome	Naples Yellow
Middle Chrome	Raw Sienna
Indian Yellow	Yellow Lake
Yellow Ochre	Cadmium Yellow
Orpiment	

PURPLES.

Purple	Purple Madder
Mauve	Dahlia Carmine
Burnt Carmine	Purple Lake
Violet Carmine	

ORANGES.

Orange Chrome	Orange Vermilion
Deep Orange Chrome	Cadmium Orange
Orange Orpiment	Mars Orange

GREENS.

- Prussian Green
- Hooker's Green (Nos. 1 & 2)
- Sap Green
- Verdigris
- Green Oxide of Chromium
- Emerald Green
- Olive Green
- Terre-Verte
- Veronese Green

BROWNS.

- Cologne Earth
- Burnt Umber
- Sepia
- Roman Sepia
- Warm Sepia
- Vandyke Brown
- Burnt Sienna
- Brown Madder
- Brown Pink
- Raw Umber
- Brown Ochre

BLACKS.

- Indian Ink (in sticks)
- Ivory Black
- Lamp Black
- Blue Black

WHITES.

- Chinese White (in Bottles, &c.)
- Flake White
- Permanent White

GREYS.

- Neutral Tint
- Ultramarine Ashes
- Payne's Grey

REMARKS.—As the whole of the colours named in this Table would never be required by the same artist, each having his especial taste both as to his style of art, and the materials he employs, we give here the contents of small, medium, and full boxes of colours adapted for landscape or landscape and figure:—

LANDSCAPE, 6 CAKE BOX (OR THE SAME COLOURS IN TUBES OR PANS).

Gamboge, Yellow Ochre, Light Red, Crimson Lake, Vandyke Brown, Indigo.

LANDSCAPE AND FIGURE, 7 COLOURS

Gamboge, Raw Sienna, Light Red, Rose Madder, Vandyke Brown, Indigo.

LANDSCAPE, 19 COLOURS.

Gamboge, Yellow Ochre, Lemon Yellow, Pale Cadmium, Deep Cadmium, Chinese Orange, Light Red, Vermilion, Orange Vermilion, Crimson Lake, Rose Madder, Purple Lake, Sepia, Brown Pink, Cobalt Indigo, Cæruleum, Payne's Grey, Terre-Verte.

LANDSCAPE AND FIGURE, 17 COLOURS.

Raw Sienna, Indian Yellow, Lemon Yellow, Italian Pink, Pale Cadmium, Deep Cadmium, Brown Ochre, Burnt Sienna, Scarlet Vermilion, Madder Lake, Indian Lake, Cologne Earth, Vandyke Brown, French Ultramarine, Ultramarine Ash, Indigo, Veronese Green.

LANDSCAPE AND FIGURE, 29 COLOURS.

Gamboge, Yellow Ochre, Raw Sienna, Lemon Yellow, Italian Pink, Indian Yellow, Middle Cadmium, Orange Cadmium, Light Red, Indian Red, Vermilion, Orange Vermilion, Carmine, Rose Madder, Madder Brown, Brown Ochre, Burnt Umber, Sepia, Cobalt, French Ultramarine, Indigo, Emerald Green, Lamp Black, Cæruleum, Ultramarine Ash, Smalt, Purple Madder, Olive Green, Veronese Green.

TABLE XII.

LIST OF POWDER COLOURS FOR PAINTING IN TEMPERA.

Burnt Carmine	Mineral Grey
Carmine	Pure Scarlet
Deep Rose	Purple Lake
Cadmium Yellow	Platina Yellow
Chinese White	Rose Madder Carmine
Flake White	Rubens' Madder
Zinc White	Smalt
Kremnitz White	Vermilion
Crimson Lake	Violet Carmine
Scarlet Lake	Yellow Carmine or Gallstone
Ultramarine	Antwerp Blue
French Ultramarine	Brown Pink
Ultramarine Ash	Indian Red
Green Oxide of Chromium	Light Red
Indian Lake	Venetian Red
Indian Yellow	Blue Black
Intense Blue	Bone Brown
Lemon Yellow	Cologne Earth
Madder Brown	Emerald Green
Madder Lake	Ivory Black
Madder Purple	Lamp Black
Malachite Green	Patent Yellow
Mars Orange	Roman Ochre
Mars Yellow	Vandyke Brown

Indigo	Chrome Yellow (pale) medium and deep
Mummy	
Italian Pink	Naples Yellow
Prussian Blue	Orpiment
Verdigris	Raw Sienna
Yellow Lake	Terre-Verte
Burnt Sienna	Yellow Ochre
Burnt Umber	

Gamboge in Lump—Drop Lake.

REMARKS.—These colours are also used for illumination and for herald painting. For the former, they are either mixed with gum-water, or may be obtained in powder with which gum in a dry condition has already been incorporated—requiring only the addition of water; and the different technical colours used in the latter may be obtained ready mixed in cups.

TABLE XIII.
OIL COLOURS IN METALLIC COLLAPSIBLE TUBES.

REDS.

Indian Red	Burnt Brown Ochre
Light Red	Burnt Roman Ochre
Venetian Red	Magenta
Indian Lake	Paladium Red
Scarlet Lake	Paladium Scarle
Vermilion	Scarlet Vermilion
Madder Lake	Rose Madder
Carmine, &c.	

BLUES.

Antwerp Blue	Chinese Blue
Permanent Blue	Prussian Blue
Indigo	Cæruleum
Cobalt	French Ultramarine
Ultramarine Ash	

YELLOWS AND ORANGES.

Chrome, Pale	Italian Ochre
Do., Middle	Italian Pink
Do., Deep	King's Yellow
Do., Orange	Naples Yellow, 1, 2, & 3
Gamboge	Orpiment
Raw Sienna	Patent Yellow
Yellow Ochre	Roman Ochre
Indian Yellow	Mars Yellow
Platina Yellow	Strontian Yellow
Mars Orange	Orange Vermilion
Cadmium Yellow	Cadmium Orange

PURPLES.

Purple Lake	Violet Carmine
Purple Madder	

GREENS.

Emerald Green	Mineral Green, Nos. 1 & 2
Olive Tint	Terre-Verte
Verdigris	Malachite
Oxide of Chromium	Veronese Green

BLACKS.

Ivory Black	Lamp Black
Blue Black	Black Lead

WHITES.

Flake White	New White
Permanent White	Silver White
Zinc White	

BROWNS.

Asphaltum	Bitumen
Bone Brown	Cappagh Brown
Indian Brown	Manganese Brown
Vandyke Brown	Verona Brown
Brown Ochre	Brown Pink
Burnt Umber	Cassel Earth
Mummy	Raw Umber
Madder Brown	Rubens' Madder
Burnt Sienna	

Mineral Grey, &c., &c.

REMARKS.—These tubes may either be purchased separately or in boxes fitted up for figure-landscape, &c.; or in any way desired by the artist. The student is advised not to purchase a large stock at once, but to obtain just enough for his immediate wants, making additions from time to time according to necessity.

PART III.

ON VEHICLES, OILS, AND VARNISHES.

CHAPTER XXIII.

ON VEHICLES, ETC.

Since colours and pigments are liable to material influence, and changes of effect, from the materials employed in painting for tempering, combining, distributing, and securing them on their grounds in the various modes of the art, the powers and properties of oils, vehicles, and varnishes are of hardly less importance than those of colours themselves; they are, therefore, an essential branch of our subject. Vehicles, which term is borrowed from pharmacy, are, indeed, among the chief materials and indispensable means of painting, and give name to its principal modes under the titles of painting, in Water, Oil, Varnish, Distemper and Fresco: we will consider them, therefore, in these respects.

It is observable that the colours of pigments bear out with effects differing according to the liquids with which they are combined, and the substances those liquids hold in solution, which in some instances obscure or depress, and in others enliven or exalt, the colours;

in the first case by the tinge and opacity of the fluid, and in the latter, by its colourless transparency, and sometimes also much more so by a refractive power; as in varnishes made of pure resinous substances, which have a very evident and peculiarly exalting effect upon colours, that continues when they are dry; because resins form a glossy transparent cement, while the media formed by expressed oils become horny, or semi-opaque. This principle applies also to aqueous and spirituous vehicles in water-painting, according to the nature of the substances they may hold in solution.

WATER VEHICLES.

The most natural or fit distribution of vehicles is into those of *water, oils,* and *varnishes;* under which heads we proceed to regard them, and the various substances employed as additions, according to the variety of practice.

As the action of AQUEOUS LIQUIDS and solvents upon colours is stronger and more immediate than that of oils and varnishes, it is of great importance to the water-colour painter that he should attend to the pureness of his water, as in all hard and impure waters colours are disposed to separate and curdle, so that it is often impossible a clear flowing wash, or gradation of colour, should be obtained with them.

As water is not sufficient to connect, bear out, and secure colours on their grounds in painting, owing to its entirely evaporating in drying, additions of permanently adhesive substances soluble therein are necessary, such as vegetable gums, mucilages, farinaceous paste, sugar, animal glues and size, glaire or white of eggs, serum of blood, milk, curd, whey, &c., and finally mineral solids, such as quick-lime, alum, borax, &c.,

and these variously mixed and compounded: whence a variety of empirical methods of painting.

Water, as a vehicle compared with *oil*, is of simple and easy use, drying readily, and being subject to little alteration of colour or effect subsequently; for, notwithstanding oils and varnishes are less chemically active upon colours than aqueous fluids, the vehicles of the oil-painter subject him to all the perplexities of their bad drying, change of colour, blooming, and cracking, —to habits varying with a variety of pigments, and to the contrariety of qualities, by which they are required to unite tenuity with strength, and to be fluid without flowing, &c.; to provide for and reconcile all which has continually exercised the ingenuity of the oil-painter.

MUCILAGES.

Gum, or some mucilaginous substance, is a necessary addition to water to give pigments their requisite cohesion, and to attach the colours to the grounds on which they are applied, as well as to give them the property of bearing out to the eye, according to the intention of the artist; upon which, and upon the pigments used, depend the proportions of gum to be employed, gum being a constituent of some pigments, while others are of textures to require it in considerable quantity to give them proper tenacity,—qualities we have adverted to in speaking of individual pigments: as a general rule, however, the proportion of gum, &c., employed with a colour should be sufficient to prevent its abrasion, but not so much as to occasion its scaling or cracking, both of which are easily determined by trial upon paper.

GUMS.

Of *Gums*, SENEGAL is the strongest and best suited to dark colours, being of a brown hue; but the light-coloured pieces may be employed for the more delicate pigments. All gums contain an acid, very unfavourable to their preservation in a fluid state; which acid requires, therefore, to be neutralised by the addition of some alkaline substance, of which we have found the carbonate of ammonia, being volatile, to be the best; a small portion of which being shaken into the dissolved gum will purify it by precipitating all its foulness, and preserve it a very long time for use, and very much improve the working of colours without occasion for gall: the gum will rarely require more than one scruple of the powdered carbonate to an ounce of the gum dissolved by maceration in two or three ounces of cold water. Solution of borax will answer the same purpose, but less eligibly.

GUM ARABIC is in general clearer and whiter than Senegal, and hence is better adapted to the brighter and more delicate colours. It should be picked and purified by solution in cold water, straining, and decanting; and should be used fresh, or preserved by addition of alcohol, or by ammonia in the manner already described.

AMMONIA, or *Gum Ammoniac*, is a gum-resin, soluble in spirit and in water, in the latter of which it forms a milky fluid that dries transparent: it has many properties which render it useful in water-painting. It is avoided by insects, is very tenacious, and affords a middle vehicle between oil and water, with some of the advantages of both. It contributes also, in the manner of a varnish, to protect the more fugitive colours over which it may be glazed, or with which it may be mixed, and on this account it is eligible in water-painting.

GUM TRAGACANTH is a strong colourless gum, soluble in hot water, and of excellent use when colours are required to lie flat, or not bear out with gloss, and also when a gelatinous texture of the vehicle is of use to prevent the flowing of the colours; *starch* as prepared by the laundress, water in which *rice* has been boiled, used by the Chinese, and *paste* of wheaten flour, are available for the same purpose. *Sugar* and *honey* have also been employed, but as they attract flies and moisture are better avoided.

SIZE

Is prepared either by long boiling the shreds of parchment, &c., or from *glue* by soaking in cold water, and subsequently dissolving by heat. The quantity to be used depends like that of gums on the quality of the pigments employed, and caution is more necessary than with the gums not to use it in excess on account of its disposition to contract in drying, and occasion the colour to crack and scale off. The lighter-coloured *fish-glue* and *isinglass* are substituted for the nicer kinds of painting; *albumen* or *white of egg*, and also the *yolk*, employed by glovers, is used in some cases; *oxgall* is useful when the surface to be painted is polished, or works greasy. Size is sometimes worked into oil colours instead of mastic varnish to gelatinize and give them crispness.

MILK OF LIME

Is commonly employed in distemper painting without size, as a white basis and cement of colours, with or without addition of drying oil, and, when dry, stands weather with considerable firmness. It is prepared by slacking lumps of white quicklime in water.

BORAX

Is a mild alkaline salt, useful for neutralising the acidity of gums, and as a substitute for animal gall in attaching colours to polished or oily surfaces. It is also valuable as a *medium* for uniting varnishes and oils with water, in an intermediate mode of painting, which after drying is insoluble in water and may be washed. In small quantity borax promotes the drying of oils.

MEDIA.

Many attempts have been made to unite the advantages of the two modes of painting—of water and oil—either by successive processes, or by the use of a vehicle of a compound or intermediate affinity to both of these fluids, and thence technically denominated a *medium;* a term otherwise properly applicable to every vehicle.

With regard to *media*, all the gelatinous substances before mentioned as additions to water vehicles may be combined with linseed and other oils, and such compounds may be employed as vehicles, and will keep their place as delivered by the brush in painting. Indeed starch, as prepared by the laundress, has been lately recommended for this purpose. Nevertheless we regard these mixtures as both chemically and mechanically inferior to the combination of lac and borax, which is equally diffusible in water and in oil, and does not contract in drying, or render the painting penetrable by moisture as farinaceous and mucilaginous substances do, nor, in the end, dispose the work to crack. It has accordingly been proposed that artists should adopt the Indian process of painting, in which lac is rendered saponaceous and miscible in water by the medium of borax; but against this process the foul colour and opacity of the vehicle have been heretofore justly objected. If, however, one part of borax be dissolved in twelve of boiling water, and the solution be added, in equal or other proportions, to white lac varnish, a perfectly transparent colourless liquid is formed, which diffuses freely in water, and may be used, with some difficulty, as a quick-drying vehicle for painting instead of oil, and, when dry, is not acted on or removable by water; add to this, that as this lac vehicle is as freely miscible with oil as it is with water, it supplies a true medium, or connecting link, between painting in water and oil, which may, in ingenious hands, unite the advantages of both.

DRYERS,

Or *Siccatives*. With respect to DESICCATION OR DRYING, the well-known additions of the acetate or *sugar of lead, litharge*, and *sulphate of zinc*, called also improperly *white copperas* and *white vitriol*, either mechanically ground or in solution, for light colours; and *japanners' gold size*, or oils boiled upon litharge for lakes, or in some cases *verdigris* and *manganese* for dark colours, may be resorted to when the colours or vehicles are not sufficiently good dryers alone: but it requires attention, that an excess of dryer renders oils saponaceous, is inimical to drying, and injurious to the permanent texture of the work. Some colours, however, dry badly from not being sufficiently edulcorated or washed, and many are improved in drying by passing through the fire, or by age. Sulphate of zinc, as a dryer, is less powerful than acetate of lead, but is preferable in use with some colours, upon which it acts less injuriously; but it is supposed, erroneously, to set the colours running; which is not positively the case, though it will not retain those disposed to it, because it wants the property the acetate of lead possesses, of gelatinizing the mixture of oil and varnish. These two dryers should not be employed together, as frequently directed, since they counteract and decompose each other by double election,—forming two new substances, the acetate of zinc, which is an ill dryer, and the sulphate of lead, which is insoluble and opaque.

It is not always that ill drying is attributable to the pigments or oils;—the states of the weather and atmosphere have great influence thereon. The oxygenating power of the direct rays of the sun renders them peculiarly active in drying oils and colours, and was probably resorted to before dryers were added to oils, and the atmosphere is imbued with the active matter of light to which its drying property may be attributed. The ground may also advance or retard drying, because some pigments, united either by mixing or glazing, are either promoted or obstructed in drying by their conjunction: artificial heat also promotes drying.

The various affinities of pigments occasion each to have its more or less appropriate dryer; and it would be a matter of useful experience if the habits of every pigment in this respect were ascertained; siccatives of less power generally than the above, such as the acetate of copper, *massicot*, *red lead*, and the oxides of manganese, to which *umber* and the Cappagh browns owe their drying quality, and others, might come into use in particular cases. Many other accidental circumstances may also affect drying. Dryers should be added to pigments only at the time of using them, because they exercise their drying property while chemically combining with the oils employed, during which the latter become thick or fatten, and render additional oil and dryer necessary when again used. *Acetate of lead*, dissolved in water, spirit, or turpentine, may be used as a dryer of oil paints with convenience and advantage in some cases.

In the employment of dryers attention is necessary —1. Not to add them uselessly to pigments that dry well in oil alone. 2. Not to employ them in excess, which retards drying. 3. Not to add them to the colour till it is to be used. 4. Not to add several kinds of dryers to the same colour: and—5. To use simple dryers in preference to nostrums recommended and vended for drying of paints. Impurity of the pigment sometimes retards drying, in which case it should be washed.

Another attention should be, that one coat of paint should be thoroughly dry before another is applied; for if the upper surface of paint dry before the surface beneath it, it will *rival* by the expansion and contraction of the under surface as the oil evaporates and dries; overloading with paint will be attended by the same evil; and if the upper surface be of varnish or brittle, *cracking* of the paint will ensue.

CHAPTER XXIV.

ON OILS, ETC.

OILS are distinguished into *Fat oils*, *Drying oils*, and *Volatile oils*; the two first are also called *fixed and expressed oils*, as the latter are *essential oils*. All oils become thickened by age, and more rapidly so by contact of air and combination with its oxygen; in which case if the oil be fat or unctuous oil, such as olive oil and all animal oils, *stearine*, or tallow, is produced and separated from the *elain*, *olain*, or fluid oil; if it be a drying oil, such as linseed and painter's oil, *caoutchouc* or gluten is, in like manner, produced; and if it be a volatile or essential oil, such as that of turpentine, solid *resin* is formed therein : a third and acid substance is formed in oils when they become rancid, called *margarine*, which is inimical to drying. *Wax* is produced by the action of oxygen on a compound fat and essential oil; wax is therefore a substance between resin and stearine or tallow. All these substances may be regarded as oxides of elain, into which oils are wholly convertible; and, finally, by the action of time, air, and heat, they approach an elementary state, suffer incipient combustion, develop hydrogen, and become ultimately carbonized and darkened ; in all which states oils are deteriorated for working freely and for painting with pureness and permanence, as the fat oils are for burning in lamps.

All oils are soluble or miscible in water by the medium of alkalis, absorbent earths, or other metallic oxides, and are therefore capable of chemical union with pigments ; they are partially soluble also in alcohol, and absorb or take up by agitation small portions of both alcohol and water, which they resign upon being heated.

LINSEED OIL.

Of the expressed or drying oils appropriate to painting "*Honest linseed*" is by far the strongest, and that which dries best, most tenaciously, and firmest under proper management; which properties it owes to its being at once resinous, glutinous, and oleaginous. Having more of the quality of a resin than a fat oil, it never totally loses its transparency while liquid, in the manner of fat oils by cold, but preserves it during the most intense frost in the manner of a resin; and, like the resins also, it becomes ultimately fixed, hard, and solid, by combining with the oxygen of the atmosphere : but it lies under the great disadvantage of acquiring, after drying, and by exclusion from light and pure air, a semi-opaque and yellow-brown colour, which darkens by age. To obviate this as much as possible, when painting with oil alone, it is best to work the colour as stiff as may be, so as to use as small a portion of the vehicle as may suffice; for it is a fact proved by direct and repeated experiments, that *little oil diffused through much colour is subject to little change* upon the canvas, and that a thin coating of linseed oil is similarly preserved by light and the action of the atmosphere.

Linseed oil varies in quality according to the goodness of the seed from which it is expressed; the best is yellow, transparent, comparatively sweet scented, and has a flavour somewhat resembling that of the cucumber: great consequence has been attributed to the cold-drawing of this oil, but it is of little or no importance in painting whether moderate heat be employed or not in expressing it. Several methods have been contrived for bleaching and purifying this oil, so as to render it perfectly colourless and limpid; but these give it mere beauty to the eye in a liquid state, without communicating any permanent advantage, since there is not any known process for preventing the discolourment we have spoken of as sequent to its drying: and it is perhaps better upon the whole that this and every vehicle should possess that colour at the time of using to which it subsequently tends, that the artist may depend upon the continuance of his tints, and use his vehicle accordingly, than that he should be betrayed by a meretricious and evanescent beauty in his vehicle to use it too freely. Linseed oil that has been long boiled upon litharge in a water-bath, to preserve it from burning, acquires colour; and is, when diluted with oil of turpentine, less disposed to run than pure linseed oil, and affords one of the most eligible vehicles of the oil-painter.

The most valuable qualities of linseed oil, as a vehicle, consist in its great strength and flexibility; some have preferred it when bleached by exposure to sun and air; others, when *new and fresh*, or that which is *cold-drawn;* but that is the best which will temper most colour in painting; and oil expressed with a heat which does not char or much discolour it, is equal in all respects to the cold-drawn.

THE DRYING OF OILS

Appears to depend on the following conditions:—the presence of oxygen which by an incipient combustion of the hydrogenous oils fixes them, whence whatever contributes oxygen to oil dries it, as it is the case with pure air, sunshine, &c. Hence all the perfect oxides of metals, including even pure earths and alkalis in due proportions, dry oils. Hence, imperfect oxides, by abstracting oxygen from oil, retard drying; hydrogenous substances are hence ill dryers in oil, hence the best dryers are those which contain oxygen in excess; and such are litharge, sugar of lead, minium, massicot manganese, umbers, sulphate of zinc or white copperas, and verdigris.

PALE DRYING OIL.

The oil should be macerated, two or three days at least, upon about an eighth of its weight of litharge, in a warm place, occasionally shaking the mixture, after which it should be left to settle and clear; or it may be prepared without heat by levigating the litharge in the oil. Acetate of lead may be substituted for litharge, being soluble with less heat, and its acid being volatile escapes during solution and bleaches the oil; to which coarse smalt may be added to clear it by subsidence, increase its drying, and neutralise its brown colour. This affords *pale drying oil* for light and bright colours, which may be preserved for use in the above-described apparatus.

BOILED OIL.

The above mixture of oil and litharge, gently and carefully boiled in an open vessel till it thickens, becomes *strong drying oil* for dark colours. Boiled oil is sometimes set on fire purposely in the making of *Printers' Varnish and Printing Ink*, and also for painting and the preparation of JAPANNERS' GOLD SIZE. As dark and transparent colours are in general comparatively ill dryers, *japanners' gold size* is sometimes employed as a powerful means of drying them. This material is very variously and fancifully prepared, often with needless, if not pernicious, ingredients; but may be simply, and to every useful purpose in painting, prepared as follows:—Powder finely of asphaltum, litharge or red lead, and burnt umber, or manganese, each one ounce; stir them into a pint of linseed oil, and simmer the mixture over a gentle fire, or on a sand-bath, till solution has taken place, scum ceases to rise, and the fluid thickens on cooling; carefully guarding it from taking fire. If the oil employed be at all acid or rancid, talc, powdered, or a small portion of chalk or magnesia, may be usefully added, and will assist the rising of the scum and the clearing of the oil, by its subsidence; and if it be kept at rest in a warm place, it will clear itself: or it may be strained through cloth and diluted with turpentine for use. *Gold size* for gilding is commonly made of boiled oil and fine Oxford ochre.

POPPY OIL

Is much celebrated in some old books under the appellations of *oil of pinks* and *oil of carnations*, as erroneously translated from the French *œillet*, or *olivet*, a local name for the poppy in districts where its oil is employed as a substitute for that of the *olive*. It is, however, inferior in strength, tenacity, and drying to linseed oil, although next to it in these respects; and though it is of a paler colour, and slower in changing, it becomes ultimately not so yellow, but nearly as brown and dusky, as linseed oil, and, therefore, is not to be preferred to it. Boiled as above, it is the *Oglio Cotto*, or the *baked oil*, of the Italians.

NUT OILS

Resemble poppy oil in painting, but with inferior powers; and the *fish oils* of the *seal* and *cod*, though sometimes used with dryers in the coarser painting, are inferior in qualities to them all, and little better than *tar* similarly employed.

MEGILP,

Or *English varnish*, &c. Half a century ago, the jellied vehicles which received the cant appellations of *magilp* and *gumtion* were the favourite nostrums of the initiated painter, and have maintained a preference with many artists to this day. These compounds of one part or more of strong mastic varnish with two of linseed or other oils rendered drying as above and coagulable by the salts and oxides of lead, were, according to the preceding intentions, improvements upon the simple oil vehicle used on impenetrable grounds, by diluting it, and giving it a gelatinous texture, which enables it, while flowing freely from the pencil, to keep its place in painting, glazing, graining, &c.

GUMTION,

Composed of not more than an eighth of the acetate or sugar of lead, with simple oil and strong varnish, which is subject to less change ultimately, particularly when the varnish abounds in the compound. In the using of sugar of lead, if the acid abound, which it does usually in the purer and more crystalline kinds, its power of drying is weakened, and it may have some injurious action upon colours, such as those of ultramarine and lakes. In this case a small addition of some of the pure oxides of lead, such as litharge, ground fine, will increase the drying property of the sugar of lead, and correct its injurious tendency. A similar composition of ground litharge rubbed with twice its quantity of nut or linseed oil, and a sixth of bees'-wax and used with mastic varnish, is called *Italian varnish*.

COPAIBA

Is a natural balsam of West Indian production in a liquid state, in which it may be employed both as a vehicle and a varnish: it being of tolerable strength in either use, and preserving its naturally pale colour, but it is entirely needless in common painting.

VOLATILE OILS,

Procured by distillation from *turpentine* and other vegetable substances, are almost destitute of the strength of the expressed oils, having hardly more cementing power in painting than water alone, and are principally useful as solvents, and media of resinous and other substances introduced into vehicles and varnishes. In drying they partly evaporate, and partly by combination with oxygen form resins and become fixed. They are not, however, liable to change colour like expressed oils of a drying nature, and, owing to their extreme fluidness, are useful diluents of the latter; they have also a bleaching quality, whereby they in some degree correct the tendency of drying and expressed oils to discolourment. Of essential oils, the most volatile, and nearest in this respect to alcohol, is the oil of *sassafras;* but that most used in painting is the

OIL OF TURPENTINE.

The rectified oil, improperly called *spirit of turpentine*, &c., is preferable only on account of its being thinner and more free from resin. By the action of oxygen upon it, water is either generated or set free, and the oil becomes thickened, but is again rendered liquid by a boiling heat upon water, in which the oxygen and resin are separated from it. When coloured by heat or otherwise, oil of turpentine may be bleached by agitating some lime powder in it, which will carry down the colour. The great use of this oil, under the cant name of *turps*, is to thin oil paints, and in the larger use thereof to *flatten* white and other colours, and to remove superfluous colour in *graining*. It however weakens paint in proportion as it prevents its bearing out, and when used entirely alone it will not fix the paint.

OIL OF LAVENDER

Is of two kinds, the fine-scented English oil, and the cheaper foreign oil, called *oil of spike:* these are rather more volatile and more powerful solvents than the oil of turpentine, which render them preferable in enamel painting, of which they are the proper vehicles; they have otherwise no advantage over the latter oil, unless they be fancied for their perfume. The other essential oils, such as oil of rosemary, thyme, &c., are very numerous; but it has not appeared that they possess any property that gives them superiority in painting over that of turpentine some of them have, however, more power in dissolving resins in the making of varnishes, as is the case also with naphtha or petroleum and the rectified oil of coal tar.

NAPHTHA

And the *Coal Oil* of our gas works are even more powerful solvents than the vegetable essential oils; but on this account, and the usual bad scent of the latter, they are less eligible for the painter's use as vehicles: the rectified coal oil may, however, be deprived of its nauseous smell by agitating it during several days with dilute sulphuric acid, and subsequently washing the oil with a little powder or milk of lime.

SPIRIT OF WINE,

Or *Alcohol*, is weaker and more dilute than essential oils, or even than water, and is so volatile as to be of use in vehicles only as a medium for combining oils with resins, &c.—as a powerful solvent in the formation of spirit varnishes, and in some degree as an innocent promoter of drying oils and colours. It affords also powerful means of removing varnishes, &c.

CHAPTER XXV.

ON VARNISHES, ETC.

The last operation of painting is *varnishing*, which completes the intention of the vehicle, by causing the design and colouring to bear out with their fullest freshness, force, and keeping; supplies, as it were, natural moisture, and a transparent atmosphere to the whole, while it forms a glazing which secures the work from injury and decay. It is especially necessary for graining, and often in ornamental and fancy works of the art.

Varnishes are prepared from an immense variety of substances, of which the *resins*, improperly called gums, afford the best, and those principally used, and a vast number of preparations thereof uselessly compounded of many ingredients and little to be depended on, are recorded in different works, wherein as usual the simplest are the best. Varnishes are best classed according to their solvents, as water varnishes, spirit varnishes, essential oil varnishes, and oil varnishes, but more usually distinguished according to the substances from which they are prepared.

RESINOUS VARNISHES

Are either *spirit varnishes, volatile oil varnishes, fixed oil varnishes, natural balsams,* or compounds of these; their usual solvents being either spirit of wine or alcohol, oil of turpentine, or linseed oil.

The principal varnishes hitherto introduced and to be preferred in painting are the following :—

MASTIC VARNISH.

It is true that other soft resins are sometimes substituted for that of mastic, and that very elaborate compounds of them have been recommended and celebrated, but none that possess any evident advantage over the simple solution of mastic in rectified oil of turpentine. Some have used a varnish of *Damas*, or *common white resin* mixed with *naphtha*. Others have employed *mastic* and *sandarach* dissolved in *nut, poppy*, or *linseed oils*, and this is evident from the difficulty of removing varnishes from very old pictures. Mastic varnish is easily prepared, by digesting in a bottle during a few hours, in a warm place, one part of the dry picked resin with three or four of the oil of turpentine. A quantity of this cleared varnish sufficient to gelatinize or set up either of the before-mentioned drying oils of linseed, constitutes the transparent *megilp* of the painter, &c. If, instead of drying oil, the simple pure linseed oil be used with about an eighth of acetate of sugar of lead dissolved in water, or ground fine, we obtain variously the opaque mixture called *gumtion*.

COPAL VARNISH.

As other soft resins are sometimes substituted for mastic, so inferior hard resins are sometimes employed in the place of copal in the composition of varnishes celebrated as copal varnishes. Copal is of difficult solution in turpentine and linseed oils, both of which enter into the composition of the ordinary copal varnishes, which are employed by the coach painter and herald painter, and afford the best varnishes used by the house painter and grainer. Combined, however, with linseed oil and oil of turpentine, copal varnish affords a vehicle superior in texture, strength, and durability to mastic and its megilp, though in its application it is a less attractive instrument, and of more difficult management. As copal swells while dissolving, so its solutions and varnish contract, and consequently crack in drying, and thence linseed oil is essential to prevent its cracking. The mixture of copal varnish and linseed oil is best effected by the medium of oil of turpentine, and for this purpose heat is sometimes requisite: strong copal varnish and oil of turpentine in equal portions with one-sixth of drying oil mixed together, hot, afford a good painter's vehicle: and if about an eighth of pure bees'-wax be melted into it, it will enable the vehicle to keep its place in the manner of magilp. Elemi, anime, and resins of inferior hardness are sometimes substituted for copal in preparing its varnish.

WHITE LAC VARNISH

Is a new varnish introduced by the author. It is prepared by dissolving in alcohol or spirit of wine the lac resin of India, deprived chemically of all colouring matter, and purified from gluten, wax, and other extraneous substances with which it is naturally combined; without which process the varnish it affords is opaque and of the dark colours of the japans and lackers of the East, but when thus purified, its varnish is brilliant, transparent, very hard, and nearly colourless. This varnish, being a spirit varnish, requires a warm temperature, which is useful in all varnishing, and it dries rapidly. Its place is usually supplied by the *light, hard varnish* of the shops, in which softer resins are used with shelllac.

LAC

Is of three principal kinds, namely, *Stick-lac, Seed-lac,* and *Shell-lac,* of dark or light amber colours, of which the last is the purest, and that of palest colour is the best for varnishes. They are all soluble in pure spirit of wine. Various compositions of *Lac* with less than a fourth of mastic or sandarach, all dissolved, without fire, in spirit of wine, afford the *French polishes,* which are applied to cabinet work by a roll of woollen list or cloth wound tight, the face of which being dipped into the varnish and covered with a fine linen rag, having a drop only of linseed oil on the centre, is used circularly as a rubber for the varnishing and polishing the plain surfaces of the work by an easy and efficacious process, the carvings and mouldings which the rubber cannot reach requiring to be varnished with the brush. The dipping of the rubber, and supplying the drop of oil, are to be repeated alternately as the work goes on, till the whole is completed.

COWDIE,

Or *Fossil Varnish*. A new resin which exudes naturally from the *Cowdie Pine* of New Zealand and Australia into the soil at the foot of the trees, from which being dug, it has obtained the improper name of *Fossil Gum*, under which it has been imported, and being a fine, transparent *resin* nearly of the hardness of copal, and of similar habits, may become a valuable substitute for the hard varnishes in decorative painting and fine art. But it has hitherto been rejected by manufacturers of varnishes, first from the want of success in forming a permanent solution, owing to its precipitating from the solvents after being dissolved, and secondly from the danger of ebullition, inflammation, and explosion of gas evolved during its solution.

This latter defect arises from the water absorbed by the resin in its growth, or in the earth, which renders it opaque, but from which it may be freed by grossly powdering and drying, when the resin becomes transparent as glass, and may be melted and dissolved with the safety of other resins; and the first-named difficulty we have effectually remedied by the following simple formula, which yields a strong varnish that dries readily and with a fine surface:—

Take of broken and dried *Cowdie Resin* one part, melt it in the ordinary vessel, with the usual caution, and stir well and gradually into it, over a fire sufficient to boil without burning it, four parts or more of hot oil of turpentine till the solution is completed, finally stir it well and keep it hot off the fire one hour to clear. In this way, strictly followed, the cowdie or fossil resin will afford an excellent varnish applicable to the purposes of the usual copal varnishes, and superior to that of mastic varnish for pictures in not cracking like copal, and being more permanent than mastic, and as easily and safely removed when requisite: but it does not magilp with drying oil, although it may be mixed and employed therewith.

We are are of opinion also that, from the abundance, cheapness, and excellence of this resin, it is especially applicable to the purposes of civil, military, and naval architecture, in whatever works a varnish may be required or can be usefully employed, to which the difficulty and danger of permanent solution have been hitherto the obstacles with manufacturers of varnishes accustomed to the old *resins* of elimi, copal, sandarach, &c., improperly called *gums;* but which objections are entirely remedied by the preceding formula. It is, we presume, for the uses here suggested that the American merchants have become great purchasers of the cowdie resin.

GENERAL REMARKS.

Upon comparing the qualities of the varnishes of mastic, cowdie, copal, and lac, it will appear that the latter are successively harder and more perfect as varnishes, and in proportion to their perfection as *varnishes* is the difficulty of using them as *vehicles;* and as it is necessary that before varnishing with any of them the picture should be thoroughly dry, to prevent subsequent cracking, this is perhaps more essential for the latter than for the former. Notwithstanding this necessity, there is one highly important advantage which seems to attend early varnishing; namely, that of preserving the colour of the vehicle used from changing, which it is observed to do when a permanent varnish is passed over colours and tints newly laid; but this it does always at the hazard, and often at the expense, of cracking, and early varnishing with soft varnish dries slowly and is more disposed to bloom.

This saving grace of early varnishing appears to arise from the circumstance that, while linseed and other oils are in progress of drying, they attract oxygen, by the power of which they entirely lose their colour; but, after becoming dry, they progressively acquire colour. It is at the mediate period between oils thus losing and acquiring colour, which commences previously to the oil becoming perfectly dry, that varnish preserves the colour of the vehicle, probably by preventing its further drying and oxidation, which latter may in the end amount to that degree which constitutes combustion and produces colour:—indeed it is an established fact that oils attract oxygen so powerfully, as in many cases to have produced spontaneous combustions and destructive fires.

It is eminently conducive to good varnishing, in all cases, that it should be performed in fair weather, whatever varnish may be employed; and that a current of cold or damp air, which chills and blooms them, should be avoided. To escape the perplexities of varnishing, some have rejected it altogether, contenting themselves with oiling-out,—a practice which, by avoiding one extreme, runs to its opposite, and subjects the work to ultimate irrecoverable dulness and obscurity.

The manufacturing processes for the varnishes now generally used have been detailed in the *Transactions of the Society of Arts, &c.*, vol. xlix. But with regard to the recipes for compounding varnishes, &c., superabounding in ancient and modern treatises, however flatteringly recommended, there are few eligible and yet fewer justifiable to art and good chemistry by the simplicity upon which certainty of effect depends, being in general quite of the class of the recipes and formulæ of the old cookery-books and dispensatories.

Presuming the decorator and painter to have acquainted himself with the principles of colours, &c., so as to apply them with taste and effect, as well as with a due knowledge of his materials, both of which are indispensable, there will yet remain to the complete mastery of his art the various modes and operations of painting, &c., in which they are to be applied, but for which he must rely upon his acquirement of skill and practice. These, therefore, we now proceed finally to describe, with such observations and additions as may appear expedient.

PART IV.

THE MODES AND OPERATIONS OF PAINTING.

CHAPTER XXVI.

OF MATERIALS, AND THE METHOD OF USING THEM.

We must assume that our student has mastered the elementary principles, and has attained some power in the practice of drawing;* we shall therefore proceed with instructions as to working with the brush, as distinct from that done with the pencil. This latter term has been applied to small brushes, such as "camel-hair" and "sable" pencils, and is generally used symbolically in relation to painting: thus Sir Joshua Reynolds says, "the pencil speaks the tongue of every land."

Still, in general terms, a brush is understood to mean the implement with which wet colour is applied, in opposition to the dry point, such as a crayon or lead pencil.

The simplest method of painting is that in which water alone is used as a medium; and we therefore

---

* For a course of elementary drawing, adapted for painters, grainers, and letter-writers, see the "Practical Manual for House-Painters, &c.," of this series.

make this a starting-point, the pigments having been previously mixed with a mucilage.

The paper on which water-colour painting is executed is of various degrees of roughness; for it will of course be understood that it is necessary that there should be some "tooth" or grain on the surface; the very smooth being only adapted for a very minute drawing which is to be very highly finished. The following are the sizes of the different drawing-papers, and these may be obtained either hot-pressed, plain, or, as it is called, "not," meaning not hot-pressed, or possessing a finely grained surface for water-colour painting generally, and rough (in various degrees) for large and bold pictures.

The following are the names of the various drawing-papers and their sizes :—

Demy	20 inches by 15
Medium	22 ,, 17
Royal	24 ,, 19
Super Royal	27 ,, 19
Imperial	30 ,, 21
Elephant	28 ,, 23
Columbier	34 ,, 23
Atlas	23 ,, 26
Double Elephant	40 ,, 26
Antiquarian	52 ,, 31

Several of these papers may be had of an extra thick quality.

The paper most generally used is the Imperial, either full size or in halves, 21 × 15, or in quarters, 15 × 11$\frac{1}{3}$.

The student will no doubt be possessed of a drawing-board; if not, he is advised to purchase one at a respectable shop, rather than to have one made, as, in the former case, he can select from a stock of boards which have been kept some time, and are therefore likely to be well seasoned, whilst, in the latter, he will run the risk of the newly made board warping twisting, or cracking. Drawing-boards are made in various ways.—1. Clamped: in these, pieces are placed across the ends, and are attached by what is called the plough-and-tongue joint ; this is a very generally adopted method, and is only open to the objection that, as the fibres of the end-pieces are in an opposite direction to those of the board itself, the latter is liable to shrink in one way, and the former in another, thus, after a while, the ends of the cross-pieces will be found to project beyond the edges of the board. This will not, however, last long, and when it has been once or twice corrected by the plane being run along the edge, it will cause no further inconvenience. 2. The cross-piece may be put on by the method called mitre-clamping, in which it is cut slantingly at its ends, the board being correspondingly cut to receive it. This is not as a rule advantageous, as, should any shrinking take place, the cross-pieces would be forced out of their mitres, and the board thus thrown out of square. 3. A very good board is made by placing rabbets across the back of the board; these should be fixed edgewise, and should be inserted into grooves, the sides of which are cut so as to slant inward, the rabbets being planed to fit; the grooves and the rabbets should be rather wider at one end than at the other, and they may thus be tightened by a blow from a hammer. They should not be glued, but should be merely attached by one screw near the end of each. Thus, whilst the board is prevented warping or twisting, it is allowed to expand or contract, and splitting or cracking is prevented. We are thus particular in relation to boards in order to avoid the annoyance ensuing from twisting and warping during the progress of a picture, of which there is the more likelihood from the frequent washes applied to the drawing, the board being thus subjected to constant alternations of wet and dry.

The paper for water-colour painting should be attached to the board by the method called "stretching." This is done in the following manner. The paper is cut so as to be slightly smaller than the board, a strip of about three-quarters of an inch being removed all round; a border of about half an inch is then to be turned up on each side. The sheet is next to be turned face downward, whilst the back is to be covered with water, which must be allowed to soak well in. The moisture should be equalised by means of a sponge, so that one part may not be more wetted than the other.

The paper is then to be turned—the wetted side towards the board—and paste is to be applied to the upturned edges, which are subsequently to be pressed down, during which operation the paper is to be stretched, the thumbs being placed against the edge of the board and the fingers on the edge of the paper whilst drawing it outward.

If whilst drying some of the blisters which naturally arise in the damp paper do not seem to decrease with sufficient rapidity they should be pricked with a needle in several places, so as to allow the air to escape; this will in most cases be found a sufficient remedy, but if not successful the surface of the paper must be again moistened all over, especially towards the edges; and if this should fail also, the paper must be taken off the board and the operation repeated altogether. The edges should be well rubbed down with the handle of a penknife or some similar article, and the paper should be placed to dry in a horizontal position.

Sketching-blocks are very convenient, as they serve the purpose of a drawing-board with a quantity of paper ready stretched upon it. They consist of a number of pieces of paper well pressed and fastened together at their edges, so as to form a compact mass or block, which is then glued down to a piece of very thick millboard. As each drawing is finished it may be removed by inserting the penknife into a small aperture specially left open and running it round the edges, by which means the sheet will become detached and another ready for the next work will be presented.

The outline having been made, the colouring is to be proceeded with, but at this stage it is necessary to warn the student that no amount of colour will ever convert a bad drawing into a good painting, and that the further the work progresses the more will the effect of incorrect outline become visible, and the more difficult will alteration become; the sketch should, therefore, be most carefully corrected before the process of painting is commenced.

Moist colours are taken from the pans on the point of the wet brush, and either transferred directly to the paper, or placed on the slab or palette, so that a quantity may be mixed with water. This is by far the safer plan, where any portion of the drawing is to be evenly covered. The moist colours in tubes are used by pressing on the lower end of the tube, when the colour, which is of some consistency, will be forced from the aperture opened by unscrewing the lid. The little pyramid of colour thus deposited, is then to be mixed with water, by means of a palette-knife, or it may be washed down by a brush. Colour of any degree of depth may thus be obtained.

Water-colours in cakes are the most old-fashioned form, but still retain their hold in the estimation of perhaps the greater number of artists, as they are for many reasons the most convenient, although for large work the pans and tubes are better, as colour may be mixed in quantities from them with greater rapidity than from the cakes. In rubbing the colour, the cake should not be dipped into the water-glass, as in that way its edges become wetted more than necessary, and cause it to crack and chip. The water should be placed on the slab by means of a brush, and the colour rubbed in it, the cake being afterwards placed on one of the edges at right angles to that which has been rubbed until it has dried, when it is to be restored to its place in the box.

When it is required to compound a tint from two colours, each of them should be rubbed separately on the slab, a space being left between them on which they should be mixed with a brush; by this means the cakes are kept unsoiled by other tints.

When a quantity of colour is required in order to cover any large surface, it should be mixed in a saucer, and having been allowed to stand for an hour or so, the colour should be carefully poured off into another vessel, leaving any sediment or particles of colour which may have broken off in the original saucer, and the rest of the colour will be smooth and clear.

This cannot, however, be done with all colours; for some of them, such as vermilion, emerald green, &c., are so heavy, that nearly the whole of the colouring matter sinks to the bottom, and the liquid poured off would be almost pure water. It is, therefore, necessary to stir such at every brushful taken; but they are not adapted for flat washes.

In order that the colour may flow easily, it should, for washing, be thin; and it must be pointed out that the safest plan which can be adopted by the student is to work in stages, keeping the picture rather too light than the opposite until it is near completion, when the finishing and spirited touches can be put in; for it is easy by repetition to darken the work, but always difficult and troublesome to lighten it if too dark.

When the colour has been laid on, it should not be touched until it has dried; should any spots then appear darker than others, they may be lightened by rubbing them with a moist brush, a piece of Indian-rubber, or bread crumbs; and any part which may be lighter than the rest may be covered with another wash, or may be as it were darned, by stippling, that is, by small dots, or separate touches, done with a brush containing only a very small quantity of colour.

The student is urged never to employ a small brush where a large one could be used. Small brushes make the work look streaky, and boldness of manipulation, so much to be desired, is only to be attained by the use of large ones. In using large brushes, however, great care is necessary in order to preserve the outline; but very fine points can be made to good brushes by drawing them along a piece of waste paper, and, when held upright, very small work can, when required, be done with them.

In laying a flat wash, care should be taken that sufficient colour is prepared for the immediate purpose, as the necessary evenness of the tint will be injured if the progress of the work be interrupted. The brush should contain as much colour as it will hold without allowing it to run down, but the point should be preserved. The work should be commenced at the top, the board being placed in a slightly inclined position.

Before commencing to work in colours, it is advisable that the student should have some practice in what is called painting in monochrome, or one colour; and for this purpose sepia is generally preferred, from the ease with which it washes.

It is a good plan to draw several squares, triangles,

and oblongs, of different sizes, and to commence by laying a flat wash over each of the smaller figures, and advancing to the larger ones, for increased practice; for it will at once be understood that the difficulty of laying a flat wash increases with the size of the surface.

When a certain amount of power in using the brush has thus been attained, figures having a greater number of angles, such as octagons, nonagons, &c., should be drawn and coloured, care being taken not to pass over the outline, but still to carry the colour into all the angles, whilst spreading it evenly over the surface. In doing this, the brush should be held as nearly upright as possible.

The tints should next be graduated, commencing pale at the top, and becoming darker towards the bottom. This is accomplished in the following manner. Mix the colour in three degrees of depth, in as many different compartments of the slab. Commence with the lightest, and when the work has proceeded about one-third of the width of the surface to be covered, remove as much as possible of the colour from the brush, either against the edge of one of the compartments of the slab or on a piece of waste paper, and with the brush in this condition carry on the work a little further, so that there may not be a quantity of colour at the edge of the strip which has been tinted. Next, take a little of the colour of the second degree of strength, and with it pass over the edge of the strip just coloured whilst the latter is still wet; the two tints will thus be easily blended, and the full brush will then be used to carry the work further; in the same way the gradation from the second to the darkest tint is to be made.

The next study should be derived from a cylindrical surface, such as a garden-roller, a barrel, a jug, &c. In subjects such as these the tone becomes gradually darker as it removes from the highest light; but the darkest portion is relieved near the edge by a reflected light. The student is urged to make several studies from objects, from which he will, by careful observation, learn much more than he could from an infinite number of drawing-copies.

The next subjects for practice should be of the spherical character, commencing with objects such as a cup or basin, which are only partially globular, and subsequently proceeding to complete spheres, such as a large ball, an orange, fruit, &c.; in fact, a group consisting of three apples, placed next to each other, with a fourth resting on them, forms an excellent study of form, and of light and shade, whilst a bunch of grapes, as was long ago asserted by Titian, is the best that could be conceived.

A certain amount of practice in the use of the brush having been thus obtained, and the student having acquired a mastery over the implement and the colour he employs, the same method of proceeding is to be applied to the colours generally.

As our instructions are intended to lead more to decorative than landscape painting, we refrain from referring to the methods of obtaining the numerous and ever-varying effects visible in nature, but we still urge that observation of these must tend to improve the eye for colour, and to elevate the taste.

The decorative artist is advised to practise flower-painting in water-colour, since flowers, rendered naturally and conventionally, form such an important element in ornamental art. But we must again urge correctness in drawing, and careful study of the natural growth and botanical features of the plant, so that it may, in being adapted to an ornamental purpose, retain its natural characteristics. It is this knowledge which enables the designer to conventionalise with such admirable effect, as we see in some of the better class of decorations; it is this knowledge by which a man rises from a mere drudge to the position of an artist; and it is by these means that he acquires the power of pleasing the eye and refining the taste of those around him.

Having for a short time painted flowers from copies, the student is advised, as soon as possible, to take nature as his model, and to paint first from a single flower or spray, and subsequently from groups.

The first tints are to be laid on as washes, the petals and leaves being subsequently worked up by stippling; but this must not by any means be overdone, but should be resorted to merely as a finishing process—to give, however inadequately, an idea of the exquisite refinement of the subject itself.

The decorative artist should also make the human figure an integral portion of his study; nor should animal forms be neglected, entering as they do into so many branches of ornamentation.

CHAPTER XXVII.

PAINTING IN TEMPERA.

This mode of painting, which is undoubtedly the most ancient, and which, in trade purposes, is called Distemper painting, derives its name from the fact that the colours are "tempered," or mixed with some liquid or medium to bind their separate particles to each other and to the surface to which the paint is to be applied.

PAINTING IN TEMPERA.

The following is quoted from "Painting popularly Explained" (*Gullick and Timbs*) :—"The Italian noun *tempera* admits of the widest application, and would include any medium, even oil; but, in its restricted and proper acceptation, it means a vehicle in which the yolk of egg, beaten sometimes with the white, is the chief ingredient, diluted as required with the milky juice expressed from the shoots of the fig-tree. This is the painting strictly termed *à novo* by the Italians. Vinegar, probably, replaced the fig-tree juice among the northern artists, from the difficulty of obtaining the latter, and in modern use vinegar is substituted.

"Haydon says vinegar should be used to prevent the putrefaction of the yolk of egg; but the early Italian painters preferred the egg-vehicle when it had been suffered to stand until it had become decomposed : hence the phrase *à putrido*.

"The artist is often compelled to have recourse to very offensive media to make known his most refined revelations. On walls, and for coarser work, such as painting on linen, warm size was occasionally used, but the egg-vehicle, undiluted, was generally preferred for altar-pieces on wood. For various purposes, and at different periods, however, milk, beer, wine, and media composed of water and more or less glutinous ingredients, soluble at first in water, such as gums, &c., have also been used. Such are the media or vehicles described by the chief Italian writers as used in the days of Cimabue, Giotto, and Fra Angelico, and by the early painters before the invention and improvement of oil painting. Pliny also mentions milk and the egg-vehicle as employed for ancient wall-paintings. The finer egg *tempera*, in dry climates, has been found to attain so firm a consistence as to withstand ordinary solvents. The use of wine in diluting these glutinous vehicles was common for a long period. Buffalmacco, of whom so many humorous stories are told by Boccaccio and Vasari, is related to have persuaded some nuns, for whom he painted, to supply him with their choicest wines, ostensibly for the purpose of diluting the colours, but really to be imbibed by the thirsty painter himself. The northern artists were sometimes obliged to content themselves with beer. In the works of the northern *tempera* painters there are, however, very marked differences observable in their *impasti*, or body colour. It is certain, therefore, that these painters employed media of different degrees of consistency. In the distemper of scene-painting the medium is weak size of glue (glue dissolved), but plaster of Paris, sufficiently diluted, is worked with the colours. The carbonate of lime, or whitening, is less active as a basis for colours than the pure lime of fresco, but it is entirely destructive of transparency. When the more viscid media were employed by the *tempera* painters the effect must, with their purer use of the colours—some of which, moreover, were transparent—have been very lustrous and powerful in comparison with modern scene-painters' "distemper;" and these qualities were heightened by the addition of a strong varnish. Still, however, *tempera* fell far short of oil painting in richness and transparency."

The carbonate of lime, or whitening, employed as a basis, is, however, less active than the pure lime of fresco. The vehicles of both modes are the same, and their practice is often combined in the same work: water is their common vehicle; and to give adhesion to the tints and colours in distemper painting, and make them keep their place, they are variously mixed with the size of glue (prepared commonly by dissolving about four ounces of glue in a gallon of water). Too much of the glue disposes the painting to crack and peel from the ground; while, with too little, it is friable and deficient of strength. In some cases the glue may be abated, or altogether dispensed with, by employing plaster of Paris sufficiently diluted and worked into the colours; by which they will acquire the consistency and appearance of oil paints, without destroying their limpidness, or allowing the colours to separate, while they will acquire a good surface, and keep their place in the dry with the strength of fresco and without being liable to mildew—to which animal glue is disposed, and to which milk, and other vehicles recommended in this mode, are also subject.

Of more difficult introduction in these modes of painting is *bees'-wax*, although it has been employed successfully in each of them, and in the encaustic of the ancients, who finished their work therein by heating the surface of the painting till the wax melted.

Tempera may be considered as opaque water-colour painting, since water enters more or less into the composition of all the media employed. The fact, however, that the colours thus mixed (with body white) are opaque constitutes the great difference; and thus whilst, as a rule, the lights in water-colour painting are obtained by leaving the white paper more or less exposed, and by washing transparent colours over it, allowing for the effect resulting from the colour being rendered lighter by the white ground underneath, all these gradations are accomplished in *tempera* by means of colours with which white is mixed in various quantities, the high lights being executed in pure white. In all these respects *tempera* agrees with oil painting, the respective vehicles alone constituting the great distinction.

This style is very important to the decorative painter, and the student is, therefore, advised to practise it. It must be borne in mind that the same facility in blending the colours does not exist in *tempera* as in water-colour painting, for if the colour were diluted with water, in order to soften it off, the gelatinous quality of the medium would be exhausted, and the colour would rub off; it is, of course, impossible to prepare as many gradations as there are tints in nature, and such as are placed next to each other dry by far too quickly to allow of their being blended together. The processes of "hatching" and "stippling" have, therefore, been employed. "Hatching" is another word for "etching," and consists in working lines in different directions so as to give the appearance of relief required. Stippling is done in dots instead of lines. The methods are often seen combined, the dots being placed in the lozenge-like spaces left by the crossings of the lines.

The method principally used in decorative painting is that by which the effect is obtained by flat tints of different gradations; and practice will soon enable the artist to blend these very successfully in the ornamental forms of which the design consists.

A beautiful set of flowers in flat tints, as studies for *tempera* painting, is published under the auspices of the Department of Science and Art, and may be obtained through Messrs. Chapman and Hall, Piccadilly.

CHAPTER XXVIII.

PAINTING IN OIL.

The various oils, megilps, varnishes, &c., used in painting in oils have already been described. It is not, however, necessary that the student should prepare these for himself, as they may all be purchased at most reasonable prices. The information in the body of the book is, however, given in order that the student may be acquainted with the composition of the different vehicles, and be able to manufacture them should circumstances at any time require him to do so.

The colours used in oil painting have been given in Table XIII. The method now adopted of supplying them in collapsible tubes is a great improvement on those of former years. In early days the artist had to grind up his own colours in oil by means of a muller, or piece of stone, on a marble slab; perhaps he had to roast the raw sienna and umber to produce the burnt sienna and burnt umber, and to pound them in a mortar; the paints were then kept in jars, or gallipots, from which they were taken with the palette-knife. At a more modern period the colours, ready ground up in oils, were tied up in pieces of bladder, like so many small puddings, a label outside denoting the contained colour. These were then termed "bladder colours," as we now speak of "tube colours." When the bladders were to be used a hole was pricked, the bladder was squeezed, the contents curled out like a handsomely coloured worm; a tack or small nail was then placed in the aperture to close it up.

The brushes used in oil painting are principally those made of hog-hair, sable, and badger—fitch and goats'-hair brushes are also employed. These brushes are made round and flat, and are mounted in tin. Flat hog-hair tools are generally preferred to round ones, as they give that squareness in the outline which contributes so much to the boldness and crispness in the work.

It is almost needless to explain that the brushes should not be cut at the ends, but that the natural point of each hair should be carefully preserved. If any special form of brush is required, in order to accomplish certain results, they may be purchased under the head of irregular-shaped tools, amongst which are the Short Hair Flat, the Long Hair Flat, the Landseer brush—especially adapted for animal painting, made of extra thin hair; the Short Hair Round; Extra Long Hair Round; the Set Brush, in which the hair is gathered into several separate tufts, with spaces between them; the Swallow-tail or Double-pointed brush; the Straight Angular Edge, in which the hair of the brush, which is a flat one, slants to a point in the middle; the Angular Brush, in which the hair slants from one side of the point to the other; the Hollow Brush, &c.

All these are, however, intended for special methods of manipulation; the student is advised to work with the usual forms, only availing himself of the above when he has obtained full mastery over the other, when he wishes to accomplish a particular effect. In decorative painting, however, this contingency is scarcely likely to occur.

The *hog-hair brushes*, although firm, should be soft and elastic, returning to their straight shape immediately after being pressed against the hand. It is a good plan to soak new brushes for an hour or two in water, thus causing the hair to swell. The ends subsequently dry, and as they are then immersed in oil-colour, the portion enclosed by the tin still retains, for some time, a certain amount of moisture; and as this dries away its place is taken by particles of paint—thus preventing, in a great degree, the annoyance caused by loose hairs working out during painting.

Sable brushes.—The hair of these is, of course, softer than the hog, and thus they may be brought to a finer point, which is still very firm. Although they go by the name of "Red Sable," the best hair is of a pale yellowish cast. The round sables are very useful in working up and finishing details. Some are set in quills and go by the name of "sable pencils;" those which bag near their insertion should be avoided.

Badger tools are differently formed from the others; they are so bound that the hairs, instead of combining to form a point, spread outward—something after the fashion of a shaving-brush. This brush enjoys the pleasant name of "softener" or "sweetener," and is used to blend the freshly laid colours together by sweeping over them.

We cannot too strongly warn the student against the too frequent use of the softener, as it is apt to produce a woolly, feeble, and (if we may use the term) unbusiness-like appearance. A little practice will enable him to blend his colours with the brushes he is using, or at most a larger tool, and he will soon learn to use the softener as a duster only. When the badger tool has been much used a certain amount of colour will adhere to the ends of the hairs, and thus will inflict a series of scratches over the colour it is intended to soften; it is therefore necessary that it should be frequently cleaned. This is done by gathering up the hairs and holding them tightly whilst rubbing them on a dry rag each time the brush has been used; and it should also be occasionally washed with soap and water and well rinsed. The water which remains after the hair has been squeezed may be got rid of by striking the brush against the edge of the easel, or against the maul-stick, and it may then be placed to dry.

All the brushes used in oil painting should be carefully cleansed; the hair should be dipped in raw linseed oil, which should be rubbed in by pressing the brush between the fingers, so that all the colour it contains may be diluted and set free from the hairs. This liquid colour should then be pinched out by drawing the brush between the finger and thumb, and it should afterwards be thoroughly washed with soap and warm water until the frothy matter formed by rubbing the brush in the hand is perfectly colourless. The brushes should then be rinsed in clean water, which should be beaten out of them in the manner already described. It is not a good plan to wipe them on a cloth, as the smallest possible piece of fibre adhering to the ends of the hair may prove a very great annoyance; the only rag which may be used for this purpose with perfect safety is an old disused silk handkerchief. Some artists use turpentine instead of linseed-oil; but turpentine is injurious to the brushes, as it renders the hair harsh and stiff; it should only be used when it is required to wash out a brush quickly during work, so that the hairs may not be soaked in it. Some painters use a mixture of nut-oil and turpentine in the first instance, and pure nut-oil afterwards, which latter they do not quite wipe out, and thus the brush is kept soft and moist for use—the nut-oil being a very slow drier. When the brushes are to be used in the same colours the next day, they need not be cleaned at night, but may be dipped in nut-oil and laid in a tin slant until wanted again. "Brush washers" are small tin cans, in which a still smaller one, the bottom of which is pierced with holes, is placed—in the same way that a glue-pot is placed in the outer pan. This inner vessel does not reach to the bottom of the outer receptacle, and has a piece of wire placed across the top; the liquid in which the brush is to be cleaned is poured in until it rises about half way in the inner vessel;

the brush is then washed in it and rubbed off against the wire; the liquid, containing the colour in suspension, drains through the pierced bottom of the vessel, and sinks by its own weight to the bottom of the outer can, whilst the liquid rises, pure and limpid, in the inner one.

The surface most generally used for painting upon is canvas. It is sold in rolls of various widths and qualities—" plain cloth," " Roman," and " ticken." The most general form, however, in which it is purchased is stretched on frames, with wedges at the angles by which it may be tightened up. These are made in certain sizes, and in proportions adapted for portraits or landscapes. Thus we have, amongst the rest, the Kit-Cat size—named after the club—the portraits of the members of which were painted by Sir Godfrey Kneller in this size, in order to fit the room in which the pictures were to be placed—this measures 36×28 inches. The following are some of the sizes used :—

	Ft.	In.		Ft.	In.
Head size	2	0	by	1	8
Whole length	7	10	,,	4	10
Half length	4	2	,,	3	4
Bishop's half length	4	8	,,	3	8
Bishop's whole length	8	10	,,	5	10

Many of the painters of old executed some of their finest works on panels of wood, and such, made of well-seasoned mahogany, are still often used: besides which we have prepared millboards, which afford an excellent surface for painting; the Academy boards, made of a thinner millboard and well adapted for sketching; and also prepared oil-paper, which is exceedingly useful, whilst it is very economical and portable. If it be desired to preserve the sketch, it may be glued on to a strained canvas. The method of painting in oil may be described as consisting of four processes—Dead Colouring, Glazing, Scumbling, and Impasting.

Dead colouring is the first, or preparatory, painting: it is so called because the colours are laid on in a dead or cold manner—to form, as it were the ground for the subsequent processes—resembling in some degree the work known amongst house-painters as "priming," the future effects being rather indicated and provided for than really attained. It is sometimes found convenient to divide the painting of a picture into certain stages, termed first, second, third, and fourth paintings, &c.

Glazing consists in spreading colour, much diluted, over the picture, or parts of it.

The, colours which when mixed with the proper vehicles become transparent, are called "glazing colours." The purpose of glazing is to deepen shadows and to give warmth or coldness to their hues, to subdue lights which may appear too strong, and to give force and richness to the picture.

"Glazing forms a distinct series of tints, without which it is impossible to represent transparent objects. By it, shadows are strengthened, and warmth or coldness given to their hue; by it, also, lights that are unduly obtrusive are subdued, or additional colour and tone given to those that are deficient in force and richness. The processes of glazing, we have observed, is generally effected by the application of diluted transparent colour; but occasionally semi-transparent colours are used when rendered sufficiently transparent, by the admixture of a large proportion of vehicle. Such glazings are useful to modify parts of the picture, or produce particular effects, such as representations of smoke, mist, dust, and the like. Glazing, when used injudiciously or in excess, produces that "horny" uniform dulness of surface and "leathery" discoloration so offensive to the eye, which, till recently, was the common characteristic of the modern Continental Schools"*

Scumbling resembles glazing, but the colours used are opaque ones. It is used to give distance to object's which appear too near, and to modify effects which are found to be too strong. The colour thus used, after a time sinks partially into that over which it is passed, producing beautiful effects. Dry-touching, or dragging, consists in the addition of a few sharp or bold touches or lights: great care should be taken so that this process may not be overdone, so as to produce what is known as a "mealy" appearance.

Impasting (Ital. *impasto*) consists in painting the highest lights solidly with opaque colours—that is to say, mixed more or less with white, and laid on thickly—not only with the brush, but often with the palette-knife. Impasting gives texture and surface. In the foreground, and in parts not intended to retire, "impasto" should be bold; but this loading of masses of colour upon the picture, so as to give actual relief to the high lights, making them project considerably from the surface, has its disadvantages; for although the parts thus mechanically raised are strongly illuminated by the light impinging on their prominences, these protuberances of paint will, of course, in certain lights, cast a shadow of their own. They also afford lodgment for dust, and, owing to the quantity of white in them, they are very liable to discolour; and thus it often occurs that they form dark or dirty patches in the very places where high lights were intended.

The easel—a ladder-like frame on which the canvas is placed during painting, so made that the picture can be raised or lowered to suit the convenience of the artist—is an important item in the furniture of the

* "Painting Popularly Explained," Gullick and Timbs.

studio, and, besides the other implements mentioned—Palettes, are indispensable. These are made of mahogany, or of satin or other light woods—the latter are to be preferred for mixing tints, the precise tones of which can be better seen on them than on the darker ones. Palettes should be light in weight, and the oblong ones will be found more useful than those of the elliptical shape, as they afford more space for colours. New palettes should be prepared for use by rubbing raw linseed-oil repeatedly over them until they will absorb no more, the last coat being allowed to dry in; the palette will not then be stained by the absorption of colour.

The palette should be carefully cleaned every day on leaving off work, and colour should not by any means be allowed to harden upon it. When all the colour has been scraped off with the palette-knife (carefully observing not to make scratches or indentations), the surface should be cleaned with a piece of silk rag dipped in nut-oil, the edges being also well attended to. We have often observed students merely cleaning off the middle of the palette, whilst round the edges there have been accumulations of hardened colour. The palette should be left each night as clean as when first used. Should it be desired to save any colour which may remain, for next day's use, it should be scraped off the palette and placed in a little heap in a saucer, and covered with water, which, when poured off, will leave the colour fresh and good, or it should be put on a piece of tinfoil, which may be closely rolled up, thus forming a temporary collapsible tube.

CHAPTER XXIX.

FRESCO.

The art of painting in Fresco is naturally adapted to decorative painting, and the zealous attention of eminent artists of the day having been turned to the revival of this grand and important mode of art, a few remarks thereon are deemed desirable.

It is hardly necessary to inform the reader that *fresco painting* is performed with pigments prepared in water, and applied upon the surface of *fresh-laid plaster* of lime and sand, with which walls are covered; and as it is that mode of painting which is least removed in practice from modelling or sculpture, it might not improperly be called *plastic* painting; for which the best lime, perfectly burnt and kept long slacked in a wet state, is most essential. As lime in an active state is the common cementing material of the ground and colours employed in fresco, it is obvious that such colours or pigments only can be used therein, as remain unchanged by lime. This need not, however, be a universal rule for painting in fresco, since other cementing materials as strong or stronger than lime may be employed, which have not the action of lime upon colours—such is calcined gypsum, of which plaster of Paris is a species; which, being neutral sulphates of lime, exceedingly unchangeable, have little or no chemical action upon colours, and would admit even Prussian blue, vegetal lakes, and the most tender colours, to be employed thereon, so as greatly to extend the sphere of colouring in fresco, adapted to its various design; this basis merits also the attention of the painter in crayons, scagliola, and distemper.

So far, too, as regards durability and strength of the ground, the compo and cements now so generally employed in architectural modellings would afford new and advantageous grounds for painting in fresco; and as they resist damp and moisture, they would be well adapted, with colours properly chosen, to situations in which paintings executed in other modes of the art, or even in ordinary fresco, would not long endure.

As these materials, and others now in use, were either unknown or unemployed by the ancient painters in fresco, their practice was necessarily limited to the pigments enumerated in the preceding Table IX.; but every art demands such a variation in practice as adapts it to circumstances and the age in which it is exercised, without attention to which it may degenerate, or, at best, remain stationary, but cannot advance.

Although differing exceedingly in their mechanical execution, the modes of fresco, distemper, and scagliola agree in their chemical relations; so far, therefore, as respects colours and pigments, the foregoing remarks apply to these arts.

From the fact that fresco is executed on the plaster whilst in a wet condition, it becomes necessary that the portion of the work begun in the morning should be finished before evening. Full-sized drawings are therefore prepared, and the portion which is to be painted in the day is transferred to the plaster, of which just a sufficient quantity has been freshly laid on. This is done either by pricking through the lines and pouncing through the apertures with red or blue dust, or by marking over the lines with a blunt point, so that a slightly indented mark is left on the plaster underneath.

The outline being thus secured on the wall, the

painting is proceeded with, and in this the artist must depend entirely on his experience and knowledge of the result his work will produce; for the tints when first applied look faint and cold, and sink into the wet plaster, so that it is necessary to go over the work repeatedly before the required effect is attained.

The colours used are principally mineral, and are ground in pure water, which is also the vehicle employed.

The wall having been previously prepared and covered with plaster made of river sand and best old lime and mixed to about the usual slackness, the *intonaco* or painting surface is to be floated on. This must be prepared of the very best old lime, perfectly free from grit. The mixture must be made about the consistency of milk, and is then passed through the hair sieve into jars in which it is allowed to settle, when the water is poured off; the sediment is then mixed with fine quartz sand well sifted, in the proportion of one part lime to two of sand. This plaster is spread by means of wooden or glass implements; but iron trowels may be used if they are perfectly free from rust, and care is taken not to press the iron into the plaster.

The rough-cast ground is now to be thoroughly wetted, and the intonaco is to be floated on in two coats, the last with rather more sand than the first; the thickness of the two should be about 3-16ths of an inch. The whole is then to be gone over with a roll of wet linen, which will remove the marks of the trowel, and prevent the surface being too smooth.

When the intonaco has acquired sufficient firmness, which may be tested by pressing it with the finger, the first colouring may be applied. Where possible, the portion of plaster laid on for the day's work should be made to end at some bold outline of the picture, or at the edges of some well-defined object. If the result of the work is not satisfactory, the artist is compelled to cut away the plaster and apply fresh; the process of fresco-painting thus becomes a slow and difficult one.

CHAPTER XXX.

USEFUL RECEIPTS.

CLEANING AND RESTORING.

OF the importance of this minor function of the art of painting a just estimate may be formed by considering that there is hardly a limit to the time which works in oil-painting may be preserved by care and attention. These are subject to deterioration and disfigurement simply by dirt,—by the failure of their grounds,—by the obscuration and discolourment of vehicles and varnishes,—by the fading and changing of colours,—by the cracking of the body and surface,—by damp, mildew, and foul air,—and by mechanical violence. The first thing necessary to be done is to restore the ground, if on canvas, by stretching or lining with new canvas. In cases of simple dirt, washing with a sponge or soft leather with soap and water, judiciously used, is sufficient. Varnishes are removed by friction or solution, or by chemical and mechanical means united, when the varnish is combined, as commonly happens, with oil and a variety of foulness.

TO REMOVE VARNISH

By friction, if it be a soft varnish, such as that of mastic, the simple rubbing of the finger-ends, with or without water, may be found sufficient; a portion of the resin attaches itself to the fingers, and by continued rubbing removes the varnish. If it be a hard varnish, such as that of copal, which is to be removed, friction with sea or river sand, the particles of which have a rotundity that prevents their scratching, will accomplish the purpose.

The solvents commonly employed for this purpose are the several alkalies, alcohol, and essential oils, used simply or combined. Of the alkalies, the volatile in its mildest state, or carbonate of ammonia, is the only one which can be safely used in removing dirt, oil, and varnish from a picture, which it does powerfully; it must therefore be much diluted with water, according to the power required, and employed with judgment and caution, stopping its action on the painting at the proper time by the use of pure water and a sponge.

Many other methods of cleaning have been recommended and employed, and in particular instances, for sufficient chemical reasons, with success; some of which we will recount, because, in art so uncertain, it is good to be rich in resources.

A thick coat of *wet fuller's earth* may be employed with safety, and, after remaining on the paint a sufficient time to soften the extraneous surface, may be removed by washing, and leave the picture pure; and an architect of the author's acquaintance has succeeded in a similar way in restoring both paintings and gilding to their original beauty by coating them with wet clay. Ox-gall is even more efficacious than soap.

In filling cracks and replacing portions of the ground, putty formed of white lead, whitening, varnish, and drying oil, tinted somewhat lighter than the local colours require, may be employed, as plaster of Paris may also in some cases; and, in restoring colours accidently removed, it should be done with a vehicle of simple varnish, because of the change of tint which takes place after drying in oil.

REMOVING PAINT,

Burning, &c. In those cases in which it is requisite to remove painting entirely from its ground, it is usual to resort to mechanical scraping, &c., or to the very dangerous operation of setting fire to the painted surface immediately after washing it over with oil of turpentine, called *turps*, for burning off the paint from old disfigured work; an operation that may be safely and more easily accomplished by laying on a thick wash or plaster of fresh-slacked quicklime mixed with soda, which may be washed off with water the following day, carrying with it the paint, grease, and other foulness, so that when clear and dry, the painting may be renewed as on fresh work. Clear-colling is sometimes resorted to over old painting, for the purpose of re-painting, in which case the surface exposed to the sun's rays or alterations of temperature is liable to become blistered and scale off.

PART V.

THE CHARACTERISTIC FEATURES OF THE VARIOUS STYLES OF ORNAMENT.

CHAPTER XXXI.

OF ORNAMENT GENERALLY.

A "DECORATIVE painter" does not mean just one who can paint decoration, but it should imply that the person so termed understands what kind of ornaments should be applied as a system; so as to carry out the admirable rule that construction should be decorated, but that decoration should not be constructed. Further, he must bear in mind that in all decoration the leading idea of the designer should be *fitness*; for, however beautiful an ornament may be in itself, that beauty is sadly deteriorated when it is out of place.

Again, the decorative artist should make himself acquainted with the styles and orders of architecture, so that his decoration may agree with them. What should we say of a dramatic writer who introduces into a play, the period of which is supposed to be that of William the Conqueror, characters, or even costumes, belonging to the reign of Charles the First? and yet we see uneducated men painting Gothic ornaments on buildings which are Greek in character, and making other blunders of a similar nature; such as rendering an ornament in the flat which was intended to be in relief, or placing a border on a curved surface when the whole beauty of the form consists in its geometrical and rectilineal character.

Ornament may, in the first place, be broadly divided into the symbolic and æsthetic; or, such as address our understanding, and those which appeal to our feelings. We may term those styles symbolic* in which the ordinary elements have been chosen for the sake of their significations as symbols of something not necessarily implied, and irrespective of their effect as works of art or arrangements of forms and colours. Those that are composed of elements derived solely from principles of symmetry of form and harmony of colour, and exclusively for their effect on our perception of the beautiful, without any further extraneous or ulterior aim, may be termed æsthetic.

Style in ornament is analogous to *hand* in writing. As every individual has some peculiarity in his mode of writing, as every man has his individual habit of thought and mode of expression, so every age or nation has been distinguished in its ornamental system, and by a certain individuality of taste, either original or borrowed.

There are two provinces of ornament—the flat and the relieved. In the relieved we have the contrast of light and shade; in the flat we have the contrast of light and dark: in both a variety of effect for the pure gratification of the sense of vision. Much of the effect is common to both; but in the flat a play of line is the main feature, whilst in the relieved a play of masses, acted upon by light, so as to produce shadows, which

* Wornum's Analysis.

materially add to the beauty of form, whilst colour may be an auxiliary to both, but it acts with greater power in the flat, as it is entirely dependent on light.

Although the varieties of ornamental systems are very numerous, they may be classed under three great periods—ancient, middle-age, and modern.

To the ancient belong Egyptian, Assyrian, Grecian, Roman; the middle-age period comprehends the Byzantine, Saracenic, and Gothic; whilst in the modern are classed the Renaissance, the Cinquecento, and the Louis Quatorze.

CHAPTER XXXII.

THE EGYPTIAN AND ASSYRIAN STYLES.

THE elements of Egyptian ornament have, as a rule, a particular meaning, being seldom, if ever, chosen for the sake of beauty of effect. The style is, therefore, very simple and limited in its arrangements in comparison with later styles, in which mere symbolism was superseded by the pure principles of art; the artist aiming at *effect* rather than meaning.

Fig. 10.

" Yet," says Mr. Wornum, " we cannot but admire the ingenuity with which the Egyptian decorator, by a mere symmetrical arrangement, has converted even the incomprehensible hieroglyphics into pleasing and tasteful ornaments."

A simple symmetrical arrangement, however, is the limit of his artistic scheming, and generally in the shape of a simple progression, whether in horizontal lines, or repeated on the principle of the diaper; that is, row upon row, horizontally or diagonally, as seen in the Tombs of the Kings at Thebes.

The Winged Globe (Fig. 10) is the most important of Egyptian ornaments; it is supposed to have been an invocation to the good spirit, Agathodemon, and was used in architecture, costume, and every kind of manufactured fabric.

In one class of ornament Egypt is eminent, independent of its skilful application of art to manufactures: it is remarkable in its complete adaptation of its own natural productions in the development of a style peculiar to itself; in its conventional treatment of the natural types of the locality, as, for instance, the Papyrus-plant (Figs. 11 and 12), and the lotus or water-lily of the Nile, the element of so many varieties of ornament. The Egyptian details are not mere crude imitations of nature, but natural objects, selected by symbolism, and fashioned by symmetry into ornamental decoration. So that we have here one great class, and the earliest systematic efforts in design in the world's history. Many of the details of the Egyptians are still popular ornaments handed down to our own times, such as the fret or key border, &c.

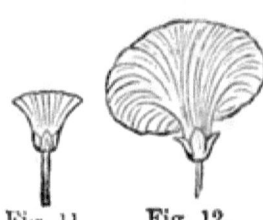

Fig. 11.   Fig. 12.

Next we have the Zigzag which was used as a type of the waters of the Nile, and is still preserved as the symbol of Aquarius, the water-bearer, in the Zodiac.

This has been a favourite ornament in all periods, and we shall again meet with it as the zigzag in the Norman, and as the dog-tooth in the early English styles.

Equal in importance to the zigzag is the Wave scroll, (Fig. 13); it typified the waves of the rising Nile, from

Fig. 13.

which Egypt derived so many benefits. It subsequently became a favourite ornament in Greece, where it no doubt suggested the idea of the scroll proper, in which the wave is alternated on each side of a serpentine line.

Next we have the lotus or water-lily of the Nile, and the papyrus-plant, both treated—as were indeed all the Egyptian ornaments—in a strictly conventional manner, as already shown in Figs. 11, 12; the former typified the fruitfulness produced by the inundations of the Nile, and was used not only as a flat, or even relief, ornament, but as a leading decoration on the Egyptian columns, around which it is frequently given as a frieze or broad band. Many of the columns are themselves founded upon its form, or rather upon the form of a bundle of the stalks banded together, with flowers on the capitals.

The Fret, or labyrinth, was the type of the Labyrinth of Lake Mœris, with its twelve palaces and three thousand chambers; representing, in their turn, the twelve signs of the Zodiac, and the three thousand years of transmigration the soul was supposed to undergo. We illustrate in the next chapter this ornament as adopted by the Greeks.

Gaudy diapers and general gaiety of colour are likewise characteristic of Egyptian taste, but the colours are generally limited to red, blue, yellow, and green, though the Egyptians were acquainted with nearly all other colours.

The Assyrian style of ornament may be said to have been contemporaneous with the Egyptian. Its chief characteristics are sculptured records of leading events, and the human-headed colossi with bodies of either bulls or lions. The Assyrian buildings were erected on terraces composed of sun-dried bricks, faced with sculptured slabs of stone, with wooden columns and super-structure, which of course decayed as time progressed; this accounts for the circumstance that we have but little data as to the cornices and internal ornamentation, whilst we have large portions of the external sculptures, pavements, &c.

Fig. 14.

The Sphinx, or composite animal, with which the Assyrian bulls (Fig. 14) must be classed, were also important objects in Egypt—whole avenues of them, interspersed with obelisks, led to the temples; and we also meet with the sphinx in Greece, and a similar animal, called the chimera, in Rome. It must, however, be noted that the Egyptian sphinx (Fig. 15) is always male and without wings, whilst the Grecian sphinx is female, with wings. It may be that the ancients—the Assyrians, at least—thought that the deities they selected to guard them should possess a combination of attributes which should render them in every way fitted for the position ascribed to them. Thus, for strength, they gave their idol the body of a bull; for wisdom, the head of a man; whilst, in order to give omnipresence, they added wings. Truly, in the words of Holy Writ, "they had mouths, but spoke not; they had eyes, but saw not; they had ears, but heard not; they had noses, but smelled not; they had hands, but handled not; they had feet, but walked not;" and have not all that made them become like unto them? For the nation has passed away, the palaces have crumbled to the dust, and these supposedly wise, powerful, and omnipresent watchmen have been buried for more than two thousand years. Armies have passed over them without dreaming of their very existence, corn has waved its golden head over them; and only in our own day have these records of the distant past been brought to light and lodged in the museums of Europe.

Fig. 16.

In addition to the sculptured histories, we find reliefs of several gods, and a peculiarly formed tree, called the sacred tree. This emblem occurs continually in Assyrian ornamentation. It is supposed to have some reference to the tree of life, so universally recognised as a sacred and mysterious symbol in the religious systems of the East. Mr. Fergusson has conjectured that it may be identified with the "grove" so frequently mentioned in the Bible. It consists of an upright central stem, with branches extending to a kind of border formed by other branches proceeding in an upright form and bending into an arch above, flowers being placed at intervals. These flowers seem to be the "open flower" (Fig. 16) mentioned in the description of Solomon's temple, and to form the prototype of the Greek honeysuckle, whilst the "chain" (Fig. 17) was also used, and seems to have been the original guilloche

Fig. 16. Fig. 17.

which afterwards became such a leading ornament in Greece. There are proofs that the ornaments were strongly coloured, and that much gilding was used.

Grandeur of proportion, simplicity of parts, and costliness of material, were the characteristics of the Egyptian style; and this love of gorgeousness prevailed in all Asiatic art, in which we find gold, silver, ivory, jewels, and colours profusely used. In the Hindoo art we find the fantastic element prevailing, and though the same jewelled richness is observed as in the Egyptian, the simplicity and grandeur are wanting.

CHAPTER XXXIII.

THE GRECIAN STYLE.

Hitherto all the ornaments have been symbolic or descriptive; but when we come to Greece we find forms introduced for their own sake, for their beauty alone; and this must be considered as a decided step in advance. Architecture had made rapid strides, and sculpture having advanced with it, the pediments of the temples were filled with beautiful groups, and the frieze on the cella of the Parthenon was sculptured with a procession consisting of horses and men, which

Fig. 18.

for grouping and execution has never been surpassed. It was placed in an elevated position in the cloister or covered walk around the building; and as the spectator was thus debarred from stepping backward to view it from a distance, the sculpture was executed in low relief, whilst full effect was still given to the roundness of the figures—which effect would have been lost from the closeness of the spectator had the work been executed in high relief, for when looking from below, the projecting parts would have hidden the others. Portions of this frieze are in the British Museum, and casts, coloured to suit the various theories as to the extent to which the ancients applied colour to sculptures, may be seen in the Crystal Palace (Greek Court). The pediments (or triangular spaces above the columns at each end, corresponding with the gable-ends of a cottage) were filled with magnificent sculptures, the positions of the figures corresponding most gracefully with the form of the space they were to

Fig. 19.

occupy. The frieze outside was filled with metopes or groups of figures and triglyphs, which were supposed to represent the ends of joists resting on the architraves. These were divided into three compartments by grooves or water-channels, and underneath are pendants, supposed to represent drops of water.

The first ornaments which we find in the Greek vases are those with which Egypt has already made us acquainted—the Zigzag, the Wave scroll, and the Labyrinth or fret (Fig. 18). The most characteristic ornaments of the period, however, are the Echinus, or horse-chestnut, popularly called the egg and tongue, and the Anthemion or honeysuckle (Fig. 19), or Palmette, both of which it in some degree resembles; it is generally alternated with the lily, or some analogous form.

The capital forms in the three Greek orders (the Doric, Corinthian, and Ionic) the distinctive architectural ornament. The Doric capital consists of a circular flat cushion, called the Echinus, from its being invariably decorated in colour with that ornament, and the order is frequently called the echinus order. In the Greek forms the curves are flat, being portions of ellipses and parabolas, not of circles. This is no doubt owing to the practice of polychromatic decoration which was universally adopted; and it has already been remarked that high relief, as producing shadows, is antagonistic to the effect of colour.

In the second, or, as it is called, the Alexandrian, period, the ornamental forms were elaborated and the simple scroll added to them: this, in its original development, consisted, as already stated, of a succession of spirals reversed alternately, and the practice of carving, instead of painting, the ornaments began; horns or volutes were added to the capital, a border of the Anthemion was often placed under them, and thus the Ionic capital was formed.

In the Corinthian capital the volutes are further developed—the body is a graceful bell, clothed with the acanthus leaf. The ordinary scroll and acanthus were only in a slight degree developed in Greece, but became leading features in the Roman system of ornamentation.

ROMAN.

The Roman system of ornamentation cannot be considered in any way original, since the only new form which appears is that of the shell, which in later periods became such an important feature in certain styles of ornament. The Romans, however, enlarged, decorated, and developed the Greek elements, which they embellished and amplified until the original refinement was lost in gorgeousness. The Greek origin is no doubt attributable to the fact that most of the artists employed were Greeks.

The chief characteristic of the Roman style, then, is great magnificence, the Acanthus being largely em-

Fig. 20.

ployed. The Composite order now appeared, made up of the echinus, the volute, and the acanthus; and the scroll and acanthus, which had both been so sparingly used in Greece, now became leading features, almost every ornamental form, indeed, being enriched with the acanthus.

The Roman acanthus is, however, distinct from the Grecian; the Greeks used the *Acanthus spinosa*, or narrow prickly acanthus, whilst the Romans adopted the *Acanthus mollis*, or soft acanthus, known to us as the Brank Ursine. But they mostly, for capitals, used conventional clusters of olive-leaves, in order to obtain the strong effects required on the pillars of their lofty temples; this modification does not, however, seem to have been adopted in any other situation. Fig. 20 is a sketch from a well-known example of a Roman scroll decorated with the acanthus.

The Tuscan capital is simply an Italian rendering of the Doric, in which the echinus is exchanged for a quarter round—an astragal, or narrow half-round moulding, taking the place of the annulets or zones underneath the Doric capital.

The Romans, as well as the Egyptians, Assyrians, and Greeks, used monsters and composite animals, such as the triton, the griffin, the chimera, &c., which may be seen on the sculptures of the period.

CHAPTER XXXIV.

BYZANTINE.

When Constantine, the first Christian emperor of Rome, removed the seat of empire to Constantinople, previously called Byzantium (about A.D. 330), he took with him the arts of the former empire—which were then in a most debased condition—and applied them to the enlargement and decoration of the new city. Thence arose that combination of Roman, Greek, and Oriental traditions which distinguish the Byzantine style (Fig. 21).

Mr. Wornum in his Analysis says: "The peculiar views of the Early Christians in matters of art had, before the establishment of Christianity by the State, no material influence in society, though the pagan idolatries found many vigorous opponents long before the time of Constantine. During the first and second centuries Christian arts were limited to symbols, and were then never applied as decoration, but as exhortations to faith and piety. All Christian decoration rests upon this foundation—the same spirit of symbolism prevailing throughout, until the return to

Fig. 21.

the heathen principle of beauty (to the æsthetic) in the period of the Renaissance."

The early Christian designers, most of them no doubt connected with the Church, seem rather to have avoided than sought beauty in these peculiar forms, from precisely the same feeling by which the Egyptians were animated. The lily (fleur-de-lis), the emblem of the Virgin and of purity, is as common as the lotus was in Egypt, though having a very different meaning, and a peculiarly angular rendering of the Greek acanthus was also used.

The reason why the beautiful forms of Greece were rejected seems to have been none other than that they were pagan in their origin. Paganism, however, consisted solely in forms, not in the colours adopted; still, as paganism itself expired, the scroll and other ornaments were admitted, the foliage being rendered in the peculiarly formal manner already described.

The chief varieties of the Romanesque are the Byzantine, the Lombard, and the Norman. Both the Lombard and the Norman may be considered in their main features as mere modifications of the Romanesque; certainly few examples of the Romanesque out of Italy were not derived directly or indirectly from Constantinople. The Norman has by most writers been considered as the first of the Gothic styles, and as such we shall class it here.

Besides the sculptured ornaments of the early Christians, their decorative effects were produced by polychromatic ornamentation, executed by means of painting and by mosaics.

The earliest paintings after the time of Constantine are to be found in the catacombs of Rome and Naples. The general characteristics of such paintings are, that the outlines are strongly defined by a very fine, firm, brown line, dark and broad; the figures are by no means well drawn; and the colours and shadows are not very forcible, although they are somewhat heavy. Byzantine mosaic work* may be classed under three heads—

---

* For much information concerning which we are indebted to the excellent account by Mr. J. B. Waring.

1. Glass mosaic, called Opus Musivum; used for both walls and vaults.
2. Glass tesselation, called generally Opus Grecanicum, conventional; generally inlaid in church furniture.
3. Marble tesselation, called indifferently Grecanicum and Alexandrinum, conventional; formed into pavements.

In the first division of mosaics we observe as a peculiarity that it was employed only to represent and reproduce the forms of existing objects, such as figures, architectural features, and conventional foliage, which were generally relieved with some slight indications of shading upon a gold ground, the whole being bedded on the cement covering the walls and vaults of the basilicas and churches.

The pieces of glass employed in the formation of this work are of very irregular shapes and sizes, of all colours and tones of colour, and the ground that almost invariably prevails is gold. The manner of execution is always large and coarse; yet, notwithstanding this, the effect of gorgeous, luxurious, and at the same time solemn decoration is unattainable by any other means as yet employed in structural ornamentation.

The second variety of Christian mosaic, the glass tesselation, or Opus Grecanicum, consisted in the insertion into grooves, cut in white marble to the depth of about half an inch, of small cubes of variously coloured and gilded "smalto," as the Italians called, and still call, the material of which mosaic is composed, and in the arrangement of these simple forms in such geometrical combinations as to compose the most elaborate patterns.

These differ from all that were produced by the former system in the essential particular of being purely conventional in style. These ornamental bands it was customary to combine with large slabs of the most precious materials—serpentine, porphyry, pavonazzetto, and other valuable marbles, and apply them to the decoration of the churches and basilicas.

The third system of mediæval mosaic, the Opus Alexandrinum, which formed the ordinary church-paving from the time of Constantine down to the thirteenth century, and has in our own day been most successfully imitated in encaustic tile pavements, may be described generally as tesselated marble-work, that is, an arrangement of small cubes, usually of porphyry or serpentine, reddish-purple and green coloured, composing geometrical patterns in grooves cut in the white marble slabs which formed the pavement. The contrast between these two colours produces a monotonous but always harmonious effect.

SARACENIC.

The Mohammedan law forbidding the introduction of the forms of either animals or plants, a peculiar system of ornamentation was developed, consisting of scroll-work interlaced with a sort of conventional form approximating to the lily, mixed with ornamental inscriptions. Closely filled diapers, gorgeously coloured and gilded, form the leading characteristics; the reliefs on these wall-diapers were coloured blue on the background, red on the edges of the reliefs, and gold on the surface.

The late Mr. Owen Jones must be accepted as the modern exponent of this style, and his great work on the Alhambra should be carefully studied by every decorative artist, since from it may be gleaned lessons of the most important character as to the correct distribution of form and space, and the principles of ornamentation. The following remarks are based on Mr. Jones's description of his reproduction of portions of the Alhambra in the Crystal Palace.

In surface decoration of the Moors, all lines flow out of a parent stem: every ornament, however distant, can be traced to its branch and root; they have the happy art of so adapting the ornament to the surface decorated, that the ornament appears as often to have suggested the general form as to have been suggested by it. In all cases we find the foliage flowing out of a parent stem (Fig. 22), and we are never offended as in modern practice by the random introduction of an ornament just dotted down without a reason for its existence. However irregular the space the Moors had to fill, they always commenced by dividing it into equal areas, and round these trunk lines, they filled in the detail, but invariably returned to the parent stem.

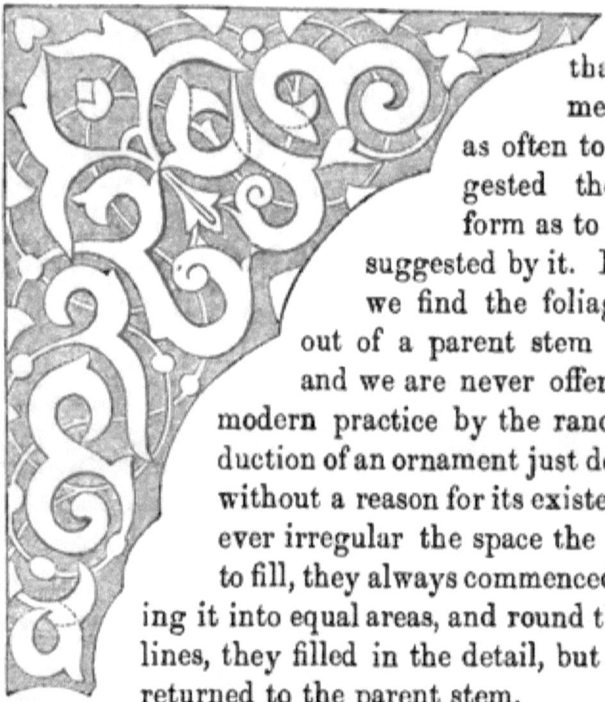

Fig. 22.

They appear in this to have worked by a process analogous to that of nature, as we see in the vine-leaf; they also followed the principle of radiation, as in the horse-chesnut, &c. (Fig. 23). We see in these examples how beautifully all these lines radiate from the parent stem; how each leaf diminishes towards the extremities; and how each area is in proportion to the leaf. The Orientals carry out this principle with marvellous perfection; so did the Greeks in their honeysuckle ornament. It may here be remarked that the Greek ornamental forms appear to follow the principle of the cactus tribe, where one leaf grows out of the other. This is generally the case with the Greek ornament; the acanthus leaf-scrolls are a series of leaves growing out of each other in a continuous line, whilst the Arabian ornaments always grow out of a continuous stem.

Another important principle in ornamentation was carried out by the Moors; namely, that all junctions of

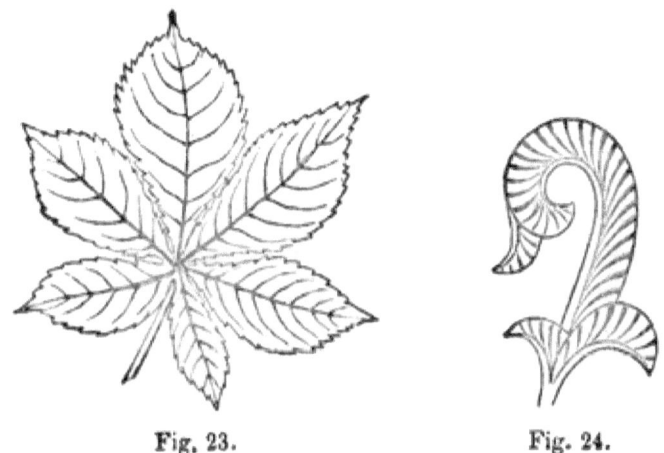

Fig. 23.   Fig. 24.

curved lines with curved, or of curved with straight (Fig. 24), should be tangential to each other. This law is found everywhere in nature, and the Oriental practice is in accordance with it. Many of the ornaments are on the principle which we observe in a feather and in the articulations of every leaf; and to this is due that additional charm found in all perfect ornamentation which we call graceful. We shall find these laws of equal distribution, radiation from a parent stem, continuity of line, and tangential curvation, ever present in natural leaves.

CHAPTER XXXV.

GOTHIC.

THIS great middle-age period has been variously divided: we adopt the simplest classification. The Saxon style, of which but few examples remain in this country, contained but few ornamental features; and although the first ecclesiastical style was Romanesque in its origin, it is characterized by the small windows with semicircular heads, the lights divided by a baluster instead of a mullion, and semicircular arching generally.

The Gothic grew out of the Byzantine, and flourished chiefly on the Rhine, in the north of France, and in England. If we consider the Norman as the first Gothic (of which it certainly was the forerunner or starting-point), the style commenced in England with the Norman invasion; it was developed in the thirteenth, and was perfected in the fourteenth century; in the fifteenth century it rapidly declined, and became extinct in this country in the sixteenth century; and has, in recent years, been revived with an amount of vigour which is so characteristic of the age we live in.

The peculiarly Norman style, such as is best known in this country, was originally developed in Sicily; it contains, of course, many Saracenic features, of which the pointed arch (introduced in the second or transition period) and the zigzag are the most prominent; for the Norman, though originally a simple Romanesque style, eventually adopted in the twelfth century the pointed arch of the Mohammedans.

The periods of Gothic may be briefly stated as follows:—

The Round Norman, or zigzag style (William I.).

The Pointed Norman, or Transition (Henry II. or first Plantagenet).

The Early English Gothic (Henry III. or second Plantagenet).

The Decorated Gothic (The Edwards, the third Plantagenet style).

The Perpendicular Gothic (Henry VII. or Lancastrian), ending in the Debased Perpendicular or Tudor (Henry VIII.), which scarcely deserves to be separately classed.

Fig. 25.

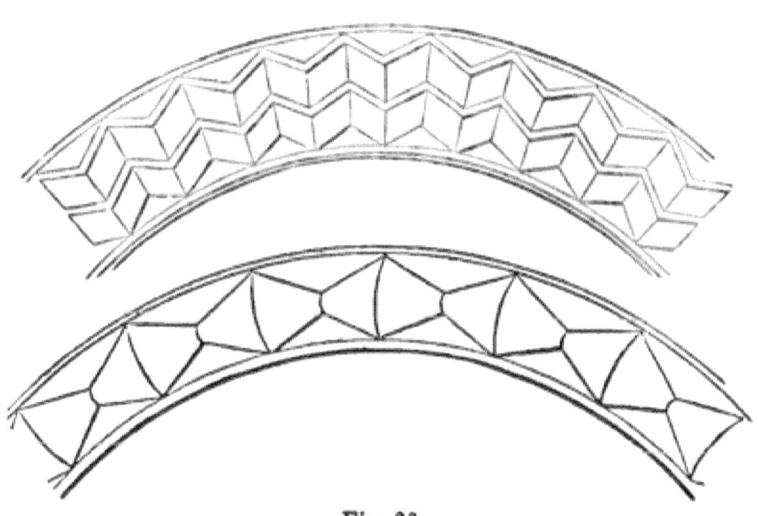

Fig. 26.

The Norman.—The chief characteristics of this style are the great solidity of its columns or piers, its semicircular arches, and its numerous ornamental borders or bands, miscalled mouldings.

The fact is, that the walls were of immense thickness, and at the soffits of arches this thickness was gradually diminished by being recessed, in order to remove the disagreeable appearance of the very wide intrados of the arch; on the perpendicular faces of the parts so recessed the ornamental bands were carved; the edges of the projections were in later periods cut away, or chamfered, and were subsequently worked into hollows and rolls, and thus we have the origin of mouldings.* Amongst these ornamental bands we have the Chevron or zigzag (Fig. 25), the Double cone (Fig. 26), the Beak's head, the Billet, the Chain, the Star, and an infinity of others; the chevron is, however, the most general, being found in every Norman building. The capital, called generally the cushion capital, is for the most part a mere block from which the lower angles are chamfered away; in some examples the lower part was fluted and otherwise ornamented.

In the *Transition* from the *Norman* to the *Early English*, we find the pointed arch, together with mouldings and other features altogether Norman. The most important form, however, introduced in the transition period was the "roll and fillet," a moulding which continued to hold a leading place in the combinations of the succeeding styles. It may be described as a narrow band or fillet set flat upon the face of the common cylindrical roll. In the earlier examples it is mostly set square upon the round member; but it is often found with the joining edges rounded off, so that the fillet merges gradually into the roll.

Early English.—The windows form very characteristic features in the Gothic style, but it is not possible here to enter deeply into that interesting subject. We will therefore only briefly mention that, in the period under consideration, the windows are for the most part long and narrow, with acutely pointed heads. These were often gathered together in two, three, five, or seven lights under one dripstone.

* For full description of mouldings, and of the Gothic style generally, see "Gothic Stonework," by Ellis A. Davidson.

It will be easily understood that when two windows of the lancet form were gathered under a dripstone rising to a point, a blank space, known as the tympanum, was formed. In process of time this was pierced with another light, in the form of a circle, ellipse, trefoil, &c. This feature was subsequently elaborated, and has been termed "plate tracery." It was the origin of the magnificent tracery which formed the leading characteristic of the next period. The capitals of

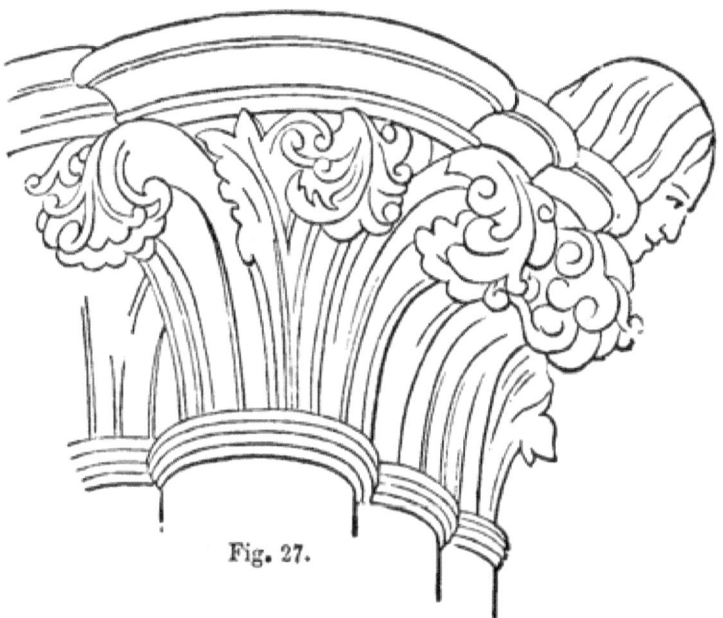

Fig. 27.

this period are bell-shaped, and are often, especially in the smaller examples, quite plain; but in the larger and richer specimens as, in Fig. 27—from Stone Church, Kent—the bell is covered with a peculiar rendering of the trefoil-leaf, springing from the neck and rising in a direct manner until it bends over in clusters; this has been called the stiff-leaved foliage: the method of thus rendering the trefoil evinces a desire to aim at the representation of natural forms, which was so well accomplished in the Decorated, and which declined in the Perpendicular period.

The most characteristic ornament of the Early English period is the Dog-tooth or "tooth" ornament (Fig. 28). It bears, however, no relation to a tooth, but is merely a solid rendering of the zigzag, and consists of a series of pyramids placed on their bases next to each other, and sometimes pierced with the trefoil ornament. It is also frequently rendered as a flower with four petals bent backwards.

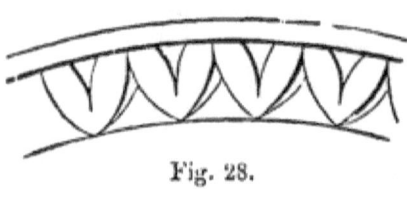

Fig. 28.

A beautiful method of ornamenting flat surfaces, which had originated with the Normans, was prevalent at this and subsequent periods; this was the manner of covering walls or portions of them with

Fig. 29.

Fig. 30.

what has been called "diapering."* The diaper consisted of a small flower, or geometrical pattern, carved in low relief, the design being repeated in separate

---

* The origin of this term has been much discussed. It is supposed to be taken from a kind of cloth worked in small square patterns, and which was then as now much used under the name of Dyaper, originally d'Ypres, the chief manufactory being at Ypres, in Belgium.

squares or other figures. Fig. 29, from Westminster Abbey, is an illustration of one of these.

The crocket and finial were also ornamental features of this and the subsequent periods. The crocket consisted, in the first place, merely of the pastoral crook, but soon became an ornament formed of the trefoil. Fig. 30 is one of the earliest, and is taken from Lincoln Cathedral. The finial consists of a bunch of crockets placed at the apex of the spires.

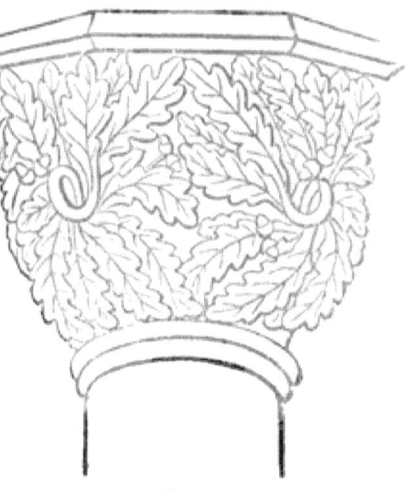

Fig. 31.

In the Decorated period we have two very distinguishing features. First, that the tracery was developed into the most beautiful patterns; and that the leading ornamentation is based on natural forms. The tracery is of two kinds: the geometrical and the flowing. In the former, the pattern consists entirely of geometrical combinations, as trefoils, quatrefoils, cinquefoils, hexafoils, &c., based on triangles, squares, pentagons, hexagons, &c. In the flowing tracery these figures, though still employed as the bases, are not completed in themselves, so as to stand out individually, but merge into each other: thus producing the most graceful forms, which have been called "flame-like" compartments.

Fig. 32.

In the *Decorated* period the capitals are either bell-shaped or octagonal, the foliage being wreathed around it instead of rising perpendicularly from the neck, as in the Early English. The leaves of the oak, maple, vine, ivy, strawberry, hazel, ferns, &c., are all so beautifully rendered as to give evidence of their having been taken directly from nature. The oak seems to have been an especial favourite. Fig. 31, which illustrates these remarks, is from York Cathedral; and this system was also carried out in the crockets and finials. One of the latter, from Cherrington, is shown in Fig. 32.

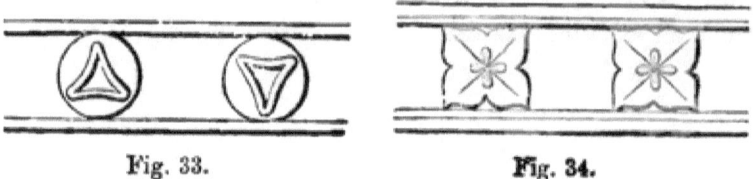

Fig. 33.   Fig. 34.

The Ball flower (Fig. 33) and Square flower (Fig. 34) were the most prevailing ornaments of the period.

The *Perpendicular style*, when fully developed, is characterized by the exuberance and redundancy of its ornaments. In the latter portion of the period it became so excessive, that the term "Florid" has been applied to it. The term Perpendicular has, however, been adopted in consequence of the peculiar arrangement of the tracery in the window heads, which form a very marked characteristic of the style. The beautiful flowing contour and curved lines of the tracery which so adorned the windows of the Decorated period, were superseded by mullions running perpendicularly from bottom to top, with transoms crossing horizontally; the roofs also were lowered, and the arch was flattened, until at last, in the Tudor period, it was drawn from four centres; and, in the Debased period, it was flattened altogether.

The capitals were either circular or octagonal, the

bell portion being mostly plain, but often covered with foliage of a harsh and conventional character, without either the freedom and boldness of the Early English or the natural grace of the Decorated period. Fig. 35, taken from the west doorway of Beverley Church, Yorkshire, will illustrate these remarks.

The leading features in the ornamentation of the Perpendicular period are—panel tra-

Fig. 35.

cery, which corresponds in some degree with the diaper work of the previous period, the patterns being, however, formed of mullions or tracery, quatrefoils, trefoils, &c.; a very rich description of vaulting, composed of pendant semicones covered with foliated panel work, called "fan tracery." The Tudor flower, the Portcullis and Rose, both badges of the Tudors, were also constantly used as ornaments; and the Angel bracket is very frequent, especially in the reign of Henry VII., angels being placed at intervals in the string courses.

The gradual decline of the Gothic style is very evident in the later churches of this period, especially in those begun in the tenth century. It will be easily understood that the Reformation formed a bar to the revival of this style; and the introduction at the same period of the Renaissance style, whilst the elements of the Gothic, though much degraded, were still in existence, led to the mixture of features, and that incongruity of style, which followed, and which has been called the Debased Gothic, in which every real principle of beauty was lost.

In Italy the Gothic was at once superseded by the classical; but in other countries it waned into what has been termed the "After-Gothic," which in its turn gradually merged into the revived Classic, which will presently be described.

Within recent years a revival of Gothic has taken place in this country, and buildings have been, and are being, erected which will bear comparison with those of the Middle Ages. We have architects, too, who in their scientific principles of construction, and in their enthusiasm, have not been surpassed at any period. Let us hope our artisans will avail themselves of the opportunities now held out to them for acquiring the skill to worthily carry out the works, and that our designers and decorators will make themselves acquainted with the principles of the architecture of different periods, so that they may understand the application, and enter into the spirit, of the system of ornamentation to be adopted in accordance with the style.

CHAPTER XXXVI.

THE RENAISSANCE.

This style was the revival and combination of the most beautiful elements of Classic art. The return to these was due to the gradually growing influence of the Saracenic, not as an absolute style, but as affording new elements of beauty, especially in its varied and intricate interlacings, which were so prominent for a while as to constitute the chief characteristic of a new style.

Fig. 36.—Bronze from Door of St. Maclou, Rouen, 1542 (Wornum).

The first step of the transition from middle age to modern art is known from its mean time (about 1300) as the *Trecento*, the great features of which are its intricate tracery or interlacings and delicate scroll-work of conventional foliage—the style being a combination of the Byzantine and Saracenic, the symbolism of both being excluded. The foliage and floriage, however, are not exclusively conventional, and it comprises a fair rendering of the classical orders with the *restoration of the round arch.**

In the *Quattrocento*, the next period of this style,

---

* For much of the above information the writer is indebted to Mr. Wornum's admirable lectures (1848, 1849, and 1850). Digests of these lectures are now published under the auspices of the Department of Science and Art, and the reader is urged to supplement the sketch here given by further study from that work.

we have a far more decided revival. The bronze gates of the Baptistry of San Giovanni, by Lorenzo Ghiberti (1425-52), exhibit one feature of this period in perfection—the prominence of simple natural imitations, which now almost entirely superseded the conventional representations of previous times. Nature no longer supplied mere suggestions, but afforded directly exact models for imitation, whether fruit or flowers, birds or other animals, all disposed with a view to the picturesque or ornamental. The selection of the details might still have some typical significance, but this had no influence on the manner of their execution, which was as purely imitative as their arrangement was ornamental. Thus, in the grand border surrounding the gates of Ghiberti, the flowers and fruit are grouped in the most luxurious manner, whilst birds and squirrels seem enjoying themselves according to their natural habits, the whole being evidently emblematic of the fulness of the Creation; yet, although some of the forms—the egg-plant, the pomegranates, the pears, and the lilies—stand out in full relief, they are so disposed that their shadows do not hide the objects by which they are surrounded, but merely serve as it were to gather them into one harmonious whole.

It appears that in the year 1401 the civic trades of Florence were formed into guilds, called "Arti," represented by deputies called "Consoli." These patriotic men resolved to open a competition for a bronze gate, to be erected at the Baptistry, that should surpass the old one by Andrea Pisano. Seven of the greatest artists of Italy entered the lists, but the prize was awarded by the competitors themselves to Lorenzo Ghiberti, who was only at the time twenty-two years of age. This great work occupied him twenty-three years; and at the completion, so great was the admiration it excited, that the consuls of the guild of merchants commissioned him to execute another corresponding door, of which, according to his own account, they placed the plan and execution in his own hands.

"They gave him full permission," says Vasari, "to proceed with the work as he should think best, and to do whatever might most effectually secure that this third door should be the richest, most highly adorned, most beautiful, and most perfect that he could possibly contrive or that could be imagined. He received more than 13,000 florins for his labour, and gained great fame and honour."

Casts of these gates are in the Art Schools of the Department of Science and Art, and may also be seen complete in the Renaissance Court of the Crystal Palace, in the hand-book to which, by Sir M. D. Wyatt and J. B. Waring, Esq., they are fully described.

The border, already described, surrounds the gates, which are divided into ten panels, representing Scripture subjects—

1. The Creation, up to the expulsion of Adam and Eve from Paradise.
2. Cain and Abel.
3. The Flood.
4. Passages in the history of Abraham.
5. The history of Esau.
6. The history of Joseph.
7. Moses on Mount Sinai.
8. The passage of the Israelites across the Jordan.
9. A battle between the Hebrews and the Philistines.
10. The meeting of the Queen of Sheba and Solomon.

"The love of nature," says Mr. Waring, "with

the first Renaissance artists became a passion, and was the basis of their style. It is this which gives such a wonderful charm to the works of that illustrious triad — Ghiberti, Donatello, and Lucca della Robbia, who, imbued with the true spirit of the antique, and an unusual sense of the beautiful, ennobled all, even the commonest subjects, which came from their hands. We are the more desirous that this should be well understood, since it is a fact too often lost sight of; and the 'Renaissance' implies not the revival of antique art only, but the return to that great school which nature keeps ever open to us."
"The artist held his place modestly, working for the sake of art and the love of truth, whilst in his productions he sought, not to astonish by his skill or science, but to infuse into others that love of nature and the antique which inspired himself."

Our own *Elizabethan* must be considered as an elaboration of the Renaissance, probably introduced from the Low Countries, the only difference being that the Elizabethan exhibits a very striking preponderance of strap and shield-work; but this was a gradual result; and what we now term Elizabethan was not thoroughly developed until the time of James I., when the pierced shields even outbalanced the strap work. The pure Elizabethan is much nearer allied to the continental styles of the true classical ornaments, but rude in detail, occasionally scroll and arabesque work, and the tracery or strap-work holding a much more prominent place than the pierced and scrolled shields. Such are the varieties of the Revival distinct from the Cinquecento, or perfect form. A design containing all the elements of this period is properly called *Renaissance*. If it contains only the tracery and foliage of the period, it would be more properly called *Trecento*. If it contains, besides these elaborate natural imitations, festoons, scroll-work, and occasional symmetrical arabesques, it is of the *Quattrocento*, the Italian Renaissance of the fifteenth century; and if it displays a decided prominence of strap-work and shield-work, it is *Elizabethan*.

The *Cinquecento* is the full development of the modern styles, and was the most prominent style of the sixteenth century; it is the real goal of the Re-

Fig. 37.—Chimney-piece, Louvre, by Germain Pilou (Wornum).

naissance, to which all the efforts of the fifteenth century tended.

The styles we have described all tended to the ultimate perfection attained in that now under consideration, which was only achieved by the artists of Italy when the glorious monuments of the ancients were excavated at the close of the fifteenth century; and, with these examples before them, Raffaelle, Julio Romano, the Lombardi, Bramante, and Michael-Angelo succeeded in developing the style until it surpassed in its beauty the very originals from which it sprang.

The leading elements of the Cinquecento may be considered to be—the arabesque scroll (Fig. 37), combining in its elements every other feature of classical art, with animals and plants rendered naturally or conventionally, the sole guiding idea being beauty of form; the beautiful variations of ancient standard forms, as the anthemion, the guilloche, the fret, the acanthus scroll, &c. ; absolute works of art introduced into the arabesques, as vases, implements, and instruments of all kinds—strap and shield work being, however, wholly excluded, as not authorised by ancient practice; the admirable play of colour in the arabesques and scrolls—the three secondary colours, orange, green, and purple, are the leading ones—thus affording a contrast to the early periods of ornamentation, in which we have already shown the primary colours were preferred.

"The Cinquecento," says Mr. Wornum, "may be considered the culminating style in ornamental art, as presenting the most perfect forms and pleasing varieties, nature and art vieing with each other in their efforts to attract and gratify the eye. It appeals only to the sense of beauty. All its efforts are made to attain the most attractive effects, without any intent to lead the mind to an ulterior end, as is the case in the Byzantine and other symbolic styles. The Cinquecento forms are supposed to be symbols of beauty alone; and it is a remarkable concession to the ancients that the moderns to attain this result were compelled to recur to their works; and it is only now, in contemplation of this consummate style, that the term Renaissance becomes quite intelligible. The Renaissance, or re-birth, of ornament is accomplished in the Cinquecento; still the term is not altogether ill appropriated to the earlier styles, because these were really the stepping-stones to the Cinquecento, and, as already explained, in them also the æsthetic was substituted for the symbolic. The principles, therefore, were identical, though, from the imperfect apprehension, elements strange to the classical period were generally admitted: it was a revival of principle, though not of element."

The great characteristic of the *Louis Quatorze* style (1643-1715) is its gilt stucco work, which almost entirely superseded decorated painting; the ornamental features being rendered in very high relief, depending

Fig. 38.—Carved Wood, Notre Dame, Paris (Wornum).

more on the play of light and shade than in the colouring; in fact, the favourite ornament, the anthemion, under a treatment which rejected flat surfaces and necessitated hollows and projections, became the hollow shell, which is perhaps the most leading ornament of this style.

The *Louis Quinze* (1715-74), Fig. 38, does not much differ from the Louis Quatorze in its elements, but yet, from a certain manner of treatment, must be considered as distinct in a discrimination of styles. It differs in this, that the merely characteristic elements of the Louis Quatorze became paramount in Louis Quinze; all its details, instead of coming direct from the Cinquecento or Renaissance, came immediately from the French schemes of the preceding reign, and the divergence from the original types thus became wider.

The infinite and fantastic play of light and shade being the great idea of the Louis Quatorze period of ornamentation, exact symmetry in the parts was no longer essential, and accordingly we find, for the first time, symmetry systematically avoided. This feature was gradually increased in the Louis Quinze style, and ultimately led to the debased system of ornamentation (if system it can properly be called) known as the *Rococo*, in which balance of separate parts, or symmetry of the whole, was entirely set aside.

INDEX.

ACANTHUS Plant, in the Grecian and Roman Styles, 190
Accordance of Colours, 6
Alphabet of Colours, 4
Analogy of Colours, 10
Angel Bracket (Perpendicular Gothic), 206
Anomalous Colours, 5
Anotta, 67
Anthemion or Honeysuckle (in Greek Ornament), 188
Antimony, Orange, 67
    White, 31
    Yellow, 28—30
Antwerp Brown, 97
    Blue, 60
Arabesque Scrolls (in Cinquecento Ornament), 212
Arabic, Gum, 130
Arrangement of Colours, 4
Arsenic, Yellow, 36
Ashes, Ultramarine, 56
Asphaltum (Bitumen), 95
Assyrian Style, Chain or Guilloche, 186
    Human-headed Colossi, 184
    Open Flower, 186
    Ornament, 184
Aureolin, 38
Azure, 54

BADGER Tools, 167
Ball Flower (Decorated Gothic), 204
Baptistry at Florence (Ghiberti's Gates), 209
Barytic White, 22

Beauty, 8
Bice, Blue, 62
    Green, 71
Bismuth (Pearl), White, 22
Bistre, 97
Bitumen (Asphaltum), 95
Black Colour, 7
Black, 102
    Blue, 106
    Bone, 105
    Chalk, 108
    Frankfort, 106
    Ivory, 105
    Lamp, 105
    Lead (Plumbago), 109
    Manganese, 108
    Mineral, 107
    Mixed, 103
    Nero di Foglio, 107
    Ochre, 108
    Peach, 106
    Pigments, 105
    Spanish, 107
    Vine, 106
Bladder Green, 75
Blanc d'Argent, 20
Blood, Dragon's, 47
Blooming of Varnishes, 149
Blue, Antwerp, 60
    Armenian, 54
    Azure, 54
    Bice, 62
    Black, 106
    Cæruleum, 62
    Cobalt, 57
    Colour, 3, 52
    Dumont's, 57

Blue,
    Enamel (Zaffre), 57
    Factitious, 56
    Haarlem, 60
    Hungary, 57
    Indigo, 60
    Intense, 61
    Mountain, 62
    Ochre (Phosphate of Iron), 101
    Pigments, 54
    Prussian, 60
    Royal, 59
    Saunders, 62
    Saxon, 57
    Schweinfurt, 62
    Smalt, 58
    Thenard's, 57
    Ultramarine, 54
    Verditer, 61
    Vienna, 58
Body, 15
Borax, 131
Bougeval White, 23
Broken Colours, 91
Brown, 5, 89
    Antwerp, 97
    Bone, 95
    Cappagh, 93
    Egyptian (Mummy), 96
    Euchrome, 93
    Ivory, 95
    Madder, 98
    Manganese, 92
    Ochre, 33, 94
    Pigments, 92
    Pink, 83
    Prussian, 98
    Rubens, 94
    Spanish, 45
    Tints, 25
    Vandyke, 92
Brunswick Green, 72
Brush, Use of, 157
Brushes used in Oil Painting, 166
    To clean, 168
Burnt Carmine, 79
    Roman Ochre, 33
    Sienna Earth, 66
    Umber, 93
    Verdigris, 88
Byzantine Style of Ornament, 191
    Mosaics, 194
    Varieties of, 193

CADMIUM Yellow, 36
Canvas for Oil-painting, 169
    Various Sizes of, 169
Capitals, Composite, 190
    Corinthian, 189
    Decorated, 203
    Doric, 189
    Early English, 201
    Ionic, 189
    Norman, 200
    Perpendicular, 205
    Tuscan, 191
Cappagh Brown, 93
Carmine, 50
    Burnt, 79
    Durable, 51
    Madder, 51
Carnations, Oil of, 139
Carucru, 67
Cassel Earth, 94
Cassius's Precipitate, 86
Cendres Blue, 62
Chain Ornament (in the Assyrian Style), 186
Chalk, Black, 108
    White, 23
Characteristic Features of the various Styles of Ornament, 179
Chica, 67
Chilling of Varnishes, 150
Chinese Vermilion, 42
    Yellow, 36
Chromate of Mercury, 65
Chromatic Equivalents, 7
Chromatics defined, 3
Chrome Green, 71
    Orange, 65
    Yellow, 29
Cinnabar, 42
Cinquecento Style of Ornament, 211
Citrine Colour, 5, 80
    Mixed, 81
    Pigments, 83
    Umber, 83
Cleaning and restoring Paintings, 175
Cobalt, Blue, 57
    Green, 72
Cochineal Lakes, 48
Cologne Earth, 94
Colour, Hues of, 5
    Influence of, 2
    Relation of, 4

INDEX.

Colour,
  Shades of, 6
  Suggestions for Studies of Harmony of, 9
Colouring, Illustrations of, 9
  Practical, 13
Colourists, 9
Colour Pigments, Qualities of, 15
Colours, Complementary, 7
  Contrasts of, 6
  Definitive Scale of, 7
  Discordant, 12
  Elements of, 1
  Evolved from Light and Shade, 2
  Expression of, 11
  How generated, 2
  Harmony of, 4
  Heraldic, 123
  Inherent and Transient, 13
  Measured, 7
  Material, 13
  Neutral, 7
  Of Flowers, 1
  Polar Elements of, 3
  Powers of, 7
  Primary, 3, 26
  Secondary, 4
  Semi-neutral, 90, 98
  Studies in Harmony of, 9
  Tables of Fresco, 118
  Tables of Heraldic, 119
  Tables of Oil, 125
  Tables of Qualities, 111—117
  Tables of Tempera, 124
  Tables of Water, 123, 124
  Tertiary, 2, 4
  Three Orders of, 4
Colours and Pigments, Difference between the Terms, 16
Complementary Colours, 7
Composition of Colours, 3
Compound Pigments, 15
  Black, 103
  Brown, 91
  Citrine, 81
  Green, 70
  Grey, 100
  Olive, 88
  Orange, 65
  Purple, 78
  Russet, 85
Constant White, 22
Contrasts of Colours, 6

Conventional rendering of Natural Elements in Egyptian Ornament, 182
Copaiba, 141
Copal Varnish, 145
Copper Greens, 72
Cowdie, or Fossil Varnish, 147
Cracking, 135, 149
Crayon Colours, 118
Crems, or Krems, White, 20
Cyanide of Iron, 59

DAMAS Varnish, 144
  Dead Colouring (in Oil-painting), 169
Debased Gothic, 206
Decorated Gothic, Capitals, 203
  Foliage, 204
  Ornaments, 204
  Tracery, 203
Definitive Scale of Colours, 7
Discordant Colours, 12
Distemper Colours, 124
  Painting, 160
Doctrine of Light and Colours, 3
Dog-tooth Ornament (Early English Gothic), 202
Doric Capital, 189
Diapers in Egyptian Ornament, 184
  In Gothic Ornament, 202
Dragon's Blood, 47
Dryers, 133, 138
Drying Oils, 138
Drawing-board, 153
Drawing Papers, Qualities and Sizes of, 152
  To stretch, 154
Dumont's Blue, 57
Durability of Colours, 15
Dutch Pink, 39

EARTH, Cassel, 94
  Cologne, 94
  Sienna, 32, 65
Early English (Gothic), 200
  Capitals, 201
  Crockets, 202
  Diapers, 202
  Finials, 203
  Foliage, 201
  Plate Tracery, 201
  Windows, 200
Easel, 171

Echinus, or Horse Chestnut (in Greek Ornament), 189
Egg-shell White, 23
Egyptian Brown (Mummy), 96
  Sphinx, 185
  Style of Ornament, 181
Elements of Colours, 1
Elizabethan Style of Ornament, 210
Emerald Green, 73
Enamel Blue (Zaffre), 57
  Colours, 117
English Pink, 39
  Red, 42
Equivalents, Scale of, 7
Essential Oils, 134, 141
Euchrome, 93
Expressed Oil, 135
Expression of Colours, 8
Eye, Effects of Colours on the, 3

FADING of Colours, 14
  Fish Oils, 140
Flake White, 20
Flat Tints, Flowers in, 164
  Washes, 157
Florentine Lake, 49
Flower Painting in Water-colours, 160
Foliage, Natural (Decorated Gothic), 202
  Stiff (Early English Gothic), 201
Frankfort Black, 106
French Green, 72
  Gray, 24
Fresco Painting, Processes of, 173
Fundamental Scale of Colours, 2

GALENA, 110
  Gall Stone, 37
Gamboge, 36
Ghiberti, Gates of, Baptistry at Florence, 208
Glass Mosaics (Byzantine), 194
  Tesselation (Byzantine), 194
Glazing in Oil-painting, 170
Golden Sulphur of Antimony, 67
Gold Purple, 78
  Size, Japanner's, 139
Gothic Style, Debased, 206
  Decorated, 203
  Early English, 200

Gothic Style,
  General Features of, 198
  Norman, 199
  Perpendicular, 204
  Transition, 200
Graduating Tints in Water-colours, 159
Graphite, 109
Gray, Anomalous Tint, 5
  Mixed, 100
  Neutral Colour, 7, 99
  Pigments, 101
Grecian Style of Ornament, 187
Green, Bice, 71
  Brunswick, 72
  Chrome, 71
  Cobalt, 72
  Copper, 72
  Emerald, 73
  French, 72
  Hooker's, 70
  Invisible, 76
  Italian, 71
  Malachite, 74
  Marine, 72
  Mineral, 74
  Mixed, 70
  Mountain, 74
  Olive, 88
  Olympian, 72
  Patent, 72
  Persian, 72
  Relations of, 4, 68, 69
  Pigments, 70
  Prussian, 75
  Rinmann's, 72
  Sap, 75
  Saxon, 72
  Scheele's, 74
  Schweinfurt's, 75
  Terre-verte, 71
  Varley's, 70
  Venetian, 76
  Verdigris, 73
  Verditer, 72, 73
  Verona, 71
  Tints, 26
Grey Tints, 25
Grinding Pigments, 14
Gum Ammonia, 130
  Arabic, 130
  Senegal, 129
  Tragacanth, 130
Gumtion, 140

INDEX.

HAARLEM Blue. 60
   Hamburg Lake, 50
Harmony of Colours, 4
   Suggestions for Studies in, 9
Hatching, 164
Heat, Effects of, on Colours, 117
Heraldic Colours, &c., Table of, 120
Hog-hair Brushes, 166
Hooker's Green, 70
Hue, Tint, and Shade distinguished, 5
Hungary Blue, 57

ILLUSTRATIONS of Colouring, 9
Impasting in Oil Painting, 71
Impurity of Pigments, 6
Indian Blue, 60
   Ink, 108
   Lake, 50
   Red, 46
   Varnish, 146
   Yellow, 38
Indigo, 60
Inherent and Transient Colours, 13
Ink, China, 108
   Indian, 108
Intense Blue, 61
   Brown, 86
Intonaco (in Fresco Painting), 175
Invisible Green, 76
Iodine, Scarlet, 43
Ionic Capital, 189
Iron, Cyanide of, 59
   Effects of, on Pigments, 115
   Yellow, 34
Irregular-shaped Brushes, 166
Italian Green, 71
   Pink, 39
Ivory Black, 105
   Brown, 95

JAPANNER'S Gold Size, 138
   Jaune Minérale, 29
   Jaune de Mars, or Jaune de Fer, 36
Jews' Pitch, 95

KERMES, Lake, 48
   King's Yellow, 36

LAC Varnish, 146
   Labyrinth, in Egyptian Ornament, or Fret, 182
   In Greek Ornament, 187
Lake, Chinese, 48, 50
   Cochineal, 49
   Field's, 48
   Florentine, 49
   Green, 72
   Hamburg, 50
   Kermes, 48
   Lac, 50
   Madder, 48
   Purple, 79
   Red, 47
   Roman, 50
   Rubric, 48
   Scarlet, 49
   Venetian, 50
   Yellow, 38
Lamp Black, 105
Laque Minérale, 65
Lavender Oil, 142
   Tints, 25
Lead. Black, 109
   Chromate of, 29
   Colour, 17
   Its effects on Colours, 18
   Orange, 67
   Red, 44
   Sulphate of, 21
   White, 18
Lensic Prism, its Power, 3
Light and Colours, 2
Light and Shade, 2, 14
Light, Elementary, 2, 14
Linseed Oil, 136
   Preserved and Purified, 139
   Rendered Drying, 139
Litharge, 133
London White, 19
Lotus, or Water Lily (in Egyptian Ornament), 182
Louis Quatorze Style of Ornament, 213
Louis Quinze Style of Ornament, 213

MADDER Brown, 98
   Carmine, 51
   Lake, 48
   Purple, 79
   Russet, 85
Malachite, 74

Manganese Brown, 92
Maps, Tinting (with Verdigris), 73
Marble Tesselation (Byzantine), 194
Marine Green, 72
Marrone, 89
Mars Orange, 66
Massicot, 31
Mastic Varnish, 144
Material Colours, 13
Maxims in Colouring, 155
Media, 132
    In Tempera Painting, 161
Megilp, 140
Melody of Colours, 12
Mercury, Chromate of, 65
    Iodide of, 43
    Sulphuret of (Vermilion), 42
Milk of Lime, 131
Mineral Black, 107
    Green, 74
    Pitch, 95
    Purple, 80
    Yellow, 36
Minium, 44
Mixed Tints, 24—26
Mixing of Colours, 156
Modan White, 23
Modes and Operations of Painting, 151, 156, 160, 164, 173
Monochrome, Painting in, 157
    Subjects for Practice in, 158
Moors—their Principles of Design, 196
Morat White, 23
Mosaics (Byzantine), 194
Mountain Blue, 62
    Green, 74
Mucilage, 129
Mummy, 96

NAPHTHA, 143
    Naples, Yellow, 30
Natural Scale of Colours, 3
Negative Colours, 17
Nero di Foglio, 107
Neutral Black, 102
    Colours, 2, 3, 17, 102
    Gray, 98
    Tint, 100
    White, 16
Neutralization of Colours, 5

Norman Style, 199
    Capitals, 200
    Ornamental Bands, 199
    Round Arch, 199
Nottingham White, 19
Numerical Proportion of Colours, 7
Nut Oils, 140

OCHRE, Black, 108
    Brown, 94
    De Rue, 33
    Indian, 45
    Orange, 66
    Purple, 80
    Red, 45
    Roman, 33
    Scarlet, 45
    Spruce, 30, 33
    Stone, 31, 33
    Yellow, 32
Oil, Boiled, 139
    Drying, 138
    Expressed, 135
    Fish, 140
    Lavender, 142
    Linseed, 136
    Nut, 140
    Of Pinks, 139
    Of Turpentine, 142
    Olive, 140
    Poppy, 139
    Spike, 112
    Volatile or Essential, 135, 141
Oil Painting, 164
Oils, 135
Olive Colour, 5
    Green, 88
    Mixed, 88
Olympian Green, 72
Opacity, 15
Open Flower (in Assyrian Ornament), 186
Orange, 4
    Antimony, 67
    Chrome, 65
    Compound, 65
    Lead, 67
    Mars, 66
    Ochre, 66
Ornament, Assyrian, 184
    Byzantine, 191
    Cinquecento, 211

Ornament,
  Egyptian, 181
  Gothic, 198
  Grecian, 187
  Louis Quatorze, 213
  Of, generally, 179
  Roman, 190
  Renaissance, 207
  Saracenic, 195
Orpiment, 35
  Orange, 67
  Red, 35
  Yellow, 35
Oxford Ochre, 32
Ox-gall, 131
Oyster-shell White, 23

PAINTING, Fresco, 173
  Modes and Operations of, 151
  Oil, 164
  Tempera, 160
  Water-colour, 156
Paint, To Remove, 178
Palette, 172
Papyrus-plant in Egyptian Ornament, 182
Paris Blue, 58
  White, 20
Parthenon Frieze (Grecian Ornament), 187
Patent Green, 72
  Yellow, 30
Peach Black, 106
Pearl White, 22
Permanence of Colours, 15
Permanent White, 22
Perpendicular Gothic Capitals, 205
  Characteristic Features, 204
  Foliage, 205
  Ornaments, 206
  Windows, 205
Persian Green, 72
  Red, 46
Phosphate of Iron, 101
Photogen and Sciogen, Elements of Light and Colours, 14
Picture-cleaning, 176
Pigments and Colours, difference between the Terms, 16
Pigments, Black, 102
  Blue, 52
  Brown, 69
  Citrine, 80

Pigments,
  Gray, 98
  Green, 68
  Mixed, 88
  Olive, 87
  Qualities of, 14
Plumbago, 102
Polarity of Light and Colours, 4
Polish, French, 146
Portcullis (Perpendicular Gothic), 206
Powers of Colours, 7
Practical Colouring, 13
Primary Colours, 3, 6
  Contrasts, 7
Prism, The Lensic, 3
Prussian Blue, 60
  Brown, 98
  Green, 75
Prussiate of Copper, 86
  Of Iron, 59
Purple, 4
  Burnt Carmine, 79
  Its Relation to other Colours, 76, 77
  Lake, 79
  Madder, 79
  Mixed, 78
  Ochre, 80
  Of Gold, 78
  Rubiate, or Field's, 79

QUALITIES of Pigments, 14
  Quattrocento Period, 207

RAW Sienna Earth, 34
  Umber, 83
Red Colours, 3, 39
  Carmine, 50
  English, 43
  Indian, 46
  Iodine Scarlet, 43
  Lake, 47
  Lake Lac, 50
  Lake Scarlet, 49
  Lead, 44
  Light, 46
  Madder Carmine, 51
  Ochre, 45
  Pigments, 42
Red, Persian, 46
  Prussian, 47
  Saturnine, 44
  Spanish, 47

Red,
    Venetian, 47
    Vermilion, 42
Refraction of Light, 3
Refrangibility of Colours, 4
Relations of Colours, 5
Renaissance Period of Ornament, 207
Repose, Principles of, 10
Retiring Colours, 10
Rinmann's Green, 72
Roman Lake, 50
    Ochre, 33
    Style of Ornament, 189
    White, 20
Rose Pink, 51
    Rubric or Madder Lake, 48
Roucou, 67
Rouen White, 23
Rough Cast Ground in Fresco Painting, 175
Royal Blue, 59
Rubens' Brown, 94
Rubiate, or Field's Purple, 79
Rubiates, 48
Rubric Lake, 48
Rue, Ochre de, 33
Russet Colour, 5, 84, 85
    Field's, 85
    Mixed, 85
    Ochre, 86

SABLE Brushes, 166
    Sap Green, 75
Satin White, 23
Saturnine Red, 44
Saunders Blue, 62
Saxon Blue, 57
    Green, 72
Scale of Colours, Primary, 3
    Contrasts, 6
    Equivalents, 7
Scarlet, Iodine, 43
    Lake, 49
    Ochre, 45
Scene Painting, 162
Scheele's Green, 74
Schweinfurt Blue, 62
    Green, 75
Science of Colours, 2
Sciogen, 14
Scroll in Grecian Ornament, 189
    Roman Ornament, 190
Scumbling (in Oil Painting), 171

Secondary Colours, 4
Semi-neutral Colours, 89
Sepia, 97
Series of Colours, 5
Shades, Tints, and Hues, 6
Shadow Colours, 10
Sky Colours, 53, 55
Siccatives (Dryers), 133
Sienna Earth, Burnt, 66
    Raw, 34
Silver White, 20
Size, 131
Smalt, 58
Spanish Black, 107
    Brown, 45
    White, 23
Spectral Colours, 3
Spike, Oil of, 142
Spirit of Wine, 143
Sphinx, Egyptian, 184
    Greek, 184
Spruce Ochre, 33
Square Flower (Decorated Gothic), 204
Stil de Grain, 39
Stippling, 164
Stone Ochre, 33
Styles of Ornament, Assyrian, 184
    Byzantine, 191
    Cinquecento, 211
    Egyptian, 181
    Elizabethan, 210
    Gothic, 198
    Grecian, 187
    Louis Quatorze, 213
    Louis Quinze, 213
    Renaissance, 207
    Roman, 190
    Saracenic, 195
Subjects for Study, 158
Sugar of Lead, 133
Sulphate of Lead, 21
Sulphuret of Antimony, 67
    Arsenic, 35
    Cadmium, 36
    Mercury or Quicksilver, 42
    Zinc, 133
Symbolic Colouring, 121
Symbols, Heraldic, 119, 123
System, Chromatic, 3

TABLES of Colours—
    Fresco Colours, 118
    Heraldic Colours, 119

INDEX.

Tables of Colours—
  Oil Colours, 125
  Tempera Colours, 124
  Various Qualities, 111, 112, 113, 114, 115, 116, 117
  Water-colours, 123, 124
Taste, 2, 5
Tempera Painting, 160
Terra Orleans, 67
Terre Blue, 62
  De Cassel, 94
  Verte, 69, 71
Tertiary Colours, 2
Tests of Lakes, 49, 51
  Ultramarine, &c., 56, 57
  Vermilion, 43
Thenard's Blue, 57
Theory of Colours, 1, 12
Time, Effects of, on Colours, 15
Tin White, 21
Tints, Brown, 25
  Green, 26
  Grey, 25
  Lavender, 25
  Mixed, 24, 25, 26
  Yellow, 26
Tints, Hues, and Shades, 6
Tiver, 94
Tragacanth, 130
Transient Colours, 13
Transition (Gothic), 200
Trecento Period, 207
Triads of Colours, 3
Troy White, 23
Tudor Flower, 206
  Rose, 206
Turpentine Oil, 142
Tuscan Capitals, 191

ULTRAMARINE, 54
  Ashes, 56, 101
  Factitious, 56
  French, 56
Umber, Burnt, 89
  Raw, 83
Useful Receipts, 176

VANDYKE Brown, 92
  Varley's Green, 70
Varnishes, 143
  Blooming of, 149
  Copal, 145
  Cowdie, or Fossil, 147
  Damas, 144

Varnishes,
  Indian, 146
  Lac, 146
  Lac, White, 146
  Mastic, 144
  Resinous, 144
  To remove, 176
Vehicles, 126
  Egg, 161
  Oil, 135—143
  Varnish, 144—149
  Water, &c., 128—132
Venetian Green, 76
  Red, 43, 45
  White, 18
Verdigris, 73
  Burnt, 88
Verditer, Blue, 61
  Green, 72, 73
Vermilion, 42
Verona Green, 71
Verte, Terre, 71
Vienna Blue, 58
Vine Black, 106
Viride Æris, 73
Vision, Effects of Colour on, 9
Volatile Oils, 135, 141

WATER-COLOURS, 155
  Painting in, 156
Water Vehicles, 128
Wave-Scroll in Egyptian Ornament, 183
Wax Painting, 163
White, 7, 16
  Barytic, 22
  Bismuth (Pearl), 22
  Bougeval, 23
  Chinese, 23
  Colours, 16
  Constant, 22
  Copperas, 133
  Egg-shell, 23
  Flake, 20
  Krems, or Kremnitz, 20
  Lead, 18
  London, 19
  Modan, 23
  Morat, 23
  Nottingham, 19
  Oyster-shell, 23
  Pearl, 22
  Roman, 20
  Rouen, 23

INDEX.

White,
   Satin, 23
   Silver, 20
   Spanish, 23
   Sulphate of Lead, 21
   Tin, 21
   Troy, 23
   Venetian, 18
   Vitriol, 131
   Zinc, 21
White Chalk, 23
Wine, Spirit of, 143
Winged Globe, The (in Egyptian Ornament), 181

YELLOW Colour, 3, 27
   Arsenic, 36
   Aureolin, 38
   Brown Ochre, 33
   Cadmium, 36
   Chinese, 36
   Chrome, 29
   Dutch Pink, 39
   English Pink, 39
   Gall-Stone, 37
   Gamboge, 36
   Indian, 38
   Iron, 34

Yellow,
   Italian Pink, 39
   Jaune de Mars, or Jaune de Fer, 34
   Jaune Minérale, 29
   King's, 36
   Lake, 38
   Massicot, 31
   Mineral (Arsenic), 36
   Montpellier, 30
   Naples, 30
   Ochre and Oxford, 32
   Orpiment, 35
   Patent, 30
   Pigments, 27
   Roman Ochre, 33
   Stil de Grain, 39
   Stone Ochre, 33
   Terra Sienna, 34
   Tints, 26

ZAFFRE, 57
   Zarnic, 35
Zigzag (in Egyptian Ornament), 182
   In Norman Ornament, 199
Zinc, Sulphate of, 133
   White, 21

THE END.

PRINTED BY J. S. VIRTUE AND CO., LIMITED, CITY ROAD, LONDON.

WEALE'S SERIES
OF
SCIENTIFIC AND TECHNICAL
WORKS.

"It is not too much to say that no books have ever proved more popular with or more useful to young engineers and others than the excellent treatises comprised in WEALE'S SERIES."—*Engineer.*

A New Classified List.

	PAGE		PAGE
CIVIL ENGINEERING AND SURVEYING	2	ARCHITECTURE AND BUILDING	6
MINING AND METALLURGY	3	INDUSTRIAL AND USEFUL ARTS	9
MECHANICAL ENGINEERING	4	AGRICULTURE, GARDENING, ETC.	10
NAVIGATION, SHIPBUILDING, ETC.	5	MATHEMATICS, ARITHMETIC, ETC	12
BOOKS OF REFERENCE AND MISCELLANEOUS VOLUMES			14

CROSBY LOCKWOOD AND SON,
7, STATIONERS' HALL COURT, LONDON, E.C.
1897.

CIVIL ENGINEERING & SURVEYING.

Civil Engineering.
By HENRY LAW, M. Inst. C.E. Including a Treatise on HYDRAULIC ENGINEERING by G. R. BURNELL, M.I.C.E. Seventh Edition, revised, with LARGE ADDITIONS by D. K. CLARK, M.I.C.E. . . . 6/6

Pioneer Engineering:
A Treatise on the Engineering Operations connected with the Settlement of Waste Lands in New Countries. By EDWARD DOBSON, A.I.C.E. With numerous Plates. Second Edition 4/6

Iron Bridges of Moderate Span:
Their Construction and Erection. By HAMILTON W. PENDRED. With 40 Illustrations 2/0

Iron (Application of) to the Construction of Bridges, Roofs, and other Works.
By FRANCIS CAMPIN, C.E. Fourth Edition 2/6

Constructional Iron and Steel Work,
as applied to Public, Private, and Domestic Buildings. By FRANCIS CAMPIN, C.E. 3/6

Tubular and other Iron Girder Bridges.
Describing the Britannia and Conway Tubular Bridges. By G. DRYSDALE DEMPSEY, C.E. Fourth Edition 2/0

Materials and Construction:
A Theoretical and Practical Treatise on the Strains, Designing, and Erection of Works of Construction. By FRANCIS CAMPIN, C.E. 3/0

Sanitary Work in the Smaller Towns and in Villages.
By CHARLES SLAGG, Assoc. M. Inst. C.E. Second Edition . . 3/0

Roads and Streets (The Construction of).
In Two Parts: I. THE ART OF CONSTRUCTING COMMON ROADS, by H. LAW, C.E., Revised by D. K. CLARK, C.E.; II. RECENT PRACTICE: Including Pavements of Wood, Asphalte, etc. By D. K. CLARK, C.E. 4/6

Gas Works (The Construction of),
And the Manufacture and Distribution of Coal Gas. By S. HUGHES, C.E. Re-written by WILLIAM RICHARDS, C.E. Eighth Edition . . 5/6

Water Works
For the Supply of Cities and Towns. With a Description of the Principal Geological Formations of England as influencing Supplies of Water. By SAMUEL HUGHES, F.G.S., C.E. Enlarged Edition 4/0

The Power of Water,
As applied to drive Flour Mills, and to give motion to Turbines and other Hydrostatic Engines. By JOSEPH GLYNN, F.R.S. New Edition . 2/0

Wells and Well-Sinking.
By JOHN GEO. SWINDELL, A.R.I.B.A., and G. R. BURNELL, C.E. Revised Edition. With a New Appendix on the Qualities of Water. Illustrated 2/0

The Drainage of Lands, Towns, and Buildings.
By G. D. DEMPSEY, C.E. Revised, with large Additions on Recent Practice, by D. K. CLARK, M.I.C.E. Second Eition, corrected . 4/6

Embanking Lands from the Sea.
With Particulars of actual Embankments, &c. By JOHN WIGGINS . 2/0

The Blasting and Quarrying of Stone,
For Building and other Purposes. With Remarks on the Blowing up of Bridges. By Gen. Sir J. BURGOYNE, K.C.B. 1/6

Foundations and Concrete Works.
With Practical Remarks on Footings, Planking, Sand, Concrete, Béton, Pile-driving, Caissons, and Cofferdams. By E. DOBSON, M.R.I.B.A. Seventh Edition 1/6

Pneumatics,
    Including Acoustics and the Phenomena of Wind Currents, for the Use of Beginners. By CHARLES TOMLINSON, F.R.S. Fourth Edition . **1/6**

Land and Engineering Surveying.
    For Students and Practical Use. By T. BAKER, C.E. Fifteenth Edition, revised and corrected by J. R. YOUNG, formerly Professor of Mathematics, Belfast College. Illustrated with Plates and Diagrams . . . **2/0**

Mensuration and Measuring.
    For Students and Practical Use. With the Mensuration and Levelling of Land for the purposes of Modern Engineering. By T. BAKER, C.E. New Edition by E. NUGENT, C.E **1/6**

MINING AND METALLURGY.

Mineralogy,
    Rudiments of. By A. RAMSAY, F.G.S. Third Edition, revised and enlarged. Woodcuts and Plates **3/6**

Coal and Coal Mining,
    A Rudimentary Treatise on. By the late Sir WARINGTON W. SMYTH, F.R.S. Seventh Edition, revised and enlarged. **3/6**

Metallurgy of Iron.
    Containing Methods of Assay, Analyses of Iron Ores, Processes of Manufacture of Iron and Steel, &c. By H. BAUERMAN, F.G.S. With numerous Illustrations. Sixth Edition, revised and enlarged . . . **5/0**

The Mineral Surveyor and Valuer's Complete Guide.
    By W. LINTERN. Third Edition, with an Appendix on Magnetic and Angular Surveying **3/6**

Slate and Slate Quarrying:
    Scientific, Practical, and Commercial. By D. C. DAVIES, F.G.S. With numerous Illustrations and Folding Plates. Third Edition . . **3/0**

A First Book of Mining and Quarrying,
    with the Sciences connected therewith, for Primary Schools and Self Instruction. By J. H. COLLINS, F.G.S. Second Edition . . . **1/6**

Subterraneous Surveying,
    with and without the Magnetic Needle. By T. FENWICK and T. BAKER, C.E. Illustrated **2/6**

Mining Tools.
    Manual of. By WILLIAM MORGANS, Lecturer on Practical Mining at the Bristol School of Mines **2/6**

Mining Tools, Atlas
    of Engravings to Illustrate the above, containing 235 Illustrations of Mining Tools, drawn to Scale. 4to. **4/6**

Physical Geology,
    Partly based on Major-General PORTLOCK's "Rudiments of Geology." By RALPH TATE, A.L.S., &c. Woodcuts **2/0**

Historical Geology,
    Partly based on Major-General PORTLOCK's "Rudiments." By RALPH TATE, A.L.S., &c. Woodcuts **2/6**

Geology, Physical and Historical.
    Consisting of "Physical Geology," which sets forth the Leading Principles of the Science; and "Historical Geology," which treats of the Mineral and Organic Conditions of the Earth at each successive epoch. By RALPH TATE, F.G.S. **4/6**

Electro-Metallurgy,
    Practically Treated. By ALEXANDER WATT. Ninth Edition, enlarged and revised, including the most Recent Processes . . . **3/6**

MECHANICAL ENGINEERING.

The Workman's Manual of Engineering Drawing.
By JOHN MAXTON, Instructor in Engineering Drawing, Royal Naval College, Greenwich. Seventh Edition. 300 Plates and Diagrams . **3/6**

Fuels: Solid, Liquid, and Gaseous.
Their Analysis and Valuation. For the Use of Chemists and Engineers. By H. J. PHILLIPS, F.C.S., formerly Analytical and Consulting Chemist to the Great Eastern Railway. Second Edition, Revised. . . **2/0**

Fuel, Its Combustion and Economy.
Consisting of an Abridgment of "A Treatise on the Combustion of Coal and the Prevention of Smoke." By C. W. WILLIAMS, A.I.C.E. With Extensive Additions by D. K. CLARK, M. Inst. C.E. Third Edition . **3/6**

The Boilermaker's Assistant
in Drawing, Templating, and Calculating Boiler Work, &c. By J. COURTNEY, Practical Boilermaker. Edited by D. K. CLARK, C.E. . **2/0**

The Boiler-Maker's Ready Reckoner,
with Examples of Practical Geometry and Templating for the Use of Platers, Smiths, and Riveters. By JOHN COURTNEY. Edited by D. K. CLARK, M.I.C.E. Second Edition, revised, with Additions . . **4/0**

* The last two Works in One Volume, half-bound, entitled "THE BOILER-MAKER'S READY-RECKONER AND ASSISTANT." By J. COURTNEY and D. K. CLARK. Price 7s.

Steam Boilers:
Their Construction and Management. By R. ARMSTRONG, C.E. Illustrated **1/6**

Steam and Machinery Management.
A Guide to the Arrangement and Economical Management of Machinery. By M. POWIS BALE, M. Inst. M.E. **2/6**

Steam and the Steam Engine,
Stationary and Portable. Being an Extension of the Treatise on the Steam Engine of Mr. J. SEWELL. By D. K. CLARK, C.E. Third Edition **3/6**

The Steam Engine,
A Treatise on the Mathematical Theory of, with Rules and Examples for Practical Men. By T. BAKER, C.E. **1/6**

The Steam Engine.
By Dr. LARDNER. Illustrated **1/6**

Locomotive Engines,
By G. D. DEMPSEY, C.E. With large Additions treating of the Modern Locomotive, by D. K. CLARK, M. Inst. C.E. **3/0**

Locomotive Engine-Driving.
A Practical Manual for Engineers in charge of Locomotive Engines. By MICHAEL REYNOLDS. Eighth Edition. 3s. 6d. limp; cloth boards **4/6**

Stationary Engine-Driving.
A Practical Manual for Engineers in charge of Stationary Engines. By MICHAEL REYNOLDS. Fourth Edition. 3s. 6d. limp; cloth boards. **4/6**

The Smithy and Forge.
Including the Farrier's Art and Coach Smithing. By W. J. E. CRANE. Second Edition, revised **2/6**

Modern Workshop Practice,
As applied to Marine, Land, and Locomotive Engines, Floating Docks, Dredging Machines, Bridges, Ship-building, &c. By J. G. WINTON. Fourth Edition, Illustrated **3/6**

Mechanical Engineering.
Comprising Metallurgy, Moulding, Casting, Forging, Tools, Workshop Machinery, Mechanical Manipulation, Manufacture of the Steam Engine, &c. By FRANCIS CAMPIN, C.E. Third Edition . . . **2/6**

Details of Machinery.
Comprising Instructions for the Execution of various Works in Iron in the Fitting-Shop, Foundry, and Boiler-Yard. By FRANCIS CAMPIN, C.E. **3/0**

Elementary Engineering:
A Manual for Young Marine Engineers and Apprentices. In the Form of Questions and Answers on Metals, Alloys, Strength of Materials, &c. By J. S. Brewer. Second Edition 2/0

Power in Motion:
Horse-power Motion, Toothed-Wheel Gearing, Long and Short Driving Bands, Angular Forces, &c. By James Armour, C.E. Third Edition 2/0

Iron and Heat,
Exhibiting the Principles concerned in the Construction of Iron Beams, Pillars, and Girders. By J. Armour, C.E. 2/6

Practical Mechanism,
And Machine Tools. By T. Baker, C.E. With Remarks on Tools and Machinery, by J. Nasmyth, C.E. 2/6

Mechanics:
Being a concise Exposition of the General Principles of Mechanical Science, and their Applications. By Charles Tomlinson, F.R.S. . . 1/6

Cranes (The Construction of),
And other Machinery for Raising Heavy Bodies for the Erection of Buildings, &c. By Joseph Glynn, F.R.S. 1/6

NAVIGATION, SHIPBUILDING, ETC.

The Sailor's Sea Book:
A Rudimentary Treatise on Navigation. By James Greenwood, B.A. With numerous Woodcuts and Coloured Plates. New and enlarged Edition. By W. H. Rosser 2/6

Practical Navigation.
Consisting of The Sailor's Sea-Book, by James Greenwood and W. H. Rosser; together with Mathematical and Nautical Tables for the Working of the Problems, by Henry Law, C.E., and Prof. J. R. Young. 7/0

Navigation and Nautical Astronomy,
In Theory and Practice. By Prof. J. R. Young. New Edition. 2/6

Mathematical Tables,
For Trigonometrical, Astronomical, and Nautical Calculations; to which is prefixed a Treatise on Logarithms. By H. Law, C.E. Together with a Series of Tables for Navigation and Nautical Astronomy. By Professor J. R. Young. New Edition 4/0

Masting, Mast-Making, and Rigging of Ships.
Also Tables of Spars, Rigging, Blocks; Chain, Wire, and Hemp Ropes, &c., relative to every class of vessels. By Robert Kipping, N.A. . 2/0

Sails and Sail-Making.
With Draughting, and the Centre of Effort of the Sails. By Robert Kipping, N.A. 2/6

Marine Engines and Steam Vessels.
By R. Murray, C.E. Eighth Edition, thoroughly Revised, with Additions by the Author and by George Carlisle, C.E. . . . 4/6

Iron Ship-Building.
With Practical Examples. By John Grantham. Fifth Edition . 4/0

Naval Architecture:
An Exposition of Elementary Principles. By James Peake . . 3/6

Ships for Ocean and River Service,
Principles of the Construction of. By Hakon A. Sommerfeldt . 1/6

Atlas of Engravings
To Illustrate the above. Twelve large folding Plates. Royal 4to, cloth 7/6

The Forms of Ships and Boats.
By W. Bland. Seventh Edition, revised, with numerous Illustrations and Models 1/6

ARCHITECTURE AND THE BUILDING ARTS

Constructional Iron and Steel Work,
as applied to Public, Private, and Domestic Buildings. By Francis Campin, C.E. **3/6**

Building Estates:
A Treatise on the Development, Sale, Purchase, and Management of Building Land. By F. Maitland. Second Edition, revised . . . **2/0**

The Science of Building:
An Elementary Treatise on the Principles of Construction. By E. Wyndham Tarn, M.A. Lond. Third Edition, revised and enlarged . **3/6**

The Art of Building:
General Principles of Construction, Strength, and Use of Materials, Working Drawings, Specifications, &c. By Edward Dobson, M.R.I.B.A. . **2/0**

A Book on Building,
Civil and Ecclesiastical. By Sir Edmund Beckett, Q.C. (Lord Grimthorpe). Second Edition **4/6**

Dwelling-Houses (The Erection of),
Illustrated by a Perspective View, Plans, and Sections of a Pair of Villas, with Specification, Quantities, and Estimates. By S. H. Brooks, Architect **2/6**

Cottage Building.
By C. Bruce Allen. Eleventh Edition, with Chapter on Economic Cottages for Allotments, by E. E. Allen, C.E. **2/0**

Acoustics in Relation to Architecture and Building:
The Laws of Sound as applied to the Arrangement of Buildings. By Professor T. Roger Smith, F.R.I.B.A. New Edition, Revised . . **1/6**

The Rudiments of Practical Bricklaying.
General Principles of Bricklaying; Arch Drawing, Cutting, and Setting; Pointing; Paving, Tiling, &c. By Adam Hammond. With 68 Woodcuts **1/6**

The Art of Practical Brick Cutting and Setting.
By Adam Hammond. With 90 Engravings **1/6**

Brickwork:
A Practical Treatise, embodying the General and Higher Principles of Bricklaying, Cutting and Setting; with the Application of Geometry to Roof Tiling, &c. By F. Walker **1/6**

Bricks and Tiles,
Rudimentary Treatise on the Manufacture of; containing an Outline of the Principles of Brickmaking. By E. Dobson, M.R.I.B.A. Additions by C. Tomlinson, F.R.S. Illustrated **3/0**

The Practical Brick and Tile Book.
Comprising: Brick and Tile Making, by E. Dobson, A.I.C.E.; Practical Bricklaying, by A. Hammond; Brickwork, by F. Walker. 550 pp. with 270 Illustrations, strongly half-bound . . . **6/0**

Carpentry and Joinery—
The Elementary Principles of Carpentry. Chiefly composed from the Standard Work of Thomas Tredgold, C.E. With Additions, and Treatise on Joinery, by E. W. Tarn, M.A. Fifth Edition, Revised . **3/6**

Carpentry and Joinery—Atlas
Of 35 Plates to accompany and illustrate the foregoing book. With Descriptive Letterpress. 4to. **6/0**

A Practical Treatise on Handrailing;
Showing New and Simple Methods. By GEO. COLLINGS. Second Edition. Revised, including a TREATISE ON STAIRBUILDING. With Plates . **2/6**

Circular Work in Carpentry and Joinery.
A Practical Treatise on Circular Work of Single and Double Curvature. By GEORGE COLLINGS. Second Edition **2/6**

Roof Carpentry:
Practical Lessons in the Framing of Wood Roofs. For the Use of Working Carpenters. By GEO. COLLINGS **2/0**

The Construction of Roofs of Wood and Iron;
Deduced chiefly from the Works of Robison, Tredgold, and Humber. By E. WYNDHAM TARN, M.A., Architect. Second Edition, revised . **1/6**

The Joints Made and Used by Builders.
By WYVILL J. CHRISTY, Architect. With 160 Woodcuts . . **3/0**

Shoring
And Its Application: A Handbook for the Use of Students. By GEORGE H. BLAGROVE. With 31 Illustrations **1/6**

The Timber Importer's, Timber Merchant's, and Builder's Standard Guide.
By R. E. GRANDY **2/0**

Plumbing:
A Text-Book to the Practice of the Art or Craft of the Plumber. With Chapters upon House Drainage and Ventilation. By WM. PATON BUCHAN. Sixth Edition, revised and enlarged, with 380 Illustrations . . **3/6**

Ventilation:
A Text Book to the Practice of the Art of Ventilating Buildings. By W. P. BUCHAN, R.P., Author of "Plumbing," &c. With 170 Illustrations **3/6**

The Practical Plasterer:
A Compendium of Plain and Ornamental Plaster Work. By W. KEMP **2/0**

House Painting, Graining, Marbling, & Sign Writing.
With a Course of Elementary Drawing, and a Collection of Useful Receipts. By ELLIS A. DAVIDSON. Sixth Edition. Coloured Plates . . **5/0**
** The above, in cloth boards, strongly bound, 6s.

A Grammar of Colouring,
Applied to Decorative Painting and the Arts. By GEORGE FIELD. New Edition, enlarged, by ELLIS A. DAVIDSON. With Coloured Plates . **3/0**

Elementary Decoration
As applied to Dwelling Houses, &c. By JAMES W. FACEY. Illustrated **2/0**

Practical House Decoration.
A Guide to the Art of Ornamental Painting, the Arrangement of Colours in Apartments, and the Principles of Decorative Design. By JAMES W. FACEY. **2/6**
** The last two Works in One handsome Vol., half-bound, entitled "HOUSE DECORATION, ELEMENTARY AND PRACTICAL," price 5s.

Warming and Ventilation
Of Domestic and Public Buildings, Mines, Lighthouses, Ships, &c. By CHARLES TOMLINSON, F.R.S. **3/0**

Portland Cement for Users.
By HENRY FAIJA, A.M. Inst. C.E. Third Edition, Corrected . **2/0**

Limes, Cements, Mortars, Concretes, Mastics, Plastering, &c.
By G. R. BURNELL, C.E. Thirteenth Edition . . . **1/6**

Masonry and Stone-Cutting.
The Principles of Masonic Projection and their application to Construction. By EDWARD DOBSON, M.R.I.B.A. 2/6

Arches, Piers, Buttresses, &c.:
Experimental Essays on the Principles of Construction. By W. BLAND. 1/6

Quantities and Measurements,
In Bricklayers', Masons', Plasterers', Plumbers', Painters', Paperhangers', Gilders', Smiths', Carpenters' and Joiners' Work. By A. C. BEATON 1/6

The Complete Measurer:
Setting forth the Measurement of Boards, Glass, Timber and Stone. By R. HORTON. Fifth Edition 4/0

* *The above, strongly bound in leather, price 5s.*

Light:
An Introduction to the Science of Optics. Designed for the Use of Students of Architecture, Engineering, and other Applied Sciences. By E. WYNDHAM TARN, M.A., Author of "The Science of Building," &c. . 1/6

Hints to Young Architects.
By GEORGE WIGHTWICK, Architect. Fifth Edition, revised and enlarged by G. HUSKISSON GUILLAUME, Architect 3/6

Architecture—Orders:
The Orders and their Æsthetic Principles. By W. H. LEEDS. Illustrated. 1/6

Architecture—Styles:
The History and Description of the Styles of Architecture of Various Countries, from the Earliest to the Present Period. By T. TALBOT BURY, F.R.I.B.A. Illustrated 2/0

* ORDERS AND STYLES OF ARCHITECTURE, *in One Vol., 3s. 6d.*

Architecture—Design:
The Principles of Design in Architecture, as deducible from Nature and exemplified in the Works of the Greek and Gothic Architects. By EDW. LACY GARBETT, Architect. Illustrated 2/6

* *The three preceding Works in One handsome Vol., half bound, entitled* "MODERN ARCHITECTURE," *price 6s.*

Perspective for Beginners.
Adapted to Young Students and Amateurs in Architecture, Painting, &c. By GEORGE PYNE 2/0

Architectural Modelling in Paper.
By T. A. RICHARDSON. With Illustrations, engraved by O. JEWITT 1/6

Glass Staining, and the Art of Painting on Glass.
From the German of Dr. GESSERT and EMANUEL OTTO FROMBERG. With an Appendix on THE ART OF ENAMELLING 2/6

Vitruvius—The Architecture of.
In Ten Books. Translated from the Latin by JOSEPH GWILT, F.S.A., F.R.A.S. With 23 Plates 5/0

N.B.—*This is the only Edition of* VITRUVIUS *procurable at a moderate price.*

Grecian Architecture,
An Inquiry into the Principles of Beauty in. With an Historical View of the Rise and Progress of the Art in Greece. By the EARL OF ABERDEEN 1/0

* *The two preceding Works in One handsome Vol., half bound, entitled* "ANCIENT ARCHITECTURE," *price 6s.*

INDUSTRIAL AND USEFUL ARTS.

Cements, Pastes, Glues, and Gums.
A Practical Guide to the Manufacture and Application of the various Agglutinants required for Workshop, Laboratory, or Office Use. With upwards of 900 Recipes and Formulæ. By H. C. STANDAGE . . **2/0**

Clocks and Watches, and Bells,
A Rudimentary Treatise on. By Sir EDMUND BECKETT, Q.C. (Lord GRIMTHORPE). Seventh Edition **4/6**

The Goldsmith's Handbook.
Containing full Instructions in the Art of Alloying, Melting, Reducing, Colouring, Collecting and Refining, Recovery of Waste, Solders, Enamels, &c., &c. By GEORGE E. GEE. Third Edition, enlarged . . **3/0**

The Silversmith's Handbook,
On the same plan as the GOLDSMITH'S HANDBOOK. By GEORGE E. GEE. Second Edition, Revised **3/0**
** *The last two Works, in One handsome Vol., half-bound, 7s.*

The Hall-Marking of Jewellery.
Comprising an account of all the different Assay Towns of the United Kingdom; with the Stamps and Laws relating to the Standards and Hall-Marks at the various Assay Offices. By GEORGE E. GEE . . **3/0**

Practical Organ Building.
By W. E. DICKSON, M.A. Second Edition, Revised, with Additions **2/6**

Coach-Building:
A Practical Treatise. By JAMES W. BURGESS. With 57 Illustrations **2/6**

The Brass Founder's Manual:
Instructions for Modelling, Pattern Making, Moulding, Turning, &c. By W. GRAHAM **2/0**

The Sheet-Metal Worker's Guide.
A Practical Handbook for Tinsmiths, Coppersmiths, Zincworkers, &c., with 46 Diagrams. By W. J. E. CRANE. Second Edition, revised . **1/6**

Sewing Machinery:
Its Construction, History, &c. With full Technical Directions for Adjusting, &c. By J. W. URQUHART, C.E. **2/0**

Gas Fitting:
A Practical Handbook. By JOHN BLACK. Second Edition, Enlarged. With 130 Illustrations **2/6**

Construction of Door Locks.
From the Papers of A. C. HOBBS. Edited by CHARLES TOMLINSON, F.R.S. With a Note upon IRON SAFES by ROBERT MALLET. Illustrated . **2/6**

The Model Locomotive Engineer, Fireman, and Engine-Boy.
Comprising an Historical Notice of the Pioneer Locomotive Engines and their Inventors. By MICHAEL REYNOLDS. Second Edition. With numerous Illustrations, and Portrait of George Stephenson . . **3/6**

The Art of Letter Painting made Easy.
By J. G. BADENOCH. With 12 full-page Engravings of Examples . **1/6**

The Art of Boot and Shoemaking.
Including Measurement, Last-fitting, Cutting-out, Closing and Making. By JOHN BEDFORD LENO. With numerous Illustrations. Third Edition **2/0**

Mechanical Dentistry:
A Practical Treatise on the Construction of the Various Kinds of Artificial Dentures. By CHARLES HUNTER. Third Edition, revised . . **3/0**

Wood Engraving:
A Practical and Easy Introduction to the Art. By W. N. BROWN . **1/6**

Laundry Management.
A Handbook for Use in Private and Public Laundries. Including Accounts of Modern Machinery and Appliances. By the EDITOR of "The Laundry Journal." With numerous Illustrations. Second Edition . **2/0**

AGRICULTURE, GARDENING, ETC.

Draining and Embanking:
A Practical Treatise. By Prof. JOHN SCOTT. With 68 Illustrations **1/6**

Irrigation and Water Supply:
A Practical Treatise on Water Meadows, Sewage Irrigation, Warping, &c.; on the Construction of Wells, Ponds, Reservoirs, &c. By Prof. JOHN SCOTT. With 34 Illustrations **1/6**

Farm Roads, Fences, and Gates:
A Practical Treatise on the Roads, Tramways, and Waterways of the Farm; the Principles of Enclosures; and the different kinds of Fences, Gates, and Stiles. By Prof. JOHN SCOTT. With 75 Illustrations . **1/6**

Farm Buildings:
A Practical Treatise on the Buildings necessary for various kinds of Farms, their Arrangement and Construction, with Plans and Estimates. By Prof. JOHN SCOTT. With 105 Illustrations **2/0**

Barn Implements and Machines:
Treating of the Application of Power and Machines used in the Threshing-barn, Stockyard, Dairy, &c. By Prof. J. SCOTT. With 123 Illustrations. **2/0**

Field Implements and Machines:
With Principles and Details of Construction and Points of Excellence, their Management, &c. By Prof. JOHN SCOTT. With 138 Illustrations **2/0**

Agricultural Surveying:
A Treatise on Land Surveying, Levelling, and Setting-out; with Directions for Valuing Estates. By Prof. J. SCOTT. With 62 Illustrations . **1/6**

Farm Engineering.
By Professor JOHN SCOTT. Comprising the above Seven Volumes in One, 1,150 pages, and over 600 Illustrations. Half-bound . . . **12/0**

Outlines of Farm Management.
Treating of the General Work of the Farm; Stock; Contract Work; Labour, &c. By R. SCOTT BURN **2/6**

Outlines of Landed Estates Management.
Treating of the Varieties of Lands, Methods of Farming, Setting-out of Farms, Roads, Fences, Gates, Drainage, &c. By R. SCOTT BURN . **2/6**

_{*} *The above Two Vols. in One, handsomely half-bound, price* **6s.**

Soils, Manures, and Crops.
(Vol. I. OUTLINES OF MODERN FARMING.) By R. SCOTT BURN . **2/0**

Farming and Farming Economy.
(Vol. II. OUTLINES OF MODERN FARMING.) By R. SCOTT BURN **3/0**

Stock: Cattle, Sheep, and Horses.
(Vol. III. OUTLINES OF MODERN FARMING.) By R. SCOTT BURN **2/6**

Dairy, Pigs, and Poultry.
(Vol. IV. OUTLINES OF MODERN FARMING.) By R. SCOTT BURN **2/0**

Utilization of Sewage, Irrigation, and Reclamation of Waste Land.
(Vol. V. OUTLINES OF MODERN FARMING.) By R. SCOTT BURN . **2/6**

Outlines of Modern Farming.
By R. SCOTT BURN. Consisting of the above Five Volumes in One, 1,250 pp., profusely Illustrated, half-bound **12/0**

Book-keeping for Farmers and Estate Owners.
A Practical Treatise, presenting, in Three Plans, a System adapted for all classes of Farms. By J. M. WOODMAN. Third Edition, revised . **2/6**

Ready Reckoner for the Admeasurement of Land.
By A. ARMAN. Third Edition, revised and extended by C. NORRIS **2/0**

Miller's, Corn Merchant's, and Farmer's Ready Reckoner.
Second Edition, revised, with a Price List of Modern Flour Mill Machinery, by W. S. HUTTON, C.E. **2/0**

The Hay and Straw Measurer.
New Tables for the Use of Auctioneers, Valuers, Farmers, Hay and Straw Dealers, &c. By JOHN STEELE **2/0**

Meat Production.
A Manual for Producers, Distributors, and Consumers of Butchers' Meat. By JOHN EWART **2/6**

Sheep:
The History, Structure, Economy, and Diseases of. By W. C. SPOONER, M.R.V.S. Fifth Edition, with fine Engravings **3/6**

Market and Kitchen Gardening.
By C. W. SHAW, late Editor of "Gardening Illustrated" . . . **3/0**

Kitchen Gardening Made Easy.
Showing the best means of Cultivating every known Vegetable and Herb, &c., with directions for management all the year round. By GEORGE M. F. GLENNY. Illustrated **1/6**

Cottage Gardening:
Or Flowers, Fruits, and Vegetables for Small Gardens. By E. HOBDAY. **1/6**

Garden Receipts.
Edited by CHARLES W. QUIN **1/6**

Fruit Trees,
The Scientific and Profitable Culture of. From the French of M. DU BREUIL. Fourth Edition, carefully Revised by GEORGE GLENNY. With 187 Woodcuts **3/6**

The Tree Planter and Plant Propagator:
With numerous Illustrations of Grafting, Layering, Budding, Implements, Houses, Pits, &c. By SAMUEL WOOD **2/0**

The Tree Pruner:
A Practical Manual on the Pruning of Fruit Trees, Shrubs, Climbers, and Flowering Plants. With numerous Illustrations. By SAMUEL WOOD **1/6**

. *The above Two Vols. in One, handsomely half-bound, price* **3s. 6d.**

The Art of Grafting and Budding.
By CHARLES BALTET. With Illustrations **2/6**

MATHEMATICS, ARITHMETIC, ETC.

Descriptive Geometry,
An Elementary Treatise on; with a Theory of Shadows and of Perspective, extracted from the French of G. MONGE. To which is added a Description of the Principles and Practice of Isometrical Projection. By J. F. HEATHER, M.A. With 14 Plates 2/0

Practical Plane Geometry:
Giving the Simplest Modes of Constructing Figures contained in one Plane and Geometrical Construction of the Ground. By J. F. HEATHER, M.A. With 215 Woodcuts 2/0

Analytical Geometry and Conic Sections,
A Rudimentary Treatise on. By JAMES HANN. A New Edition, re-written and enlarged by Professor J. R. YOUNG 2/0

Euclid (The Elements of).
With many Additional Propositions and Explanatory Notes; to which is prefixed an Introductory Essay on Logic. By HENRY LAW, C.E. . 2/6

*** *Sold also separately, viz:—*

Euclid. The First Three Books. By HENRY LAW, C.E. . . . 1/6
Euclid. Books 4, 5, 6, 11, 12. By HENRY LAW, C.E. . . . 1/6

Plane Trigonometry,
The Elements of. By JAMES HANN 1/6

Spherical Trigonometry,
The Elements of. By JAMES HANN. Revised by CHARLES H. DOWLING, C.E. 1/0

*** *Or with "The Elements of Plane Trigonometry," in One Volume, 2s. 6d.*

Differential Calculus,
Elements of the. By W. S. B. WOOLHOUSE, F.R.A.S., &c. . . 1/6

Integral Calculus.
By HOMERSHAM COX, B.A. 1/0

Algebra,
The Elements of. By JAMES HADDON, M.A. With Appendix, containing Miscellaneous Investigations, and a collection of Problems . 2/0

A Key and Companion to the Above.
An extensive repository of Solved Examples and Problems in Algebra. By J. R. YOUNG. 1/6

Commercial Book-keeping.
With Commercial Phrases and Forms in English, French, Italian, and German. By JAMES HADDON, M.A. 1/6

Arithmetic,
A Rudimentary Treatise on. With full Explanations of its Theoretical Principles, and numerous Examples for Practice. For the Use of Schools and for Self-Instruction. By J. R. YOUNG, late Professor of Mathematics in Belfast College. Eleventh Edition 1/6

A Key to the Above.
By J. R. YOUNG 1/6

Equational Arithmetic,
Applied to Questions of Interest, Annuities, Life Assurance, and General Commerce; with various Tables by which all Calculations may be greatly facilitated. By W. HIPSLEY 2/0

Arithmetic,
Rudimentary, for the Use of Schools and Self-Instruction. By JAMES HADDON, M.A. Revised by ABRAHAM ARMAN . . . 1/6

A Key to the Above.
A. ARMAN 1/6

Mathematical Instruments
Their Construction, Adjustment, Testing, and Use concisely explained. By J. F. HEATHER, M.A., of the Royal Military Academy, Woolwich. Fourteenth Edition, Revised, with Additions, by A. T. WALMISLEY, M.I.C.E. Original Edition, in 1 vol., Illustrated . . . **2/0**

, *In ordering the above, be careful to say "Original Edition," or give the number in the Series (32), to distinguish it from the Enlarged Edition in 3 vols. (Nos. 168-9-70).*

Drawing and Measuring Instruments.
Including—I. Instruments employed in Geometrical and Mechanical Drawing, and in the Construction, Copying, and Measurement of Maps and Plans. II. Instruments used for the purposes of Accurate Measurement, and for Arithmetical Computations. By J. F. HEATHER, M.A. . **1/6**

Optical Instruments.
Including (more especially) Telescopes, Microscopes, and Apparatus for producing copies of Maps and Plans by Photography. By J. F. HEATHER, M.A. Illustrated **1/6**

Surveying and Astronomical Instruments.
Including—I. Instruments used for Determining the Geometrical Features of a portion of Ground. II. Iustruments employed in Astronomical Observations. By J. F. HEATHER, M.A. Illustrated . . . **1/6**

, *The above three volumes form an enlargement of the Author's original work, "Mathematical Instruments;" price 2s. (See No. 32 in the Series.)*

Mathematical Instruments:
Their Construction, Adjustment, Testing and Use. Comprising Drawing, Measuring, Optical, Surveying, and Astronomical Instruments. By J. F. HEATHER, M.A. Enlarged Edition, for the most part entirely re-written. The Three Parts as above, in One thick Volume . . . **4/6**

The Slide Rule, and How to Use It.
Containing full, easy, and simple Instructions to perform all Business Calculations with unexampled rapidity and accuracy. By CHARLES HOARE, C.E. With a Slide Rule, in tuck of cover. Fifth Edition . . **2/6**

Logarithms.
With Mathematical Tables for Trigonometrical, Astronomical, and Nautical Calculations. By HENRY LAW, C.E. Revised Edition. (Forming part of the above work.) **3/0**

Compound Interest and Annuities (Theory of).
With Tables of Logarithms for the more Difficult Computations of Interest, Discount, Annuities, &c., in all their Applications and Uses for Mercantile and State Purposes. By FEDOR THOMAN, Paris. Fourth Edition . **4/0**

Mathematical Tables,
For Trigonometrical, Astronomical, and Nautical Calculations; to which is prefixed a Treatise on Logarithms. By H. LAW, C.E. Together with a Series of Tables for Navigation and Nautical Astronomy. By Professor J. R. YOUNG. New Edition **4/0**

Mathematics,
As applied to the Constructive Arts. By FRANCIS CAMPIN, C.E., &c. Second Edition **3/0**

Astronomy.
By the late Rev. ROBERT MAIN, F.R.S. Third Edition, revised and corrected to the Present Time. By W. T. LYNN, F.R.A.S. . **2/0**

Statics and Dynamics,
The Principles and Practice of. Embracing also a clear development of Hydrostatics, Hydrodynamics, and Central Forces. By T. BAKER, C.E. Fourth Edition **1/6**

BOOKS OF REFERENCE AND MISCELLANEOUS VOLUMES.

A Dictionary of Painters, and Handbook for Picture Amateurs.
Being a Guide for Visitors to Public and Private Picture Galleries, and for Art-Students, including Glossary of Terms, Sketch of Principal Schools of Painting, &c. By PHILIPPE DARYL, B.A. **2/6**

Painting Popularly Explained.
By T. J. GULLICK, Painter, and JOHN TIMBS, F.S.A. Including Fresco, Oil, Mosaic, Water Colour, Water-Glass, Tempera, Encaustic, Miniature, Painting on Ivory, Vellum, Pottery, Enamel, Glass, &c. Fifth Edition **5/0**

A Dictionary of Terms used in Architecture, Building, Engineering, Mining, Metallurgy, Archæology, the Fine Arts, &c.
By JOHN WEALE. Sixth Edition. Edited by ROBT. HUNT, F.R.S. Numerous Illustrations **5/0**

Music:
A Rudimentary and Practical Treatise. With numerous Examples. By CHARLES CHILD SPENCER **2/6**

Pianoforte,
The Art of Playing the. With numerous Exercises and Lessons. By CHARLES CHILD SPENCER **1/6**

The House Manager.
Being a Guide to Housekeeping, Practical Cookery, Pickling and Preserving, Household Work, Dairy Management, Cellarage of Wines, Home-brewing and Wine-making, Stable Economy, Gardening Operations, &c. By AN OLD HOUSEKEEPER **3/6**

Manual of Domestic Medicine.
By R. GOODING M.D. Intended as a Family Guide in all cases of Accident and Emergency Third Edition, carefully revised . . **2/0**

Management of Health.
A Manual of Home and Personal Hygiene. By Rev. JAMES BAIRD **1/0**

Natural Philosophy,
For the Use of Beginners. By CHARLES TOMLINSON, F.R.S. . . **1/6**

The Electric Telegraph,
Its History and Progress. With Descriptions of some of the Apparatus. By R. SABINE, C.E., F.S.A., &c. **3/0**

Handbook of Field Fortification.
By Major W. W. KNOLLYS, F.R.G.S. With 163 Woodcuts . . **3/0**

Logic,
Pure and Applied. By S. H. EMMENS. Third Edition . . **1/6**

Locke on the Human Understanding,
Selections from. With Notes by S. H. EMMENS . . . **1/6**

The Compendious Calculator
(*Intuitive Calculations*). Or Easy and Concise Methods of Performing the various Arithmetical Operations required in Commercial and Business Transactions; together with Useful Tables, &c. By DANIEL O'GORMAN. Twenty-seventh Edition, carefully revised by C. NORRIS . . **2/6**

Measures, Weights, and Moneys of all Nations.
With an Analysis of the Christian, Hebrew, and Mahometan Calendars. By W. S. B. WOOLHOUSE, F.R.A.S., F.S.S. Seventh Edition . **2/6**

Grammar of the English Tongue,
Spoken and Written. With an Introduction to the Study of Comparative Philology. By HYDE CLARKE, D.C.L. Fifth Edition. . . . **1/6**

Dictionary of the English Language,
As Spoken and Written. Containing above 100,000 Words. By HYDE CLARKE, D.C.L. **3/6**
    Complete with the GRAMMAR **5/6**

Composition and Punctuation,
Familiarly Explained for those who have neglected the Study of Grammar. By JUSTIN BRENAN. 18th Edition **1/6**

French Grammar.
With Complete and Concise Rules on the Genders of French Nouns. By G. L. STRAUSS, Ph.D. **1/6**

French-English Dictionary.
Comprising a large number of New Terms used in Engineering, Mining, &c. By ALFRED ELWES **1/6**

English-French Dictionary.
By ALFRED ELWES **2/0**

French Dictionary.
The two Parts, as above, complete in One Vol. . . . **3/0**
    ** *Or with the* GRAMMAR, **4/6**.

French and English Phrase Book.
Containing Introductory Lessons, with Translations, Vocabularies of Words, Collection of Phrases, and Easy Familiar Dialogues . . . **1/6**

German Grammar.
Adapted for English Students, from Heyse's Theoretical and Practical Grammar, by Dr. G. L. STRAUSS **1/6**

German Triglot Dictionary.
By N. E. S. A. HAMILTON. Part I. German-French-English. Part II. English-German-French. Part III. French-German-English . **3/0**

German Triglot Dictionary
(As above). Together with German Grammar in One Volume . **5/0**

Italian Grammar
Arranged in Twenty Lessons, with Exercises. By ALFRED ELWES. **1/6**

Italian Triglot Dictionary,
Wherein the Genders of all the Italian and French Nouns are carefully noted down. By ALFRED ELWES. Vol. 1. Italian-English-French. **2/6**

Italian Triglot Dictionary.
By ALFRED ELWES. Vol. 2. English-French-Italian . . **2/6**

Italian Triglot Dictionary.
By ALFRED ELWES. Vol. 3. French-Italian-English . . **2/6**

Italian Triglot Dictionary
(As above). In One Vol. **7/6**

Spanish Grammar.
In a Simple and Practical Form. With Exercises. By ALFRED ELWES **1/6**

Spanish-English and English-Spanish Dictionary.
Including a large number of Technical Terms used in Mining, Engineering, &c., with the proper Accents and the Gender of every Noun. By ALFRED ELWES **4/0**
    ** *Or with the* GRAMMAR, **6/0**.

Portuguese Grammar,
In a Simple and Practical Form. With Exercises. By ALFRED ELWES **1/6**

Portuguese-English and English-Portuguese Dictionary.
Including a large number of Technical Terms used in Mining, Engineering, &c., with the proper Accents and the Gender of every Noun. By ALFRED ELWES. Third Edition, revised **5/0**

*** *Or with the* GRAMMAR, **7/0**.

Animal Physics,
Handbook of. By DIONYSIUS LARDNER, D.C.L. With 520 Illustrations. In One Vol. (732 pages), cloth boards **7/6**

*** *Sold also in Two Parts, as follows:—*

ANIMAL PHYSICS. By Dr. LARDNER. Part I., Chapters I.—VII. **4/0**

ANIMAL PHYSICS. By Dr. LARDNER. Part II., Chapters VIII.—XVIII. **3/0**

STATIONERS' HALL COURT, LONDON, E.C.
September, 1896.

A CATALOGUE OF BOOKS

INCLUDING NEW AND STANDARD WORKS IN
ENGINEERING: CIVIL, MECHANICAL, AND MARINE;
ELECTRICITY AND ELECTRICAL ENGINEERING;
MINING, METALLURGY; ARCHITECTURE,
BUILDING, INDUSTRIAL AND DECORATIVE ARTS;
SCIENCE, TRADE AND MANUFACTURES;
AGRICULTURE, FARMING, GARDENING;
AUCTIONEERING, VALUING AND ESTATE AGENCY;
LAW AND MISCELLANEOUS.

PUBLISHED BY

CROSBY LOCKWOOD & SON.

MECHANICAL ENGINEERING, etc.

D. K. Clark's Pocket-Book for Mechanical Engineers.
THE MECHANICAL ENGINEER'S POCKET-BOOK OF TABLES, FORMULÆ, RULES AND DATA. A Handy Book of Reference for Daily Use in Engineering Practice. By D. KINNEAR CLARK, M.Inst.C.E., Author of "Railway Machinery," "Tramways," &c. Third Edition, Revised. Small 8vo, 700 pages, 6s. bound in flexible leather cover, rounded corners.

SUMMARY OF CONTENTS.

MATHEMATICAL TABLES.—MEASUREMENT OF SURFACES AND SOLIDS.—ENGLISH WEIGHTS AND MEASURES.—FRENCH METRIC WEIGHTS AND MEASURES.—FOREIGN WEIGHTS AND MEASURES.—MONEYS.—SPECIFIC GRAVITY, WEIGHT AND VOLUME.—MANUFACTURED METALS.—STEEL PIPES.—BOLTS AND NUTS.—SUNDRY ARTICLES IN WROUGHT AND CAST IRON, COPPER, BRASS, LEAD, TIN, ZINC.—STRENGTH OF MATERIALS.—STRENGTH OF TIMBER.—STRENGTH OF CAST IRON.—STRENGTH OF WROUGHT IRON.—STRENGTH OF STEEL.—TENSILE STRENGTH OF COPPER, LEAD, ETC.—RESISTANCE OF STONES AND OTHER BUILDING MATERIALS.—RIVETED JOINTS IN BOILER PLATES.—BOILER SHELLS.—WIRE ROPES AND HEMP ROPES.—CHAINS AND CHAIN CABLES.—FRAMING.—HARDNESS OF METALS, ALLOYS AND STONES.—LABOUR OF ANIMALS.—MECHANICAL PRINCIPLES.—GRAVITY AND FALL OF BODIES.—ACCELERATING AND RETARDING FORCES.—MILL GEARING, SHAFTING, ETC.—TRANSMISSION OF MOTIVE POWER.—HEAT.—COMBUSTION: FUELS.—WARMING, VENTILATION, COOKING STOVES.—STEAM.—STEAM ENGINES AND BOILERS.—RAILWAYS.—TRAMWAYS.—STEAM SHIPS.—PUMPING STEAM ENGINES AND PUMPS.—COAL GAS, GAS ENGINES, ETC.—AIR IN MOTION.—COMPRESSED AIR.—HOT AIR ENGINES.—WATER POWER.—SPEED OF CUTTING TOOLS.—COLOURS.—ELECTRICAL ENGINEERING.

*** OPINIONS OF THE PRESS.

"Mr. Clark manifests what is an innate perception of what is likely to be useful in a pocket-book, and he is really unrivalled in the art of condensation. Very frequently we find the information on a given subject is supplied by giving a summary description of an experiment, and a statement of the results obtained. There is a very excellent steam table, occupying five and-a-half pages; and there are rules given for several calculations, which rules cannot be found in other pocket-books, as, for example, that on page 497, for getting at the quantity of water in the shape of priming in any known weight of steam. It is very difficult to hit upon any mechanical engineering subject concerning which this work supplies no information, and the excellent index at the end adds to its utility. In one word, it is an exceedingly handy and efficient tool, possessed of which the engineer will be saved many a wearisome calculation, or yet more wearisome hunt through various text-books and treatises, and, as such, we can heartily recommend it to our readers, who must not run away with the idea that Mr. Clark's Pocket-book is only Molesworth in another form. On the contrary, each contains what is not to be found in the other; and Mr. Clark takes more room and deals at more length with many subjects than Molesworth possibly could."—*The Engineer*.

"It would be found difficult to compress more matter within a similar compass, or produce a book of 650 pages which should be more compact or convenient for pocket reference. . . . Will be appreciated by mechanical engineers of all classes."—*Practical Engineer*.

"Just the kind of work that practical men require to have near to them."—*English Mechanic*.

MR. HUTTON'S PRACTICAL HANDBOOKS.

Handbook for Works' Managers.

THE WORKS' MANAGER'S HANDBOOK OF MODERN RULES, TABLES, AND DATA. For Engineers, Millwrights, and Boiler Makers; Tool Makers, Machinists, and Metal Workers; Iron and Brass Founders, &c. By W. S. HUTTON, Civil and Mechanical Engineer, Author of "The Practical Engineer's Handbook." Fifth Edition, carefully Revised, with Additions. In One handsome Volume, medium 8vo, price 15s. strongly bound. *[Just published.*

☞ The Author having compiled Rules and Data for his own use in a great variety of modern engineering work, and having found his notes extremely useful, decided to publish them—revised to date—believing that a practical work, suited to the DAILY REQUIREMENTS OF MODERN ENGINEERS, would be favourably received.

In the Fourth Edition the First Section has been re-written and improved by the addition of numerous Illustrations and new matter relating to STEAM ENGINES and GAS ENGINES. The Second Section has been enlarged and Illustrated, and throughout the book a great number of emendations and alterations have been made, with the object of rendering the book more generally useful.

** OPINIONS OF THE PRESS.

"The author treats every subject from the point of view of one who has collected workshop notes for application in workshop practice, rather than from the theoretical or literary aspect. The volume contains a great deal of that kind of information which is gained only by practical experience, and is seldom written in books."—*Engineer.*

"The volume is an exceedingly useful one, brimful with engineers' notes, memoranda, and rules, and well worthy of being on every mechanical engineer's bookshelf."—*Mechanical World.*

"The information is precisely that likely to be required in practice. . . . The work forms a desirable addition to the library not only of the works' manager, but of anyone connected with general engineering."—*Mining Journal.*

"A formidable mass of facts and figures, readily accessible through an elaborate Index . . . Such a volume will be found absolutely necessary as a book of reference in all sorts of 'works' connected with the metal trades."—*Ryland's Iron Trades Circular.*

"Brimful of useful information, stated in a concise form, Mr. Hutton's books have met a pressing want among engineers. The book must prove extremely useful to every practical man possessing a copy."—*Practical Engineer.*

New Manual for Practical Engineers.

THE PRACTICAL ENGINEER'S HAND-BOOK. Comprising a Treatise on Modern Engines and Boilers: Marine, Locomotive and Stationary. And containing a large collection of Rules and Practical Data relating to recent Practice in Designing and Constructing all kinds of Engines, Boilers, and other Engineering work. The whole constituting a comprehensive Key to the Board of Trade and other Examinations for Certificates of Competency in Modern Mechanical Engineering. By WALTER S. HUTTON, Civil and Mechanical Engineer, Author of "The Works' Manager's Handbook for Engineers," &c. With upwards of 370 Illustrations. Fifth Edition, Revised, with Additions. Medium 8vo, nearly 500 pp., price 18s. Strongly bound. *[Just published.*

☞ This work is designed as a companion to the Author's "WORKS' MANAGER'S HAND-BOOK." *It possesses many new and original features, and contains, like its predecessor, a quantity of matter not originally intended for publication, but collected by the author for his own use in the construction of a great variety of* MODERN ENGINEERING WORK.

The information is given in a condensed and concise form, and is illustrated by upwards of 370 Woodcuts; and comprises a quantity of tabulated matter of great value to all engaged in designing, constructing, or estimating for ENGINES, BOILERS, *and* OTHER ENGINEERING WORK.

** OPINIONS OF THE PRESS.

"We have kept it at hand for several weeks, referring to it as occasion arose, and we have not on a single occasion consulted its pages without finding the information of which we were in quest."—*Athenæum.*

"A thoroughly good practical handbook, which no engineer can go through without learning something that will be of service to him."—*Marine Engineer.*

"An excellent book of reference for engineers, and a valuable text-book for students of engineering."—*Scotsman.*

"This valuable manual embodies the results and experience of the leading authorities on mechanical engineering."—*Building News.*

"The author has collected together a surprising quantity of rules and practical data, and has shown much judgment in the selections he has made. . . . There is no doubt that this book is one of the most useful of its kind published, and will be a very popular compendium."—*Engineer.*

"A mass of information, set down in simple language, and in such a form that it can be easily referred to at any time. The matter is uniformly good and well chosen and is greatly elucidated by the illustrations. The book will find its way on to most engineers' shelves, where it will rank as one of the most useful books of reference."—*Practical Engineer.*

"Full of useful information and should be found on the office shelf of all practical engineers."—*English Mechanic.*

MR. HUTTON'S PRACTICAL HANDBOOKS—*continued.*

Practical Treatise on Modern Steam-Boilers.

STEAM-BOILER CONSTRUCTION. A Practical Handbook for Engineers, Boiler-Makers, and Steam Users. Containing a large Collection of Rules and Data relating to Recent Practice in the Design, Construction, and Working of all Kinds of Stationary, Locomotive, and Marine Steam-Boilers. By WALTER S. HUTTON, Civil and Mechanical Engineer, Author of "The Works' Manager's Handbook," "The Practical Engineer's Handbook," &c. With upwards of 300 Illustrations. Second Edition. Medium 8vo, 18s. cloth.

☞ *This work is issued in continuation of the Series of Handbooks written by the Author, viz :—"*THE WORKS' MANAGER'S HANDBOOK*" and "*THE PRACTICAL ENGINEER'S HANDBOOK,*" which are so highly appreciated by Engineers for the practical nature of their information; and is consequently written in the same style as those works.*

The Author believes that the concentration, in a convenient form for easy reference, of such a large amount of thoroughly practical information on Steam-Boilers, will be of considerable service to those for whom it is intended, and he trusts the book may be deemed worthy of as favourable a reception as has been accorded to its predecessors.

*** OPINIONS OF THE PRESS.

"Every detail, both in boiler design and management, is clearly laid before the reader. The volume shows that boiler construction has been reduced to the condition of one of the most exact sciences; and such a book is of the utmost value to the *fin de siècle* Engineer and Works' Manager."—*Marine Engineer.*

"There has long been room for a modern handbook on steam boilers; there is not that room now, because Mr. Hutton has filled it. It is a thoroughly practical book for those who are occupied in the construction, design, selection, or use of boilers."—*Engineer.*

"The book is of so important and comprehensive a character that it must find its way into the libraries of everyone interested in boiler using or boiler manufacture if they wish to be thoroughly informed. We strongly recommend the book for the intrinsic value of its contents."—*Machinery Market.*

"The value of this book can hardly be over-estimated. The author's rules, formulæ &c., are all very fresh, and it is impossible to turn to the work and not find what you want. No practical engineer should be without it."—*Colliery Guardian.*

Hutton's "Modernised Templeton."

THE PRACTICAL MECHANICS' WORKSHOP COMPANION. Comprising a great variety of the most useful Rules and Formulæ in Mechanical Science, with numerous Tables of Practical Data and Calculated Results for Facilitating Mechanical Operations. By WILLIAM TEMPLETON, Author of "The Engineer's Practical Assistant," &c. &c. Seventeenth Edition, Revised, Modernised, and considerably Enlarged by WALTER S. HUTTON, C.E., Author of "The Works' Manager's Handbook," "The Practical Engineer's Handbook," &c. Fcap. 8vo, nearly 500 pp., with 8 Plates and upwards of 250 Illustrative Diagrams, 6s., strongly bound for workshop or pocket wear and tear.

*** OPINIONS OF THE PRESS.

"In its modernised form Hutton's 'Templeton' should have a wide sale, for it contains much valuable information which the mechanic will often find of use, and not a few tables and notes which he might look for in vain in other works. This modernised edition will be appreciated by all who have learned to value the original editions of 'Templeton.'"—*English Mechanic.*

"It has met with great success in the engineering workshop, as we can testify; and there are a great many men who, in a great measure, owe their rise in life to this little book."—*Building News.*

"This familiar text-book—well known to all mechanics and engineers—is of essential service to the every-day requirements of engineers, millwrights, and the various trades connected with engineering and building. The new modernised edition is worth its weight in gold."—*Building News.* (Second Notice.)

"This well-known and largely-used book contains information, brought up to date, of the sort so useful to the foreman and draughtsman. So much fresh information has been introduced as to constitute it practically a new book. It will be largely used in the office and workshop."—*Mechanical World.*

"The publishers wisely entrusted the task of revision of this popular, valuable, and useful book to Mr. Hutton, than whom a more competent man they could not have found."—*Iron.*

Templeton's Engineer's and Machinist's Assistant.

THE ENGINEER'S, MILLWRIGHT'S, and MACHINIST'S PRACTICAL ASSISTANT. A collection of Useful Tables, Rules and Data. By WILLIAM TEMPLETON. 7th Edition, with Additions. 18mo, 2s. 6d. cloth.

*** OPINIONS OF THE PRESS.

"Occupies a foremost place among books of this kind. A more suitable present to an apprentice to any of the mechanical trades could not possibly be made."—*Building News.*

"A deservedly popular work. It should be in the 'drawer' of every mechanic."—*English Mechanic.*

Foley's Office Reference Book for Mechanical Engineers.

THE MECHANICAL ENGINEER'S REFERENCE BOOK, for Machine and Boiler Construction. In Two Parts. Part I. GENERAL ENGINEERING DATA. Part II. BOILER CONSTRUCTION. With 51 Plates and numerous Illustrations. By NELSON FOLEY, M.I.N.A. Second Edition, Revised throughout and much Enlarged. Folio, £3 3s. net half-bound. [*Just published.*

SUMMARY OF CONTENTS.

PART I.

MEASURES.—CIRCUMFERENCES AND AREAS, &c., SQUARES, CUBES, FOURTH POWERS.—SQUARE AND CUBE ROOTS.—SURFACE OF TUBES—RECIPROCALS.—LOGARITHMS.— MENSURATION. — SPECIFIC GRAVITIES AND WEIGHTS.—WORK AND POWER.—HEAT.—COMBUSTION.—EXPANSION AND CONTRACTION.—EXPANSION OF GASES.—STEAM.—STATIC FORCES.—GRAVITATION AND ATTRACTION.—MOTION AND COMPUTATION OF RESULTING FORCES.—ACCUMULATED WORK.—CENTRE AND RADIUS OF GYRATION.—MOMENT OF INERTIA.—CENTRE OF OSCILLATION.—ELECTRICITY.—STRENGTH OF MATERIALS.—ELASTICITY. — TEST SHEETS OF METALS.— FRICTION.—TRANSMISSION OF POWER.—FLOW OF LIQUIDS.—FLOW OF GASES.—AIR PUMPS, SURFACE CONDENSERS, &c.—SPEED OF STEAMSHIPS.—PROPELLERS. — CUTTING TOOLS.—FLANGES. — COPPER SHEETS AND TUBES.—SCREWS, NUTS, BOLT HEADS, &c.—VARIOUS RECIPES AND MISCELLANEOUS MATTER.

WITH DIAGRAMS FOR VALVE-GEAR, BELTING AND ROPES, DISCHARGE AND SUCTION PIPES, SCREW PROPELLERS, AND COPPER PIPES.

PART II.

TREATING OF, POWER OF BOILERS.— USEFUL RATIOS.—NOTES ON CONSTRUCTION. — CYLINDRICAL BOILER SHELLS. — CIRCULAR FURNACES. — FLAT PLATES. — STAYS. — GIRDERS. — SCREWS. — HYDRAULIC TESTS. — RIVETING.—BOILER SETTING, CHIMNEYS, AND MOUNTINGS.—FUELS, &c.—EXAMPLES OF BOILERS AND SPEEDS OF STEAMSHIPS.—NOMINAL AND NORMAL HORSE POWER.

WITH DIAGRAMS FOR ALL BOILER CALCULATIONS AND DRAWINGS OF MANY VARIETIES OF BOILERS.

*** OPINIONS OF THE PRESS.

"The book is one which every mechanical engineer may, with advantage to himself add to his library."—*Industries.*

"Mr. Foley is well fitted to compile such a work. . . . The diagrams are a great feature of the work. . . . Regarding the whole work, it may be very fairly stated that Mr. Foley has produced a volume which will undoubtedly fulfil the desire of the author and become indispensable to all mechanical engineers."—*Marine Engineer.*

"We have carefully examined this work, and pronounce it a most excellent reference book for the use of marine engineers."—*Journal of American Society of Naval Engineers.*

"A veritable monument of industry on the part of Mr. Foley, who has succeeded in producing what is simply invaluable to the engineering profession."—*Steamship.*

Coal and Speed Tables.

A POCKET BOOK OF COAL AND SPEED TABLES, *for Engineers and Steam-users.* By NELSON FOLEY, Author of "The Mechanical Engineer's Reference Book." Pocket-size, 3s. 6d. cloth.

"These tables are designed to meet the requirements of every-day use; they are of sufficient scope for most practical purposes, and may be commended to engineers and users of steam."—*Iron.*

"This pocket-book well merits the attention of the practical engineer. Mr. Foley has compiled a very useful set of tables, the information contained in which is frequently required by engineess, coal consumers and users of steam."—*Iron and Coal Trades Review.*

Steam Engine.

TEXT-BOOK ON THE STEAM ENGINE. With a Supplement on Gas Engines, and PART II. on HEAT ENGINES. By T. M. GOODEVE, M.A., Barrister-at-Law, Professor of Mechanics at the Royal College of Science, London; Author of "The Principles of Mechanics," "The Elements of Mechanism," &c. Twelfth Edition, Enlarged. With numerous Illustrations. Crown 8vo, 6s. cloth.

"Professor Goodeve has given us a treatise on the steam engine which will bear comparison with anything written by Huxley or Maxwell, and we can award it no higher praise."—*Engineer.*

"Mr. Goodeve's text-book is a work of which every young engineer should possess his. elf. —*Mining Journal.*

Gas Engines.

ON GAS-ENGINES. With Appendix describing a Recent Engine with Tube Igniter. By T. M. GOODEVE, M.A. Crown 8vo, 2s. 6d. cloth. [*Just published.*

"Like all Mr. Goodeve's writings, the present is no exception in point of general excellence it is a valuable little volume."—*Mechanical World.*

Steam Engine Design.

A HANDBOOK ON THE STEAM ENGINE, with especial Reference to Small and Medium-sized Engines. For the Use of Engine-Makers, Mechanical Draughtsmen, Engineering Students and Users of Steam Power. By HERMAN HAEDER, C.E. English Edition, Re-edited by the Author from the Second German Edition, and Translated, with considerable Additions and Alterations, by H. H. P. POWLES, A.M.I.C.E., M.I.M.E. With nearly 1,100 Illustrations. Crown 8vo, 9s. cloth.

"A perfect encyclopædia of the steam engine and its details, and one which must take a permanent place in English drawing-offices and workshops."—*A Foreman Pattern-maker.*

"This is an excellent book, and should be in the hands of all who are interested in the construction and design of medium sized stationary engines. . . . A careful study of its contents and the arrangement of the sections leads to the conclusion that there is probably no other book like it in this country. The volume aims at showing the results of practical experience, and it certainly may claim a complete achievement of this idea."—*Nature.*

"There can be no question as to its value. We cordially commend it to all concerned in the design and construction of the steam engine."—*Mechanical World.*

Steam Boilers.

A TREATISE ON STEAM BOILERS: *Their Strength, Construction, and Economical Working.* By ROBERT WILSON, C.E. Fifth Edition. 12mo, 6s. cloth.

"The best treatise that has ever been published on steam boilers."—*Engineer.*

"The author shows himself perfect master of his subject, and we heartily recommend all employing steam power to possess themselves of the work."—*Ryland's Iron Trade Circular.*

Boiler Chimneys.

BOILER AND FACTORY CHIMNEYS: *Their Draught-Power and Stability.* With a Chapter on *Lightning Conductors.* By ROBERT WILSON, A.I.C.E., Author of "A Treatise on Steam Boilers," &c. Second Edition. Crown 8vo, 3s. 6d. cloth.

"A valuable contribution to the literature of scientific building."—*The Builder.*

Boiler Making.

THE BOILER-MAKER'S READY RECKONER & ASSISTANT. With Examples of Practical Geometry and Templating, for the Use of Platers, Smiths and Riveters. By JOHN COURTNEY. Edited by D. K. CLARK, M.I.C.E. Third Edition, 480 pp., with 140 Illusts. Fcap. 8vo, 7s. half-bound.

"No workman or apprentice should be without this book."—*Iron Trade Circular.*

Locomotive Engine Development.

THE LOCOMOTIVE ENGINE AND ITS DEVELOPMENT. A Popular Treatise on the Gradual Improvements made in Railway Engines between 1803 and 1896. By CLEMENT E. STRETTON, C.E., Author of "Safe Railway Working," &c. Fifth Edition, Revised and Enlarged. With 120 Illustrations. Crown 8vo, 3s. 6d. cloth gilt. [*Just published.*

"Students of railway history and all who are interested in the evolution of the modern locomotive will find much to attract and entertain in this volume."—*The Times.*

"The author of this work is well known to the railway world, and no one probably has a better knowledge of the history and development of the locomotive. The volume before us should be of value to all connected with the railway system of this country."—*Nature.*

Estimating for Engineering Work, &c.

ENGINEERING ESTIMATES, COSTS AND ACCOUNTS: A Guide to Commercial Engineering. With numerous Examples of Estimates and Costs of Millwright Work, Miscellaneous Productions, Steam Engines and Steam Boilers; and a Section on the Preparation of Costs Accounts. By A GENERAL MANAGER. Demy 8vo, 12s. cloth.

"This is an excellent and very useful book, covering subject-matter in constant requisition to every factory and workshop. . . . The book is invaluable, not only to the young engineer, but also to the estimate department of every works."—*Builder.*

"We accord the work unqualified praise. The information is given in a plain, straightforward manner and bears throughout evidence of the intimate practical acquaintance of the author with every phase of commercial engineering."—*Mechanical World.*

Fire Engineering.

FIRES, FIRE-ENGINES, AND FIRE-BRIGADES. With a History of Fire-Engines, their Construction, Use, and Management; Remarks on Fire-Proof Buildings, and the Preservation of Life from Fire; Statistics of the Fire Appliances in English Towns; Foreign Fire Systems; Hints on Fire-Brigades, &c. &c. By CHARLES F. T. YOUNG, C.E. With numerous Illustrations. 544 pp., demy 8vo, £1 4s. cloth.

"To those interested in the subject of fires and fire apparatus, we most heartily commend this book. It is the only English work we now have upon the subject."—*Engineering*.

Boilermaking.

PLATING AND BOILERMAKING: A Practical Handbook for Workshop Operations. By JOSEPH G. HORNER, A.M.I.M.E. (Foreman Pattern-Maker), Author of "Pattern Making," &c. 380 pages, with 338 Illustrations. Crown 8vo, 7s. 6d. cloth. [*Just published*.

"The latest production from the pen of this writer is characterised by that evidence of close acquaintance with workshop methods which will render the book exceedingly acceptable to the practical hand. We have no hesitation in commending the work as a serviceable and practical handbook on a subject which has not hitherto received much attention from those qualified to deal with it in a satisfactory manner."—*Mechanical World*.

Engineering Construction.

PATTERN-MAKING: *A Practical Treatise*, embracing the Main Types of Engineering Construction, and including Gearing, both Hand and Machine made, Engine Work, Sheaves and Pulleys, Pipes and Columns, Screws, Machine Parts, Pumps and Cocks, the Moulding of Patterns in Loam and Greensand, &c., together with the methods of Estimating the weight of Castings; to which is added an Appendix of Tables for Workshop Reference. By JOSEPH G. HORNER, A.M.I.M.E. (Foreman Pattern-Maker). Second Edition, thoroughly Revised and much Enlarged. With upwards of 450 Illustrations. Crown 8vo, 7s. 6d. cloth. [*Just published*.

"A well-written technical guide, evidently written by a man who understands and has practised what he has written about. . . . We cordially recommend it to engineering students, young journeymen, and others desirous of being initiated into the mysteries of pattern-making."—*Builder*.

"More than 450 illustrations help to explain the text, which is, however, always clear and explicit, thus rendering the work an excellent *vade mecum* for the apprentice who desires to become master of his trade."—*English Mechanic*.

Dictionary of Mechanical Engineering Terms.

LOCKWOOD'S DICTIONARY OF TERMS USED IN THE PRACTICE OF MECHANICAL ENGINEERING, embracing those current in the Drawing Office, Pattern Shop, Foundry, Fitting, Turning, Smith's and Boiler Shops, &c. &c. Comprising upwards of 6,000 Definitions. Edited by JOSEPH G. HORNER, A.M.I.M.E. (Foreman Pattern-Maker), Author of "Pattern Making." Second Edition, Revised. Crown 8vo, 7s. 6d. cloth.

"Just the sort of handy dictionary required by the various trades engaged in mechanical engineering. The practical engineering pupil will find the book of great value in his studies, and every foreman engineer and mechanic should have a copy."—*Building News*.

"Not merely a dictionary, but, to a certain extent, also a most valuable guide. It strikes us as a happy idea to combine with a definition of the phrase useful information on the subject of which it treats."—*Machinery Market*.

Mill Gearing.

TOOTHED GEARING: A Practical Handbook for Offices and Workshops. By JOSEPH G. HORNER, A.M.I.M.E. (Foreman Pattern-Maker), Author of "Pattern Making," &c. With 184 Illustrations. Crown 8vo, 6s. cloth. [*Just published*.

SUMMARY OF CONTENTS.

CHAP. I. PRINCIPLES.—II. FORMATION OF TOOTH PROFILES.—III. PROPORTIONS OF TEETH.—IV. METHODS OF MAKING TOOTH FORMS.—V. INVOLUTE TEETH.—VI. SOME SPECIAL TOOTH FORMS.—VII. BEVEL WHEELS.—VIII. SCREW GEARS.—IX. WORM GEARS.—X. HELICAL WHEELS.—XI. SKEW BEVELS.—XII. VARIABLE AND OTHER GEARS.—XIII. DIAMETRICAL PITCH.—XIV. THE ODONTOGRAPH.—XV. PATTERN GEARS.—XVI. MACHINE MOULDING GEARS.—XVII. MACHINE CUT GEARS.—XVIII. PROPORTION OF WHEELS.

"We must give the book our unqualified praise for its thoroughness of treatment, and we can heartily recommend it to all interested as the most practical book on the subject yet written."—*Mechanical World*.

Stone-working Machinery.

STONE-WORKING MACHINERY, and the Rapid and Economical Conversion of Stone. With Hints on the Arrangement and Management of Stone Works. By M. POWIS BALE, M.I.M.E. With Illusts. Crown 8vo, 9s.

"The book should be in the hands of every mason or student of stone-work."—*Colliery Guardian.*

"A capital handbook for all who manipulate stone for building or ornamental purposes."—*Machinery Market.*

Pump Construction and Management.

PUMPS AND PUMPING: A Handbook for Pump Users. Being Notes on Selection, Construction and Management. By M. POWIS BALE, M.I.M.E., Author of "Woodworking Machinery," "Saw Mills," &c. Second Edition, Revised. Crown 8vo, 2s. 6d. cloth.

"The matter is set forth as concisely as possible. In fact, condensation rather than diffuseness has been the author's aim throughout; yet he does not seem to have omitted anything likely to be of use."—*Journal of Gas Lighting.*

"Thoroughly practical and simply and clearly written."—*Glasgow Herald.*

Milling Machinery, etc.

MILLING MACHINES AND PROCESSES: A Practical Treatise on Shaping Metals by Rotary Cutters, including Information on Making and Grinding the Cutters. By PAUL N. HASLUCK, Author of "Lathe-work," "Handybooks for Handicrafts," &c. With upwards of 300 Engravings, including numerous Drawings by the Author. Large crown 8vo, 352 pages, 12s. 6d. cloth.

"A new departure in engineering literature. . . . We can recommend this work to all interested in milling machines; it is what it professes to be—a practical treatise."—*Engineer.*

"A capital and reliable book, which will no doubt be of considerable service, both to those who are already acquainted with the process as well as to those who contemplate its adoption."—*Industries.*

Turning.

LATHE-WORK: A Practical Treatise on the Tools, Appliances, and Processes employed in the Art of Turning. By PAUL N. HASLUCK. Fifth Edition, Revised and Enlarged. Cr. 8vo, 5s. cloth.

"Written by a man who knows, not only how work ought to be done, but who also knows how to do it, and how to convey his knowledge to others. To all turners this book would be valuable."—*Engineering.*

"We can safely recommend the work to young engineers. To the amateur it will simply be invaluable. To the student it will convey a great deal of useful information."—*Engineer.*

Screw-Cutting.

SCREW THREADS: And Methods of Producing Them. With Numerous Tables, and complete directions for using Screw-Cutting Lathes. By PAUL N. HASLUCK, Author of "Lathe-Work," &c. With Seventy-four Illustrations. Third Edition, Revised and Enlarged. Waistcoat-pocket size, 1s. 6d. cloth.

"Full of useful information, hints and practical criticism. Taps, dies and screwing-tools generally are illustrated and their action described."—*Mechanical World.*

"It is a complete compendium of all the details of the screw-cutting lathe; in fact a *multum in parvo* on all the subjects it treats upon."—*Carpenter and Builder.*

Smith's Tables for Mechanics, etc.

TABLES, MEMORANDA, AND CALCULATED RESULTS, FOR MECHANICS, ENGINEERS. ARCHITECTS. BUILDERS, etc. Selected and Arranged by FRANCIS SMITH. Sixth Edition, Revised, including ELECTRICAL TABLES, FORMULÆ, and MEMORANDA. Waistcoat-pocket size, 1s. 6d. limp leather. [*Just published.*

"It would, perhaps, be as difficult to make a small pocket-book selection of notes and formulæ to suit ALL engineers as it would be to make a universal medicine; but Mr. Smith's waistcoat-pocket collection may be looked upon as a successful attempt."—*Engineer.*

"The best example we have ever seen of 270 pages of useful matter packed into the dimensions of a card-case."—*Building News.* "A veritable pocket treasury of knowledge."—*Iron.*

French-English Glossary for Engineers, etc.

A POCKET GLOSSARY of TECHNICAL TERMS: ENGLISH-FRENCH, FRENCH-ENGLISH; with Tables suitable for the Architectural, Engineering, Manufacturing and Nautical Professions. By JOHN JAMES FLETCHER, Engineer and Surveyor. Second Edition, Revised and Enlarged, 200 pp. Waistcoat-pocket size, 1s. 6d. limp leather.

"It is a very great advantage for readers and correspondents in France and England to have so large a number of the words relating to engineering and manufacturers collected in a liliputian volume. The little book will be useful both to students and travellers."—*Architect.*

"The glossary of terms is very complete, and many of the tables are new and well arranged We cordially commend the book."—*Mechanical World.*

Year-Book of Engineering Formulæ, &c.

THE ENGINEER'S YEAR-BOOK FOR 1896. Comprising Formulæ, Rules, Tables, Data and Memoranda in Civil, Mechanical, Electrical, Marine and Mine Engineering. By H. R. KEMPE, A.M. Inst.C.E., M.I.E.E., Technical Officer of the Engineer-in-Chief's Office, General Post Office, London, Author of "A Handbook of Electrical Testing," "The Electrical Engineer's Pocket-Book," &c. With 800 Illustrations, specially Engraved for the work. Crown 8vo, 670 pages, 8s. leather. [*Just published.*

"Represents an enormous quantity of work and forms a desirable book of reference."—*The Engineer.*
"The book is distinctly in advance of most similar publications in this country."—*Engineering.*
"This valuable and well-designed book of reference meets the demands of all descriptions of engineers."—*Saturday Review.*
"Teems with up-to-date information in every branch of engineering and construction."—*Building News.*
"The needs of the engineering profession could hardly be supplied in a more admirable, complete and convenient form. To say that it more than sustains all comparisons is praise of the highest sort, and that may justly be said of it."—*Mining Journal.*
"There is certainly room for the new comer, which supplies explanations and directions, as well as formulæ and tables. It deserves to become one of the most successful of the technical annuals."—*Architect.*
"Brings together with great skill all the technical information which an engineer has to use day by day. It is in every way admirably equipped, and is sure to prove successful."—*Scotsman.*
"The up-to-dateness of Mr. Kempe's compilation is a quality that will not be lost on the busy people for whom the work is intended."—*Glasgow Herald.*

Portable Engines.

THE PORTABLE ENGINE; ITS CONSTRUCTION AND MANAGEMENT. A Practical Manual for Owners and Users of Steam Engines generally. By WILLIAM DYSON WANSBROUGH. With 90 Illustrations. Crown 8vo, 3s. 6d. cloth.

"This is a work of value to those who use steam machinery. . . . Should be read by everyone who has a steam engine, on a farm or elsewhere."—*Mark Lane Express.*
"We cordially commend this work to buyers and owners of steam engines, and to those who have to do with their construction or use."—*Timber Trades Journal.*
"Such a general knowledge of the steam engine as Mr. Wansbrough furnishes to the reader should be acquired by all intelligent owners and others who use the steam engine."—*Building News.*
"An excellent text-book of this useful form of engine. 'The Hints to Purchasers' contain a good deal of commonsense and practical wisdom."—*English Mechanic.*

Iron and Steel.

"IRON AND STEEL": A Work for the Forge, Foundry, Factory, and Office. Containing ready, useful, and trustworthy Information for Ironmasters and their Stock-takers; Managers of Bar, Rail, Plate, and Sheet Rolling Mills; Iron and Metal Founders; Iron Ship and Bridge Builders; Mechanical, Mining, and Consulting Engineers; Architects, Contractors, Builders, and Professional Draughtsmen. By CHARLES HOARE, Author of "The Slide Rule," &c. Ninth Edition. 32mo, 6s. leather.

"For comprehensiveness the book has not its equal."—*Iron.*
"One of the best of the pocket books."—*English Mechanic.*
"We cordially recommend this book to those engaged in considering the details of all kinds of iron and steel works."—*Naval Science.*

Elementary Mechanics.

CONDENSED MECHANICS. A Selection of Formulæ, Rules, Tables, and Data for the Use of Engineering Students, Science Classes, &c. In Accordance with the Requirements of the Science and Art Department. By W. G. CRAWFORD HUGHES, A.M.I.C.E. Crown 8vo, 2s. 6d. cloth.

"The book is well fitted for those who are either confronted with practical problems in their work, or are preparing for examination and wish to refresh their knowledge by going through their formulæ again."—*Marine Engineer.*
"It is well arranged, and meets the wants of those for whom it is intended."—*Railway News.*

Steam.

THE SAFE USE OF STEAM. Containing Rules for Unprofessional Steam-users. By an ENGINEER. Seventh Edition. Sewed, 6d.

"If steam-users would but learn this little book by heart, boiler explosions would become sensations by their rarity."—*English Mechanic.*

Warming.

HEATING BY HOT WATER; with Information and Suggestions on the best Methods of Heating Public, Private and Horticultural Buildings. By WALTER JONES. Second Edition. With 96 Illustrations. Crown 8vo, 2s. 6d. net.

"We confidently recommend all interested in heating by hot water to secure a copy of this valuable little treatise."—*The Plumber and Decorator.*

CIVIL ENGINEERING, SURVEYING, etc.

Light Railways.

LIGHT RAILWAYS FOR THE UNITED KINGDOM, INDIA, AND THE COLONIES: A Practical Handbook setting forth the Principles on which Light Railways should be Constructed, Worked and Financed; and detailing the cost of Construction, Equipment, Revenue, and Working Expences of Local Railways already established in the above-mentioned Countries, and in Belgium, France, Switzerland, &c. By JOHN CHARLES MACKAY, F.G.S., A.M.Inst.C.E. Illustrated with 40 Photographic Plates and other Diagrams. Medium 8vo, 15s. cloth. [*Just published.*

"Exactly what has been long wanted, and sure to have a wide sale."—*Railway News.*

Water Supply and Water-Works.

THE WATER SUPPLY OF TOWNS AND THE CONSTRUCTION OF WATER-WORKS: A Practical Treatise for the Use of Engineers and Students of Engineering. By W. K. BURTON, A.M.Inst.C.E., Professor of Sanitary Engineering in the Imperial University, Tokyo, Japan, and Consulting Engineer to the Tokyo Water-works. With an Appendix on **The Effects of Earthquakes on Waterworks**, by JOHN MILNE, F.R.S., Professor of Mining in the Imperial University of Japan. With numerous Plates and Illustrations. Super-royal 8vo, 25s. buckram. [*Just published.*

"The whole art of waterworks construction is dealt with in a clear and comprehensive fashion in this handsome volume. . . . Mr. Burton's practical treatise shows in all its sections the fruit of independent study and individual experience. It is largely based upon his own practice in the branch of engineering of which it treats, and with such a basis a treatise can scarcely fail to be suggestive and useful."—*Saturday Review.*

"Professor Burton's book is sure of a warm welcome among engineers. It is written in clear and vigorous language and forms an exhaustive treatise on a branch of engineering the claims of which it would be difficult to over-estimate."—*Scotsman.*

"The subjects seem to us to be ably discussed, with a practical aim to meet the requirements of all its probable readers. The volume is well got up, and the illustrations are excellent."
—*The Lancet.*

Water Supply of Cities and Towns.

A COMPREHENSIVE TREATISE on the WATER-SUPPLY OF CITIES AND TOWNS. By WILLIAM HUMBER, A.M.Inst.C.E., and M. Inst. M.E., Author of "Cast and Wrought Iron Bridge Construction," &c. &c. Illustrated with 50 Double Plates, 1 Single Plate, Coloured Frontispiece, and upwards of 250 Woodcuts, and containing 400 pages of Text. Imp. 4to, £6 6s. elegantly and substantially half-bound in morocco.

"The most systematic and valuable work upon water supply hitherto produced in English or in any other language. . . . Mr. Humber's work is characterised almost throughout by an exhaustiveness much more distinctive of French and German than of English technical treatises."
—*Engineer.*

"We can congratulate Mr. Humber on having been able to give so large an amount of information on a subject so important as the water supply of cities and towns. The plates, fifty in number, are mostly drawings of executed works, and alone would have commanded the attention of every engineer whose practice may lie in this branch of the profession."—*Builder.*

Water Supply.

RURAL WATER SUPPLY: A Practical Handbook on the Supply of Water and Construction of Waterworks for small Country Districts. By ALLAN GREENWELL, A.M.I.C.E., and W. T. CURRY, A.M.I.C.E., F.G.S. With Illustrations. Crown 8vo, 5s. cloth. [*Just published.*

"We conscientiously recommend it as a very useful book for those concerned in obtaining water for small districts, giving a great deal of practical information in a small compass."—*Builder.*

"The volume contains valuable information upon all matters connected with water supply. . . It is full of details on points which are continually before waterworks' engineers."—*Nature.*

Hydraulic Tables.

HYDRAULIC TABLES, CO-EFFICIENTS, and FORMULÆ *for finding the Discharge of Water from Orifices, Notches, Weirs, Pipes, and Rivers.* By JOHN NEVILLE, Civil Engineer, M.R.I.A. Third Ed., carefully Revised, with considerable Additions. Numerous Illusts. Cr. 8vo, 14s. cloth.

"Alike valuable to students and engineers in practice; its study will prevent the annoyance of avoidable failures, and assist them to select the readiest means of successfully carrying out any given work connected with hydraulic engineering."—*Mining Journal.*

"It is, of all English books on the subject, the one nearest to completeness,".—*Architect.*

Hydraulics.

HYDRAULIC MANUAL. Consisting of Working Tables and Explanatory Text. Intended as a Guide in Hydraulic Calculations and Field Operations. By LOWIS D'A. JACKSON, Author of "Aid to Survey Practice," "Modern Metrology," &c. Fourth Edition, Enlarged. Large cr. 8vo, 16s. cl.

"The author has had a wide experience in hydraulic engineering and has been a careful observer of the facts which have come under his notice, and from the great mass of material at his command he has constructed a manual which may be accepted as a trustworthy guide to this branch of the engineer's profession. We can heartily recommend this volume to all who desire to be acquainted with the latest development of this important subject."—*Engineering.*

"The standard-work in this department of mechanics."—*Scotsman.*

"The most useful feature of this work is its freedom from what is superannuated, and its thorough adoption of recent experiments; the text is, in fact, in great part a short account of the great modern experiments."—*Nature.*

Water Storage, Conveyance, and Utilisation.

WATER ENGINEERING: A Practical Treatise on the Measurement, Storage, Conveyance, and Utilisation of Water for the Supply of Towns, for Mill Power, and for other Purposes. By CHARLES SLAGG, A.M.Inst.C.E., Author of "Sanitary Work in the Smaller Towns, and in Villages," &c. Second Edition. With numerous Illustrations. Crown 8vo, 7s. 6d. cloth.

"As a small practical treatise on the water supply of towns, and on some applications of water-power, the work is in many respects excellent."—*Engineering.*

"The author has collated the results deduced from the experiments of the most eminent authorities, and has presented them in a compact and practical form, accompanied by very clear and detailed explanations. . . . The application of water as a motive power is treated very carefully and exhaustively."—*Builder.*

"For anyone who desires to begin the study of hydraulics with a consideration of the practical applications of the science there is no better guide."—*Architect.*

Drainage.

ON THE DRAINAGE OF LANDS, TOWNS, AND BUILDINGS. By G. D. DEMPSEY, C.E., Author of "The Practical Railway Engineer," &c. Revised, with large Additions on RECENT PRACTICE IN DRAINAGE ENGINEERING, by D. KINNEAR CLARK, M.Inst.C.E. Author of "Tramways: Their Construction and Working," "A Manual of Rules, Tables, and Data for Mechanical Engineers," &c. Third Edition. Small crown 8vo, 4s. 6d. cloth. [*Just published.*

"The new matter added to Mr. Dempsey's excellent work is characterised by the comprehensive grasp and accuracy of detail for which the name of Mr. D. K. Clark is a sufficient voucher."—*Athenæum.*

"As a work on recent practice in drainage engineering, the book is to be commended to all who are making that branch of engineering science their special study."—*Iron.*

"A comprehensive manual on drainage engineering, and a useful introduction to the student."—*Building News.*

River Engineering.

RIVER BARS: *The Causes of their Formation, and their Treatment by "Induced Tidal Scour;"* with a Description of the Successful Reduction by this Method of the Bar at Dublin. By I. J. MANN, Assist. Eng. to the Dublin Port and Docks Board. Royal 8vo, 7s. 6d. cloth.

"We recommend all interested in harbour works—and, indeed, those concerned in the improvements of rivers generally—to read Mr. Mann's interesting work on the treatment of river bars."—*Engineer.*

Tramways and their Working.

TRAMWAYS: THEIR CONSTRUCTION AND WORKING. Embracing a Comprehensive History of the System; with an exhaustive Analysis of the various Modes of Traction, including Horse-Power, Steam, Cable Traction, Electric Traction, &c.; a Description of the Varieties of Rolling Stock; and ample Details of Cost and Working Expenses. New Edition, Thoroughly Revised, and Including the Progress recently made in Tramway Construction, &c. &c. By D. KINNEAR CLARK. M.Inst.C.E. With numerous Illustrations and Folding Plates. In One Volume, 8vo, 780 pages, price 28s., bound in buckram. [*Just published.*

"All interested in tramways must **refer to it, as all railway engineers have** turned to the author's work 'Railway Machinery.'"—*Engineer.*

"An exhaustive and practical work on tramways, in which the history of this kind of locomotion, and a description and cost of the various modes of laying tramways, are to be found.'—*Building News.*

"The best form of rails, the best mode of construction, and the best mechanical appliances are so fairly indicated in the work under review, that any engineer about to construct a tramway will be enabled at once to obtain the practical information which will be of most service to him."—*Athenæum.*

CIVIL ENGINEERING, SURVEYING, etc.

Student's Text-Book on Surveying.

PRACTICAL SURVEYING: A Text-Book for Students preparing for Examination or for Survey-work in the Colonies. By GEORGE W. USILL, A.M.I.C.E., Author of "The Statistics of the Water Supply of Great Britain." With Four Lithographic Plates and upwards of 330 Illustrations. Fourth Edition, Revised, including Tables of Natural Sines, Tangents, Secants, &c. Crown 8vo, 7s. 6d. cloth; or, on THIN PAPER, bound in limp leather, gilt edges, rounded corners, for pocket use, 12s. 6d.

"The best forms of instruments are described as to their construction, uses and modes of employment, and there are innumerable hints on work and equipment such, as the author, in his experience as surveyor, draughtsman, and teacher, has found necessary, and which the student in his inexperience will find most serviceable."—*Engineer.*

"The latest treatise in the English language on surveying, and we have no hesitation in saying that the student will find it a better guide than any of its predecessors . . . . Deserves to be recognised as the first book which should be put in the hands of a pupil of Civil Engineering, and every gentleman of education who sets out for the Colonies would find it well to have a copy."—*Architect.*

Survey Practice.

AID TO SURVEY PRACTICE, for Reference in Surveying, Levelling, and Setting-out; and in Route Surveys of Travellers by Land and Sea. With Tables, Illustrations, and Records. By LOWIS D'A. JACKSON, A.M.I.C.E., Author of "Hydraulic Manual," "Modern Metrology," &c. Second Edition, Enlarged. Large crown 8vo, 12s. 6d. cloth.

"A valuable vade-mecum for the surveyor. We can recommend this book as containing an admirable supplement to the teaching of the accomplished surveyor."—*Athenæum.*

"As a text-book we should advise all surveyors to place it in their libraries, and study well the matured instructions afforded in its pages."—*Colliery Guardian.*

"The author brings to his work a fortunate union of theory and practical experience which, aided by a clear and lucid style of writing, renders the book a very useful one."—*Builder.*

Surveying, Land and Marine.

LAND AND MARINE SURVEYING, in Reference to the Preparation of Plans for Roads and Railways; Canals, Rivers, Towns' Water Supplies; Docks and Harbours. With Description and Use of Surveying Instruments. By W. D. HASKOLL, C.E., Author of "Bridge and Viaduct Construction," &c. Second Edition, Revised, with Additions. Large cr. 8vo, 9s. cl.

"This book must prove of great value to the student. We have no hesitation in recommending it, feeling assured that it will more than repay a careful study."—*Mechanical World.*

"A most useful and well arranged book. We can strongly recommend it as a carefully-written and valuable text-book. It enjoys a well-deserved repute among surveyors."—*Builder.*

"This volume cannot fail to prove of the utmost practical utility. It may be safely recommended to all students who aspire to become clean and expert surveyors."—*Mining Journal.*

Field-Book for Engineers.

THE ENGINEER'S, MINING SURVEYOR'S, AND CONTRACTOR'S FIELD-BOOK. Consisting of a Series of Tables, with Rules, Explanations of Systems, and use of Theodolite for Traverse Surveying and Plotting the Work with minute accuracy by means of Straight Edge and Set Square only; Levelling with the Theodolite, Casting-out and Reducing Levels to Datum, and Plotting Sections in the ordinary manner; setting-out Curves with the Theodolite by Tangential Angles and Multiples, with Right and Left-hand Readings of the Instrument: Setting-out Curves without Theodolite, on the System of Tangential Angles by sets of Tangents and Offsets; and Earthwork Tables to 80 feet deep, calculated for every 6 inches in depth. By W. D. HASKOLL, C.E. Fourth Edition. Crown 8vo, 12s. cloth.

"The book is very handy; the separate tables of sines and tangents to every minute will make it useful for many other purposes, the genuine traverse tables existing all the same."—*Athenæum.*

"Every person engaged in engineering field operations will estimate the importance of such a work and the amount of valuable time which will be saved by reference to a set of reliable tables prepared with the accuracy and fulness of those given in this volume."—*Railway News.*

Levelling.

A TREATISE ON THE PRINCIPLES AND PRACTICE OF LEVELLING. Showing its Application to purposes of Railway and Civil Engineering, in the Construction of Roads; with Mr. TELFORD'S Rules for the same. By FREDERICK W. SIMMS, F.G.S., M.Inst.C.E. Seventh Edition, with the addition of LAW'S Practical Examples for Setting-out Railway Curves, and TRAUTWINE'S Field Practice of Laying-out Circular Curves. With 7 Plates and numerous Woodcuts. 8vo, 8s. 6d. cloth.   **** TRAUTWINE on Curves may be had separate, 5s.

"The text-book on levelling in most of our engineering schools and colleges. . . . The publishers have rendered a substantial service to the profession, especially to the younger members, by bringing out the present edition of Mr. Simms's useful book."—*Engineer.*

Trigonometrical Surveying.

AN OUTLINE OF THE METHOD OF CONDUCTING A TRIGONOMETRICAL SURVEY, for the Formation of Geographical and Topographical Maps and Plans, Military Reconnaissance, Levelling, &c., with Useful Problems, Formulæ, and Tables. By Lieut.-General FROME, R.E. Fourth Edition, Revised and partly Re-written by Major General Sir CHARLES WARREN, G.C.M.G., R.E. With 19 Plates and 115 Woodcuts. Royal 8vo, 16s. cloth.

"The simple fact that a fourth edition has been called for is the best testimony to its merits No words of praise from us can strengthen the position so well and so steadily maintained by this work. Sir Charles Warren has revised the entire work, and made such additions as were necessary to bring every portion of the contents up to the present date."—*Broad Arrow*.

Curves, Tables for Setting-out.

TABLES OF TANGENTIAL ANGLES AND MULTIPLES for Setting-out Curves from 5 to 200 Radius. By ALEXANDER BEAZELEY, M.Inst.C.E. Fourth Edition. Printed on 48 Cards, and sold in a cloth box, waistcoat-pocket size, 3s. 6d.

"Each table is printed on a small card, which, being placed on the theodolite, leaves the hand free to manipulate the instrument—no small advantage as regards the rapidity of work."—*Engineer*.

"Very handy: a man may know that all his day's work must fall on two of these cards, which he puts into his own card-case, and leaves the rest behind."—*Athenæum*.

Earthwork.

HANDY GENERAL EARTHWORK TABLES. Giving the Contents in Cubic Yards of Centre and Slopes of Cuttings and Embankments from 3 inches to 80 feet in Depth or Height, for use with either 66 feet Chain or 100 feet Chain. By J. H. WATSON BUCK, M.Inst.C.E. On a Sheet mounted in cloth case, 3s. 6d. [*Just published*.

Earthwork.

EARTHWORK TABLES. Showing the Contents in Cubic Yards of Embankments, Cuttings, &c., of Heights or Depths up to an average of 80 feet. By JOSEPH BROADBENT, C.E., and FRANCIS CAMPIN, C.E. Crown 8vo, 5s. cloth.

"The way in which accuracy is attained, by a simple division of each cross section into three elements, two of which are constant and one variable, is ingenious."—*Athenæum*.

Earthwork, Measurement of.

A MANUAL ON EARTHWORK. By ALEX. J. S. GRAHAM, C.E. With numerous Diagrams. Second Edition. 18mo, 2s. 6d. cloth.

"A great amount of practical information, very admirably arranged, and available for rough estimates, as well as for the more exact calculations required in the engineer's and contractor's offices."—*Artisan*.

Tunnelling.

PRACTICAL TUNNELLING. Explaining in detail the Setting-out of the works, Shaft-sinking and Heading-driving, Ranging the Lines and Levelling underground, Sub-Excavating, Timbering, and the Construction of the Brickwork of Tunnels, with the amount of Labour required for, and the Cost of, the various portions of the work. By FREDERICK W. SIMMS, M.Inst. C.E. Fourth Edition, Revised and Further Extended, including the Most Recent (1895) Examples of Sub-aqueous and other Tunnels, by D. KINNEAR CLARK, M.Inst. C.E. Imperial 8vo, with 34 Folding Plates and other Illustrations, £2 2s. cloth. [*Just published.*

"The estimation in which Mr. Simms's book on tunnelling has been held for over thirty years cannot be more truly expressed than in the words of the late Prof. Rankine:—'The best source of Information on the subject of tunnels is Mr. F. W. Simms's work on Practical Tunnelling.'"—*Architect*.

"It has been regarded from the first as a text-book of the subject. . . . Mr. Clark has added immensely to the value of the book."—*Engineer*.

Tunnel Shafts.

THE CONSTRUCTION OF LARGE TUNNEL SHAFTS: A Practical and Theoretical Essay. By J. H. WATSON BUCK, M.Inst.C.E., Resident Engineer, London and North-Western Railway. Illustrated with Folding Plates. Royal 8vo, 12s. cloth.

"Many of the methods given are of extreme practical value to the mason; and the observations on the form of arch, the rules for ordering the stone, and the construction of the templates will be found of considerable use. We commend the book to the engineering profession."—*Building News*.

"Will be regarded by civil engineers as of the utmost value, and calculated to save much time and obviate many mistakes."—*Colliery Guardian*.

Oblique Bridges.

A PRACTICAL AND THEORETICAL ESSAY ON OBLIQUE BRIDGES. With 13 large Plates. By the late GEORGE WATSON BUCK, M.I.C.E. Fourth Edition, revised by his Son, J. H. WATSON BUCK, M.I.C.E. and with the addition of Description to Diagrams for Facilitating the Construction of Oblique Bridges, by W. H. BARLOW, M.I.C.E. Roy. 8vo, 12s. cl.

"The standard text-book for all engineers regarding skew arches is Mr. Buck's treatise, and it would be impossible to consult a better."—*Engineer.*

"Mr. Buck's treatise is recognised as a standard text-book, and his treatment has divested the subject of many of the intricacies supposed to belong to it. As a guide to the engineer and architect, on a confessedly difficult subject, Mr. Buck's work is unsurpassed."—*Building News.*

Cast and Wrought Iron Bridge Construction.

A COMPLETE AND PRACTICAL TREATISE ON CAST AND WROUGHT IRON BRIDGE CONSTRUCTION, including Iron Foundations. In Three Parts—Theoretical, Practical, and Descriptive. By WILLIAM HUMBER, A.M.Inst.C.E., and M.Inst.M.E. Third Edition, Revised and much improved, with 115 Double Plates (20 of which now first appear in this edition), and numerous Additions to the Text. In Two Vols., imp. 4to, £6 16s. 6d. half-bound in morocco.

"A very valuable contribution to the standard literature of civil engineering. In addition to elevations, plans and sections, large scale details are given which very much enhance the instructive worth of those illustrations."—*Civil Engineer and Architect's Journal.*

Iron Bridges.

IRON BRIDGES OF MODERATE SPAN: Their Construction and Erection. By HAMILTON WELDON PENDRED, late Inspector of Ironwork to the Salford Corporation. With 40 Illustrations. 12mo, 2s. cloth.

"Students and engineers should obtain this book for constant and practical use."—*Colliery Guardian.*

Oblique Arches.

A PRACTICAL TREATISE ON THE CONSTRUCTION OF OBLIQUE ARCHES. By JOHN HART. Third Edition, with Plates. Imperial 8vo, 8s. cloth.

Statics, Graphic and Analytic.

GRAPHIC AND ANALYTIC STATICS, in their Practical Application to the Treatment of Stresses in Roofs, Solid Girders, Lattice, Bowstring and Suspension Bridges, Braced Iron Arches and Piers, and other Frameworks. By R. HUDSON GRAHAM, C.E. Containing Diagrams and Plates to Scale. With numerous Examples, many taken from existing Structures. Specially arranged for Class-work in Colleges and Universities. Second Edition, Revised and Enlarged. 8vo, 16s. cloth.

"Mr. Graham's book will find a place wherever graphic and analytic statics are used or studied."—*Engineer.*

"The work is excellent from a practical point of view, and has evidently been prepared with much care. The directions for working are ample, and are illustrated by an abundance of well-selected examples. It is an excellent text-book for the practical draughtsman."—*Athenæum.*

Girders, Strength of.

GRAPHIC TABLE FOR FACILITATING THE COMPUTATION OF THE WEIGHTS OF WROUGHT IRON AND STEEL GIRDERS, etc., for Parliamentary and other Estimates. By J. H. WATSON BUCK, M.Inst.C.E. On a Sheet, 2s. 6d.

Strains, Calculation of.

A HANDY BOOK FOR THE CALCULATION OF STRAINS IN GIRDERS AND SIMILAR STRUCTURES, AND THEIR STRENGTH. Consisting of Formulæ and Corresponding Diagrams, with numerous details for Practical Application, &c. By WILLIAM HUMBER, A.M.Inst.C.E., &c. Fifth Edition. Crown 8vo, nearly 100 Woodcuts and 3 Plates, 7s. 6d. cloth.

"The formulæ are neatly expressed, and the diagrams good."—*Athenæum.*

"We heartily commend this really *handy* book to our engineer and architect readers."—*English Mechanic.*

Trusses.

TRUSSES OF WOOD AND IRON. *Practical Applications of Science in Determining the Stresses, Breaking Weights, Safe Loads, Scantlings, and Details of Construction,* with Complete Working Drawings. By WILLIAM GRIFFITHS, Surveyor, Assistant Master, Tranmere School of Science and Art. Oblong 8vo, 4s. 6d. cloth.

"This handy little book enters so minutely into every detail connected with the construction of roof trusses, that no student need be ignorant of these matters."—*Practical Engineer.*

Strains in Ironwork.

THE STRAINS ON STRUCTURES OF IRONWORK; with Practical Remarks on Iron Construction. By F. W. SHEILDS, M.Inst.C.E. Second Edition, with 5 Plates. Royal 8vo, 5s. cloth.

"The student cannot find a better little book on this subject."—*Engineer.*

Barlow's Strength of Materials, enlarged by Humber.

A TREATISE ON THE STRENGTH OF MATERIALS; with Rules for Application in Architecture, the Construction of Suspension Bridges, Railways, &c. By PETER BARLOW, F.R.S. A New Edition, Revised by his Sons, P. W. BARLOW, F.R.S., and W. H. BARLOW, F.R.S.; to which are added, Experiments by HODGKINSON, FAIRBAIRN, and KIRKALDY; and Formulæ for Calculating Girders, &c. Arranged and Edited by WM. HUMBER, A-M.Inst.C.E. Demy 8vo, 400 pp., with 19 large Plates and numerous Woodcuts, 18s. cloth.

"Valuable alike to the student, tyro, and the experienced practitioner, it will always rank in future, as it has hitherto done, as the standard treatise on that particular subject."—*Engineer.*

"There is no greater authority than Barlow."—*Building News.*

"As a scientific work of the first class, it deserves a foremost place on the bookshelves of every civil engineer and practical mechanic."—*English Mechanic.*

Cast Iron and other Metals, Strength of.

A PRACTICAL ESSAY ON THE STRENGTH OF CAST IRON AND OTHER METALS. By THOMAS TREDGOLD, C.E. Fifth Edition, including HODGKINSON's Experimental Researches. 8vo, 12s. cloth.

Railway Working.

SAFE RAILWAY WORKING. *A Treatise on Railway Accidents: Their Cause and Prevention; with a Description of Modern Appliances and Systems.* By CLEMENT E. STRETTON, C.E. With Illustrations and Coloured Plates. Third Edition, Enlarged. Crown 8vo, 3s. 6d.

"A book for the engineer, the directors, the managers; and, in short, all who wish for information on railway matters will find a perfect encyclopædia in 'Safe Railway Working.'"—*Railway Review.*

"We commend the remarks on railway signalling to all railway managers, especially where a uniform code and practice is advocated."—*Herepath's Railway Journal.*

"The author may be congratulated on having collected, in a very convenient form, much valuable information on the principal questions affecting the safe working of railways."—*Railway Engineer.*

Heat, Expansion by.

EXPANSION OF STRUCTURES BY HEAT. By JOHN KEILY, C.E., late of the Indian Public Works and Victorian Railway Departments. Crown 8vo, 3s. 6d. cloth.

SUMMARY OF CONTENTS.

Section I. FORMULAS AND DATA.	Section VI. MECHANICAL FORCE OF HEAT.
Section II. METAL BARS.	
Section III. SIMPLE FRAMES.	Section VII. WORK OF EXPANSION AND CONTRACTION.
Section IV. COMPLEX FRAMES AND PLATES.	
Section V. THERMAL CONDUCTIVITY.	Section VIII. SUSPENSION BRIDGES.
	Section IX. MASONRY STRUCTURES.

"The aim the author has set before him, viz., to show the effects of heat upon metallic and other structures, is a laudable one, for this is a branch of physics upon which the engineer or architect can find but little reliable and comprehensive data in books."—*Builder.*

"Whoever is concerned to know the effect of changes of temperature on such structures as suspension bridges and the like, could not do better than consult Mr. Keily's valuable and handy exposition of the geometrical principles involved in these changes."—*Scotsman.*

Field Fortification.

A TREATISE ON FIELD FORTIFICATION, THE ATTACK OF FORTRESSES, MILITARY MINING, AND RECONNOITRING. By Colonel I. S. MACAULAY, late Professor of Fortification in the R.M.A., Woolwich. Sixth Edition. Crown 8vo, with separate Atlas of 12 Plates, 12s. cloth.

MR. HUMBER'S GREAT WORK ON MODERN ENGINEERING.

Complete in Four Volumes, imperial 4to, price £12 12s., half-morocco. Each Volume sold separately as follows:—

A RECORD OF THE PROGRESS OF MODERN ENGINEERING. First Series. Comprising Civil, Mechanical, Marine, Hydraulic, Railway, Bridge, and other Engineering Works, &c. By William Humber, A·M. Inst. C.E., &c. Imp. 4to, with 36 Double Plates, drawn to a large scale, Photographic Portrait of John Hawkshaw, C.E., F.R.S., &c., and copious descriptive Letterpress, Specifications, &c., £3 3s. half-morocco.

List of the Plates and Diagrams.

Victoria Station and Roof, L. B. & S. C. R. (6 plates); Southport Pier (2 plates); Victoria Station and Roof, L. C. & D. and G. W. R. (6 plates); Roof of Cremorne Music Hall; Bridge over G. N. Railway; Roof of Station, Dutch Rhenish Rail (2 plates); Bridge over the Thames, West London Extension Railway (5 plates); Armour Plates; Suspension Bridge, Thames (4 plates); The Allen Engine; Suspension Bridge, Avon (3 plates); Underground Railway (3 plates).

"Handsomely lithographed and printed. It will find favour with many who desire to preserve in a permanent form copies of the plans and specifications prepared for the guidance of the contractors for many important engineering works."—*Engineer.*

HUMBER'S PROGRESS OF MODERN ENGINEERING. Second Series. Imp. 4to, with 36 Double Plates, Photographic Portrait of Robert Stephenson, C.E., M.P., F.R.S., &c., and copious descriptive Letterpress, Specifications, &c., £3 3s. half-morocco.

List of the Plates and Diagrams.

Birkenhead Docks, Low Water Basin (15 plates); Charing Cross Station Roof, C. C. Railway (3 plates); Digswell Viaduct, Great Northern Railway; Robbery Wood Viaduct, Great Northern Railway; Iron Permanent Way; Clydach Viaduct, Merthyr, Tredegar, and Abergavenny Railway; Ebbw Viaduct, Merthyr, Tredegar, and Abergavenny Railway; College Wood Viaduct, Cornwall Railway; Dublin Winter Palace Roof (3 plates); Bridge over the Thames, L. C. & D. Railway (6 plates); Albert Harbour, Greenock (4 plates).

"Mr. Humber has done the profession good and true service, by the fine collection of examples he has here brought before the profession and the public."—*Practical Mechanic's Journal.*

HUMBER'S PROGRESS OF MODERN ENGINEERING. Third Series. Imp. 4to, with 40 Double Plates, Photographic Portrait of J. R. M'Clean, late Pres. Inst. C.E., and copious descriptive Letterpress, Specifications, &c., £3 3s. half-morocco.

List of the Plates and Diagrams.

MAIN DRAINAGE, METROPOLIS.—*North Side.*—Map showing Interception of Sewers; Middle Level Sewer (2 plates); Outfall Sewer, Bridge over River Lea (3 plates); Outfall Sewer, Bridge over Marsh Lane, North Woolwich Railway, and Bow and Barking Railway Junction; Outfall Sewer, Bridge over Bow and Barking Railway (3 plates); Outfall Sewer, Bridge over East London Waterworks' Feeder (2 plates); Outfall Sewer, Reservoir (2 plates); Outfall Sewer, Tumbling Bay and Outlet; Outfall Sewer, Penstocks. *South Side.*—Outfall Sewer, Bermondsey Branch (2 plates); Outfall Sewer, Reservoir and Outlet (4 plates); Outfall Sewer, Filth Hoist; Sections of Sewers (North and South Sides).

THAMES EMBANKMENT.—Section of River Wall; Steamboat Pier, Westminster (2 plates); Landing Stairs between Charing Cross and Waterloo Bridges; York Gate (2 plates); Overflow and Outlet at Savoy Street Sewer (3 plates); Steamboat Pier, Waterloo Bridge (3 plates); Junction of Sewers, Plans and Sections; Gullies, Plans and Sections; Rolling Stock; Granite and Iron Forts.

"The drawings have a constantly increasing value, and whoever desires to possess clear representations of the two great works carried out by our Metropolitan Board will obtain Mr. Humber's volume."—*Engineer.*

HUMBER'S PROGRESS OF MODERN ENGINEERING. Fourth Series. Imp. 4to, with 36 Double Plates, Photographic Portrait of John Fowler, late Pres. Inst. C.E., and copious descriptive Letterpress, Specifications, &c., £3 3s. half-morocco.

List of the Plates and Diagrams.

Abbey Mills Pumping Station, Main Drainage, Metropolis (4 plates); Barrow Docks (5 plates); Manquis Viaduct, Santiago and Valparaiso Railway (2 plates); Adam's Locomotive, St. Helen's Canal Railway (2 plates); Cannon Street Station Roof, Charing Cross Railway (3 plates); Road Bridge over the River Moka (2 plates); Telegraphic Apparatus for Mesopotamia; Viaduct over the River Wye, Midland Railway (3 plates); St. Germans Viaduct, Cornwall Railway (2 plates); Wrought-Iron Cylinder for Diving Bell; Millwall Docks (6 plates); Milroy's Patent Excavator; Metropolitan District Railway (6 plates); Harbours, Ports, and Breakwaters (3 plates).

"We gladly welcome another year's issue of this valuable publication from the able pen of Mr. Humber. The accuracy and general excellence of this work are well known, while its usefulness in giving the measurements and details of some of the latest examples of engineering, as carried out by the most eminent men in the profession, cannot be too highly prized."—*Artisan.*

THE POPULAR WORKS OF MICHAEL REYNOLDS
("THE ENGINE DRIVER'S FRIEND").

Locomotive-Engine Driving.

LOCOMOTIVE-ENGINE DRIVING: *A Practical Manual for Engineers in charge of Locomotive Engines.* By MICHAEL REYNOLDS, Member of the Society of Engineers, formerly Locomotive Inspector L. B. and S. C. R. Ninth Edition. Including a KEY TO THE LOCOMOTIVE ENGINE. With Illustrations and Portrait of Author. Crown 8vo, 4s. 6d. cloth.

"Mr. Reynolds has supplied a want, and has supplied it well. We can confidently recommend the book, not only to the practical driver, but to everyone who takes an interest in the performance of locomotive engines."—*The Engineer.*

"Mr. Reynolds has opened a new chapter in the literature of the day. Of the practical utility of this admirable treatise, we have to speak in terms of warm commendation."—*Athenæum.*

"Evidently the work of one who knows his subject thoroughly."—*Railway Service Gazette.*

"Were the cautions and rules given in the book to become part of the every-day working of our engine-drivers, we might have fewer distressing accidents to deplore."—*Scotsman.*

Stationary Engine Driving.

STATIONARY ENGINE DRIVING: *A Practical Manual for Engineers in charge of Stationary Engines.* By MICHAEL REYNOLDS. Fifth Edition. Enlarged. With Plates and Woodcuts. Crown 8vo, 4s. 6d. cloth.

"The author is thoroughly acquainted with his subjects, and his advice on the various points treated is clear and practical. . . . He has produced a manual which is an exceedingly useful one for the class for whom it is specially intended."—*Engineering.*

"Our author leaves no stone unturned. He is determined that his readers shall not only know something about the stationary engine, but all about it."—*Engineer.*

"An engineman who has mastered the contents of Mr. Reynolds's book will require but little actual experience with boilers and engines before he can be trusted to look after them."—*English Mechanic.*

The Engineer, Fireman, and Engine-Boy.

THE MODEL LOCOMOTIVE ENGINEER, FIREMAN, and ENGINE-BOY. Comprising a Historical Notice of the Pioneer Locomotive Engines and their Inventors. By MICHAEL REYNOLDS. Second Edition, with Revised Appendix. With numerous Illustrations and Portrait of George Stephenson. Crown 8vo, 4s. 6d. cloth. [*Just published.*

"From the technical knowledge of the author it will appeal to the railway man of to-day more forcibly than anything written by Dr. Smiles. . . . The volume contains information of a technical kind, and facts that every driver should be familiar with."—*English Mechanic.*

"We should be glad to see this book in the possession of everyone in the kingdom who has ever laid, or is to lay, hands on a locomotive engine."—*Iron.*

Continuous Railway Brakes.

CONTINUOUS RAILWAY BRAKES: *A Practical Treatise on the several Systems in Use in the United Kingdom; their Construction and Performance.* With copious Illustrations and numerous Tables. By MICHAEL REYNOLDS. Large crown 8vo, 9s. cloth.

"A popular explanation of the different brakes. It will be of great assistance in forming public opinion, and will be studied with benefit by those who take an interest in the brake."—*English Mechanic.*

"Written with sufficient technical detail to enable the principle and relative connection of the various parts of each particular brake to be readily grasped."—*Mechanical World.*

Engine-Driving Life.

ENGINE-DRIVING LIFE: *Stirring Adventures and Incidents in the Lives of Locomotive-Engine Drivers.* By MICHAEL REYNOLDS. Third and Cheaper Edition. Crown 8vo, 1s. 6d. cloth.

"From first to last perfectly fascinating. Wilkie Collins's most thrilling conceptions are thrown into the shade by true incidents, endless in their variety, related in every page."—*North British Mail.*

"Anyone who wishes to get a real insight into railway life cannot do better than read 'Engine-Driving Life' for himself; and if he once take it up he will find that the author's enthusiasm and real love of the engine-driving profession will carry him on till he has read every page."—*Saturday Review.*

Pocket Companion for Enginemen.

THE ENGINEMAN'S POCKET COMPANION AND PRACTICAL EDUCATOR FOR ENGINEMEN, BOILER ATTENDANTS, AND MECHANICS. By MICHAEL REYNOLDS. With Forty-five Illustrations and numerous Diagrams. Third Edition, Revised. Royal 18mo, 3s. 6d., strongly bound for pocket wear.

"This admirable work is well suited to accomplish its object, being the honest workmanship of a competent engineer."—*Glasgow Herald.*

"A most meritorious work, giving in a succinct and practical form all the information an engineminder desirous of mastering the scientific principles of his daily calling would require."—*The Miller.*

"A boon to those who are striving to become efficient mechanics."—*Daily Chronicle.*

MARINE ENGINEERING, SHIPBUILDING, NAVIGATION, etc.

Pocket-Book for Naval Architects and Shipbuilders.

THE NAVAL ARCHITECT'S AND SHIPBUILDER'S POCKET-BOOK of Formulæ, Rules, and Tables, and MARINE ENGINEER'S AND SURVEYOR'S Handy Book of Reference. By CLEMENT MACKROW, Member of the Institution of Naval Architects, Naval Draughtsman. Sixth Edition, Revised. 700 pages, with upwards of 300 Illustrations. Fcap., 12s. 6d. strongly bound in leather. [Just published.

SUMMARY OF CONTENTS.

SIGNS AND SYMBOLS, DECIMAL FRACTIONS.— TRIGONOMETRY. — PRACTICAL GEOMETRY. — MENSURATION. — CENTRES AND MOMENTS OF FIGURES.— MOMENTS OF INERTIA AND RADII OF GYRATION.— ALGEBRAICAL EXPRESSIONS FOR SIMPSON'S RULES.— MECHANICAL PRINCIPLES. — CENTRE OF GRAVITY.—LAWS OF MOTION.—DISPLACEMENT, CENTRE OF BUOYANCY.— CENTRE OF GRAVITY OF SHIP'S HULL. —STABILITY CURVES AND METACENTRES.—SEA AND SHALLOW-WATER WAVES.— ROLLING OF SHIPS.— PROPULSION AND RESISTANCE OF VESSELS. —SPEED TRIALS.—SAILING, CENTRE OF EFFORT.—DISTANCES DOWN RIVERS, COAST LINES.—STEERING AND RUDDERS OF VESSELS.—LAUNCHING CALCULATIONS AND VELOCITIES.—WEIGHT OF MATERIAL AND GEAR.—GUN PARTICULARS AND WEIGHT.—STANDARD GAUGES.—RIVETED JOINTS AND RIVETING.—STRENGTH AND TESTS OF MATERIALS. — BINDING AND SHEARING STRESSES, ETC.—STRENGTH OF SHAFTING, PILLARS, WHEELS, ETC. — HYDRAULIC DATA, ETC.—CONIC SECTIONS, CATENARIAN CURVES.—MECHANICAL POWERS, WORK.— BOARD OF TRADE REGULATIONS FOR BOILERS AND ENGINES. — BOARD OF TRADE REGULATIONS FOR SHIPS.—LLOYD'S RULES FOR BOILERS.—LLOYD'S WEIGHT OF CHAINS.—LLOYD'S SCANTLINGS FOR SHIPS.—DATA OF ENGINES AND VESSELS. - SHIPS' FITTINGS AND TESTS.— SEASONING PRESERVING TIMBER.— MEASUREMENT OF TIMBER.—ALLOYS, PAINTS, VARNISHES. — DATA FOR STOWAGE. — ADMIRALTY TRANSPORT REGULATIONS. — RULES FOR HORSE-POWER, SCREW PROPELLERS, ETC.— PERCENTAGES FOR BUTT STRAPS, ETC. —PARTICULARS OF YACHTS. — MASTING AND RIGGING VESSELS.—DISTANCES OF FOREIGN PORTS. — TONNAGE TABLES. — VOCABULARY OF FRENCH AND ENGLISH TERMS. — ENGLISH WEIGHTS AND MEASURES.—FOREIGN WEIGHTS AND MEASURES.—DECIMAL EQUIVALENTS. — FOREIGN MONEY.— DISCOUNT AND WAGE TABLES.—USEFUL NUMBERS AND READY RECKONERS —TABLES OF CIRCULAR MEASURES.— TABLES OF AREAS OF AND CIRCUMFERENCES OF CIRCLES.—TABLES OF AREAS OF SEGMENTS OF CIRCLES.— TABLES OF SQUARES AND CUBES AND ROOTS OF NUMBERS. — TABLES OF LOGARITHMS OF NUMBERS.—TABLES OF HYPERBOLIC LOGARITHMS.—TABLES OF NATURAL SINES, TANGENTS, ETC.— TABLES OF LOGARITHMIC SINES, TANGENTS, ETC.

"In these days of advanced knowledge a work like this is of the greatest value. It contains a vast amount of information. We unhesitatingly say that it is the most valuable compilation for its specific purpose that has ever been printed. No naval architect, engineer, surveyor, or seaman, wood or iron shipbuilder, can afford to be without this work."—*Nautical Magazine.*

"Should be used by all who are engaged in the construction or designs of vessels. . . . Will be found to contain the most useful tables and formulæ required by shipbuilders, carefully collected from the best authorities, and put together in a popular and simple form."—*Engineer.*

"The professional shipbuilder has now, in a convenient and accessible form, reliable data for solving many of the numerous problems that present themselves in the course of his work."—*Iron.*

"There is no doubt that a pocket-book of this description must be a necessity in the ship-building trade. . . . The volume contains a mass of useful information clearly expressed and presented in a handy form."—*Marine Engineer.*

Marine Engineering.

MARINE ENGINES AND STEAM VESSELS (A Treatise on). By ROBERT MURRAY, C.E. Eighth Edition, thoroughly Revised, with considerable Additions by the Author and by GEORGE CARLISLE, C.E., Senior Surveyor to the Board of Trade at Liverpool. 12mo, 5s. cloth boards.

"Well adapted to give the young steamship engineer or marine engine and boiler maker a general introduction into his practical work."—*Mechanical World.*

"We feel sure that this thoroughly revised edition will continue to be as popular in the future as it has been in the past, as, for its size, it contains more useful information than any similar treatise."—*Industries.*

"As a compendious and useful guide to engineers of our mercantile and royal naval services, we should say it cannot be surpassed."—*Building News.*

"The information given is both sound and sensible, and well qualified to direct young sea-going hands on the straight road to the extra chief's certificate. . . . Most useful to surveyors, inspectors, draughtsmen, and young engineers."—*Glasgow Herald.*

c

English-French Dictionary of Sea Terms.

TECHNICAL DICTIONARY OF SEA TERMS, PHRASES AND WORDS USED IN THE ENGLISH & FRENCH LANGUAGES. (English-French, French-English). For the Use of Seamen, Engineers, Pilots, Ship-builders, Ship-owners and Ship-brokers. Compiled by W. PIRRIE, late of the African Steamship Company. Fcap. 8vo, 5s. cloth limp.
[Just published.

"This volume will be highly appreciated by seamen, engineers, pilots, shipbuilders and shipowners. It will be found wonderfully accurate and complete."—*Scotsman.*
"A very useful dictionary, which has long been wanted by French and English engineers, masters, officers and others."—*Shipping World.*

Pocket-Book for Marine Engineers.

A POCKET-BOOK OF USEFUL TABLES AND FORMULÆ FOR MARINE ENGINEERS. By FRANK PROCTOR, A.I.N.A. Third Edition. Royal 32mo, leather, gilt edges, with strap, 4s.

"We recommend it to our readers as going far to supply a long-felt want."—*Naval Science.*
"A most useful companion to all marine engineers."—*United Service Gazette.*

Introduction to Marine Engineering.

ELEMENTARY ENGINEERING: A Manual for Young Marine Engineers and Apprentices. In the Form of Questions and Answers on Metals, Alloys, Strength of Materials, Construction and Management of Marine Engines and Boilers, Geometry, &c. &c. With an Appendix of Useful Tables. By JOHN SHERREN BREWER, Government Marine Surveyor, Hongkong. Third Edition. Small crown 8vo, 1s. 6d. cloth.

"Contains much valuable information for the class for whom it is intended, especially in the chapters on the management of boilers and engines."—*Nautical Magazine.*
"A useful introduction to the more elaborate text-books."—*Scotsman.*
"To a student who has the requisite desire and resolve to attain a thorough knowledge, Mr. Brewer offers decidedly useful help."—*Athenæum.*

Navigation.

PRACTICAL NAVIGATION. Consisting of THE SAILOR'S SEA-BOOK, by JAMES GREENWOOD and W. H. ROSSER; together with the requisite Mathematical and Nautical Tables for the Working of the Problems, by HENRY LAW, C.E., and Professor J. R. YOUNG. Illustrated. 12mo, 7s. strongly half-bound.

Sailmaking.

THE ART AND SCIENCE OF SAILMAKING. By SAMUEL B. SADLER, Practical Sailmaker, late in the employment of Messrs. Ratsey and Lapthorne, of Cowes and Gosport. With Plates and other Illustrations. Small 4to, 12s. 6d. cloth.

"This work is very ably written, and is illustrated by diagrams and carefully-worked calculations. The work should be in the hands of every sailmaker, whether employer or employed, as it cannot fail to assist them in the pursuit of their important avocations."—*Isle of Wight Herald.*
"This extremely practical work gives a complete education in all the branches of the manufacture cutting out, roping, seaming, and goring. It is copiously illustrated, and will form a first-rate text-book and guide."—*Portsmouth Times.*
"The author of this work has rendered a distinct service to all interested in the art of sailmaking. The subject of which he treats is a congenial one. Mr. Sadler is a practical sailmaker and has devoted years of careful observation and study to the subject; and the results of the experience thus gained he has set forth in the volume before us."—*Steamship.*

Chain Cables.

CHAIN CABLES AND CHAINS. Comprising Sizes and Curves of Links, Studs, &c., Iron for Cables and Chains, Chain Cable and Chain Making, Forming and Welding Links, Strength of Cables and Chains, Certificates for Cables, Marking Cables, Prices of Chain Cables and Chains, Historical Notes, Acts of Parliament, Statutory Tests, Charges for Testing, List of Manufacturers of Cables, &c. &c. By THOMAS W. TRAILL, F.E.R.N., M. Inst. C.E., Engineer Surveyor in Chief, Board of Trade, Inspector of Chain Cable and Anchor Proving Establishments, and General Superintendent, Lloyd's Committee on Proving Establishments. With numerous Tables, Illustrations and Lithographic Drawings. Folio, £2 2s. cloth.

"It contains a vast amount of valuable information. Nothing seems to be wanting to make it complete and standard work of reference on the subject."—*Nautical Magazine.*

MINING AND METALLURGY.

Mining Machinery.

MACHINERY FOR METALLIFEROUS MINES: A Practical Treatise for Mining Engineers, Metallurgists, and Managers of Mines. By E. HENRY DAVIES, M.E., F.G.S. Crown 8vo, 580 pp., with upwards of 300 Illustrations, 12s. 6d. cloth. [*Just published.*

"Mr. Davies, in this handsome volume, has done the advanced student and the manager of mines good service. Almost every kind of machinery in actual use is carefully described, and the woodcuts and plates are good."—*Athenæum.*

"From cover to cover the work exhibits all the same characteristics which excite the confidence and attract the attention of the student as he peruses the first page. The work may safely be recommended. By its publication the literature connected with the industry will be enriched, and the reputation of its author enhanced."—*Mining Journal.*

"Mr. Davies has endeavoured to bring before his readers the best of everything in modern mining appliances. His work carries internal evidence of the author's impartiality, and this constitutes one of the great merits of the book. Throughout his work the criticisms are based on his own or other reliable experience.'—*Iron and Steel Trades' Journal.*

"The work deals with nearly every class of machinery or apparatus likely to be met with or required in connection with metalliferous mining, and is one which we have every confidence in recommending."—*Practical Engineer.*

Metalliferous Minerals and Mining.

A TREATISE ON METALLIFEROUS MINERALS AND MINING. By D. C. DAVIES, F.G.S., Mining Engineer, &c., Author of "A Treatise on Slate and Slate Quarrying." Fifth Edition, thoroughly Revised and much Enlarged, by his Son, E. HENRY DAVIES, M.E., F.G.S. With about 150 Illustrations. Crown 8vo, 12s. 6d. cloth.

"Neither the practical miner nor the general reader interested in mines can have a better book for his companion and his guide."—*Mining Journal.* [*Mining World.*

"We are doing our readers a service in calling their attention to this valuable work."

"A book that will not only be useful to the geologist, the practical miner, and the metallurgist but also very interesting to the general public."—*Iron.*

"As a history of the present state of mining throughout the world this book has a real value, and it supplies an actual want."—*Athenæum.*

Earthy Minerals and Mining.

A TREATISE ON EARTHY & OTHER MINERALS AND MINING. By D. C. DAVIES, F.G.S., Author of "Metalliferous Minerals," &c. Third Edition, revised and Enlarged, by his Son, E. HENRY DAVIES M.E., F.G.S. With about 100 Illustrations. Crown 8vo, 12s. 6d. cloth.

"We do not remember to have met with any English work on mining matters that contains the same amount of information packed in equally convenient form."—*Academy.*

"We should be inclined to rank it as among the very best of the handy technical and trades manuals which have recently appeared."—*British Quarterly Review.*

Metalliferous Mining in the United Kingdom.

BRITISH MINING: A Treatise on the History, Discovery, Practical Development, and Future Prospects of Metalliferous Mines in the United Kingdom. By ROBERT HUNT, F.R.S., Editor of "Ure's Dictionary of Arts, Manufactures, and Mines," &c. Upwards of 950 pp., with 230 Illustrations. Second Edition, Revised. Super-royal 8vo, £2 2s. cloth.

"One of the most valuable works of reference of modern times. Mr. Hunt, as Keeper of Mining Records of the United Kingdom, has had opportunities for such a task not enjoyed by anyone else and has evidently made the most of them. . . . The language and style adopted are good, and the treatment of the various subjects laborious, conscientious, and scientific."—*Engineering.*

"The book is, in fact, a treasure-house of statistical information on mining subjects, and we know of no other work embodying so great a mass of matter of this kind. Were this the only merit of Mr. Hunt's volume, it would be sufficient to render it indispensable in the library of everyone interested in the development of the mining and metallurgical industries of this country.'' —*Athenæum.*

"A mass of information not elsewhere available, and of the greatest value to those who may be interested in our great mineral industries."—*Engineer.*

Underground Pumping Machinery.

MINE DRAINAGE. Being a Complete and Practical Treatise on Direct-Acting Underground Steam Pumping Machinery, with a Description of a large number of the best known Engines, their General Utility and the Special Sphere of their Action, the Mode of their Application, and their merits compared with other forms of Pumping Machinery. By STEPHEN MICHELL. 8vo, 15s. cloth.

"Will be highly esteemed by colliery owners and lessees, mining engineers, and students generally who require to be acquainted with the best means of securing the drainage of mines. It is a most valuable work, and stands almost alone in the literature of steam pumping machinery."— *Colliery Guardian.*

"Much valuable information is given, so that the book is thoroughly worthy of an extensive circulation amongst practical men and purchasers of machinery."—*Mining Journal.*

Prospecting for Gold and other Metals.

THE PROSPECTOR'S HANDBOOK: A Guide for the Prospector and Traveller in Search of Metal-Bearing or other Valuable Minerals. By J. W. ANDERSON, M.A. (Camb.), F.R.G.S., Author of "Fiji and New Caledonia." Sixth Edition, thoroughly Revised and much Enlarged. Small crown 8vo, 3s. 6d. cloth; or, 4s. 6d. leather, pocket-book form, with tuck.
[*Just published.*]

"Will supply a much felt want, especially among Colonists, in whose way are so often thrown many mineralogical specimens the value of which it is difficult to determine."—*Engineer.*

"How to find commercial minerals, and how to identify them when they are found, are the leading points to which attention is directed. The author has managed to pack as much practical detail into his pages as would supply material for a book three times its size."—*Mining Journal.*

Mining Notes and Formulæ.

NOTES AND FORMULÆ FOR MINING STUDENTS. By JOHN HERMAN MERIVALE, M.A., Certificated Colliery Manager, Professor of Mining in the Durham College of Science, Newcastle-upon-Tyne. Third Edition, Revised and Enlarged. Small crown 8vo, 2s. 6d. cloth.

"Invaluable to anyone who is working up for an examination on mining subjects."—*Iron and Coal Trades Review.*

"The author has done his work in an exceedingly creditable manner, and has produced a book that will be of service to students, and those who are practically engaged in mining operations."—*Engineer.*

Handybook for Miners.

THE MINER'S HANDBOOK: A Handy Book of Reference on the Subjects of Mineral Deposits, Mining Operations, Ore Dressing, &c. For the Use of Students and others interested in Mining matters. Compiled by JOHN MILNE, F.R.S., Professor of Mining in the Imperial University of Japan. Revised Edition. Fcap. 8vo, 7s. 6d. leather. [*Just published.*]

"Professor Milne's handbook is sure to be received with favour by all connected with mining, and will be extremely popular among students."—*Athenæum.*

Miners' and Metallurgists' Pocket-Book.

A POCKET-BOOK FOR MINERS AND METALLURGISTS. Comprising Rules, Formulæ, Tables, and Notes, for Use in Field and Office Work. By F. DANVERS POWER, F.G.S., M.E. Fcap. 8vo, 9s. leather.

"This excellent book is an admirable example of its kind, and ought to find a large sale amongst English-speaking prospectors and mining engineers."—*Engineering.*

"A useful *vade-mecum* containing a mass of rules, formulæ, tables, and various other information, necessary for daily eference."—*Iron.*

Mineral Surveying and Valuing.

THE MINERAL SURVEYOR AND VALUER'S COMPLETE GUIDE, comprising a Treatise on Improved Mining Surveying and the Valuation of Mining Properties, with New Traverse Tables. By WM. LINTERN. Third Edition, Enlarged. 12mo, 4s. cloth.

"A valuable and thoroughly trustworthy guide."—*Iron and Coal Trades Review.*

Asbestos and its Uses.

ASBESTOS: Its Properties, Occurrence, and Uses. With some Account of the Mines of Italy and Canada. By ROBERT H. JONES. With Eight Collotype Plates and other Illustrations. Crown 8vo, 12s. 6d. cloth.

"An interesting and invaluable work."—*Colliery Guardian.*

Iron, Metallurgy of.

METALLURGY OF IRON. Containing History of Iron Manufacture, Methods of Assay, and Analyses of Iron Ores, Processes of Manufacture of Iron and Steel, &c. By H. BAUERMAN, F.G.S., A.R.S.M. With numerous Illustrations. Sixth Edition, Enlarged. 12mo, 5s. 6d. cloth.

"Carefully written, it has the merit of brevity and conciseness, as to less important points; while all material matters are very fully and thoroughly entered into."—*Standard.*

Slate Quarrying, &c.

SLATE AND SLATE QUARRYING, Scientific, Practical and Commercial. By D. C. DAVIES, F.G.S., Mining Engineer, &c. With numerous Illustrations and Folding Plates. Third Edition, 12mo, 3s. cloth.

"One of the best and best-balanced treatises on a special subject that we have met with."—*Engineer.*

Colliery Management.

THE COLLIERY MANAGER'S HANDBOOK: A Comprehensive Treatise on the Laying-out and Working of Collieries, Designed as a Book of Reference for Colliery Managers, and for the Use of Coal-Mining Students preparing for First-class Certificates. By CALEB PAMELY, Mining Engineer and Surveyor; Member of the North of England Institute of Mining and Mechanical Engineers; and Member of the South Wales Institute of Mining Engineers. With nearly 700 Plans, Diagrams, and other Illustrations. Third Edition, Revised and Enlarged. Medium 8vo. about 900 pages. Price £1 5s. strongly bound. [*Just published.*

SUMMARY OF CONTENTS.

GEOLOGY.—SEARCH FOR COAL.—MINERAL LEASES AND OTHER HOLDINGS.—SHAFT SINKING.—FITTING UP THE SHAFT AND SURFACE ARRANGEMENTS.—STEAM BOILERS AND THEIR FITTINGS.—TIMBERING AND WALLING.—NARROW WORK AND METHODS OF WORKING.—UNDERGROUND CONVEYANCE.—DRAINAGE.—THE GASES MET WITH IN MINES; VENTILATION.—ON THE FRICTION OF AIR IN MINES.— THE PRIESTMAN OIL ENGINE; PETROLEUM AND NATURAL GAS—SURVEYING AND PLANNING.—LIGHTING; SAFETY LAMPS AND FIRE DAMP DETECTORS.—SUNDRY AND INCIDENTAL OPERATIONS AND APPLIANCES.—COLLIERY EXPLOSIONS.—MISCELLANEOUS QUESTIONS AND ANSWERS.

Appendix: SUMMARY OF REPORT OF H.M. COMMISSIONERS ON ACCIDENTS IN MINES.

"There can be no doubt that it is the best book on coal-mining."—J. T. ROBSON, Esq., *H.M.'s Inspector of Mines, South Wales District.*

"Mr. Pamely's work is eminently suited to the purpose for which it is intended—being clear, interesting, exhaustive, rich in detail, and up to date, giving descriptions of the very latest machines in every department. . . . A mining engineer could scarcely go wrong who followed this work."—*Colliery Guardian.*

"This is the most complete 'all round' work on coal-mining published in the English language. . . . No library of coal-mining books is complete without it."—*Colliery Engineer* (Scranton, Pa., U.S.A.).

"Mr. Pamely's work is in all respects worthy of our admiration. No person in any responsible position connected with mines should be without a copy."—*Westminster Review.*

Coal and Iron.

THE COAL AND IRON INDUSTRIES OF THE UNITED KINGDOM. Comprising a Description of the Coal Fields, and of the Principal Seams of Coal, with Returns of their Produce and its Distribution, and Analyses of Special Varieties. Also an Account of the occurrence of Iron Ores in Veins or Seams; Analyses of each Variety; and a History of the Rise and Progress of Pig Iron Manufacture. By RICHARD MEADE, Assistant Keeper of Mining Records. With Maps. 8vo, £1 8s. cloth.

"The book is one which must find a place on the shelves of all interested in coal and iron production, and in the iron, steel, and other metallurgical industries."—*Engineer.*

"Of this book we may unreservedly say that it is the best of its class which we have ever met. . . . A book of reference which no one engaged in the iron or coal trades should omit from his library."—*Iron and Coal Trades Review.*

Coal Mining.

COAL AND COAL MINING: A *Rudimentary Treatise on.* By the late Sir WARINGTON W. SMYTH, M.A., F.R.S., Chief Inspector of the Mines of the Crown. Seventh Edition, Revised and Enlarged. With numerous Illustrations. 12mo, 4s. cloth boards.

"As an outline is given of every known coal-field in this and other countries, as well as of the principal methods of working, the book will doubtless interest a very large number of readers."—*Mining Journal.*

Subterraneous Surveying.

SUBTERRANEOUS SURVEYING, *Elementary and Practical Treatise on,* with and without the Magnetic Needle. By THOMAS FENWICK, Surveyor of Mines, and THOMAS BAKER, C.E. Illust. 12mo, 3s. cloth boards.

Granite Quarrying.

GRANITES AND OUR GRANITE INDUSTRIES. By GEORGE F. HARRIS, F.G.S., Membre de la Société Belge de Géologie, Lecturer on Economic Geology at the Birkbeck Institution, &c. With Illustrations. Crown 8vo, 2s. 6d. cloth.

"A clearly and well-written manual on the granite industry."—*Scotsman.*

"An interesting work, which will be deservedly esteemed."—*Colliery Guardian.*

"An exceedingly interesting and valuable monograph on a subject which has hitherto received unaccountably little attention in the shape of systematic literary treatment."—*Scottish Leader.*

Gold, Metallurgy of.

THE METALLURGY OF GOLD: A Practical Treatise on the Metallurgical Treatment of Gold-bearing Ores. Including the Processes of Concentration, Chlorination and Extraction by Cyanide, and the Assaying, Melting, and Refining of Gold. By M. EISSLER, Mining Engineer and Metallurgical Chemist, formerly Assistant Assayer of the U.S. Mint, San Francisco. Fourth Edition, Enlarged. With about 250 Illustrations and numerous Folding Plates and Working Drawings. 8vo, 16s. cloth. [*Just published*.

"This book thoroughly deserves its title of a 'Practical Treatise.' The whole process of gold milling, from the breaking of the quartz to the assay of the bullion, is described in clear and orderly narrative and with much, but not too much, fulness of detail."—*Saturday Review*.

"The work is a storehouse of information and valuable data, and we strongly recommend it to all professional men engaged in the gold-mining industry."—*Mining Journal*.

Gold Extraction.

THE CYANIDE PROCESS OF GOLD EXTRACTION: and its Practical Application on the Witwatersrand Gold Fields in South Africa. By M. EISSLER, M.E., Mem. Inst. Mining and Metallurgy, Author of "The Metallurgy of Gold," &c. With Diagrams and Working Drawings. Large crown 8vo, 7s. 6d. cloth. [*Just published*.

"This book is just what was needed to acquaint mining men with the actual working of a process which is not only the most popular, but is, as a general rule, the most successful for the extraction of gold from tailings."—*Mining Journal*.

"The work will prove invaluable to all interested in gold mining, whether metallurgists or as investors."—*Chemical News*.

Silver, Metallurgy of.

THE METALLURGY OF SILVER: A Practical Treatise on the Amalgamation, Roasting, and Lixiviation of Silver Ores. Including the Assaying, Melting and Refining, of Silver Bullion. By M. EISSLER, Author of "The Metallurgy of Gold," &c. Third Edition. With 150 Illustrations. Crown 8vo, 10s. 6d. cloth. [*Just published*.

"A practical treatise, and a technical work which we are convinced will supply a long-felt want amongst practical men, and at the same time be of value to students and others indirectly connected with the industries."—*Mining Journal*.

"From first to last the book is thoroughly sound and reliable."—*Colliery Guardian*.

"For chemists, practical miners, assayers, and investors alike, we do not know of any work on the subject so handy and yet so comprehensive."—*Glasgow Herald*.

Lead, Metallurgy of.

THE METALLURGY OF ARGENTIFEROUS LEAD: A Practical Treatise on the Smelting of Silver-Lead Ores and the Refining of Lead Bullion. Including Reports on various Smelting Establishments and Descriptions of Modern Smelting Furnaces and Plants in Europe and America. By M. EISSLER, M.E., Author of "The Metallurgy of Gold," &c. Crown 8vo, 400 pp., with 183 Illustrations, 12s. 6d. cloth.

"The numerous metallurgical processes, which are fully and extensively treated of, embrace all the stages experienced in the passage of the lead from the various natural states to its issue from the refinery as an article of commerce."—*Practical Engineer*.

"The present volume fully maintains the reputation of the author. Those who wish to obtain a thorough insight into the present state of this industry cannot do better than read this volume, and all mining engineers cannot fail to find many useful hints and suggestions in it."—*Industries*.

"It is most carefully written and illustrated with capital drawings and diagrams. In fact, it is the work of an expert for experts, by whom it will be prized as an indispensable text-book."—*Bristol Mercury*.

Iron Mining.

THE IRON ORES OF GREAT BRITAIN AND IRELAND: Their Mode of Occurrence, Age, and Origin, and the Methods of Searching for and Working them, with a Notice of some of the Iron Ores of Spain. By J. D. KENDALL, F.G.S., Mining Engineer. Crown 8vo, 16s. cloth.

"The author has a thorough practical knowledge of his subject, and has supplemented a careful study of the available literature by unpublished information derived from his own observations. The result is a very useful volume which cannot fail to be of value to all interested in the iron industry of the country."—*Industries*.

"'Mr. Kendall is a great authority on this subject and writes from personal observation.'—*Colliery Guardian*.

"Mr. Kendall's book is thoroughly well done. In it there are the outlines of the history of ore mining in every centre and there is everything that we want to know as to the character of the ores of each district, their commercial value and the cost of working them."—*Iron and Steel Trades Journal*.

ELECTRICITY, ELECTRICAL ENGINEERING, etc.

Dynamo Management.

THE MANAGEMENT OF DYNAMOS: A Handybook of Theory and Practice for the Use of Mechanics, Engineers, Students and others in Charge of Dynamos. By G. W. LUMMIS PATERSON. With numerous Illustrations. Crown 8vo, 3s. 6d. cloth. [*Just published.*

"An example which deserves to be taken as a model by other authors. The subject is treated in a manner which any intelligent man who is fit to be entrusted with charge of an engine should be able to understand. It is a useful book to all who make, tend or employ electric machinery."—*Architect.*

"A most satisfactory book from a practical point of view. We strongly commend it to the attention of every electrical engineering student."—*Daily Chronicle.*

Electrical Engineering.

THE ELECTRICAL ENGINEER'S POCKET-BOOK OF MODERN RULES, FORMULÆ, TABLES, AND DATA. By H. R. KEMPE, M.Inst.E.E., A.M.Inst.C.E., Technical Officer, Postal Telegraphs, Author of "A Handbook of Electrical Testing," &c. Second Edition, thoroughly Revised, with Additions. Royal 32mo, oblong, 5s. leather.

"There is very little in the shape of formulæ or data which the electrician is likely to want in a hurry which cannot be found in its pages."—*Practical Engineer.*

"A very useful book of reference for daily use in practical electrical engineering and its various applications to the industries of the present day."—*Iron.*

"It is the best book of its kind."—*Electrical Engineer.*

"Well arranged and compact. The 'Electrical Engineer's Pocket-Book' is a good one."—*Electrician.* [*Review.*

"Strongly recommended to those engaged in the various electrical industries."—*Electrical*

Electric Lighting.

ELECTRIC LIGHT FITTING: A Handbook for Working Electrical Engineers, embodying Practical Notes on Installation Management. By JOHN W. URQUHART, Electrician, Author of "Electric Light," &c. With numerous Illustrations. Second Edition, Revised, with Additional Chapters. Crown 8vo, 5s. cloth.

"This volume deals with what may be termed the mechanics of electric lighting, and is addressed to men who are already engaged in the work or are training for it. The work traverses a great deal of ground, and may be read as a sequel to the same author's useful work on 'Electric Light.'"—*Electrician.*

"The book is well worth the perusal of the workmen for whom it is written."—*Electrical Review.*

"We have read this book with a good deal of pleasure. We believe that the book will be of use to practical workmen, who will not be alarmed by finding mathematical formulæ which they are unable to understand."—*Electrical Plant.*

Electric Light.

ELECTRIC LIGHT: *Its Production and Use.* Embodying Plain Directions for the Treatment of Dynamo-Electric Machines, Batteries, Accumulators, and Electric Lamps. By J. W. URQUHART, C.E., Author of "Electric Light Fitting," "Electroplating," &c. Fifth Edition, carefully Revised, with Large Additions and 145 Illustrations. Crown 8vo, 7s. 6d. cloth.

"The whole ground of electric lighting is more or less covered and explained in a very clear and concise manner."—*Electrical Review.*

"Contains a good deal of very interesting information, especially in the parts where the author gives dimensions and working costs."—*Electrical Engineer.*

"A miniature *vade-mecum* of the salient facts connected with the science of electric lighting."—*Electrician.*

"You cannot have a better book than 'Electric Light,' by Urquhart."—*Engineer.*

"The book is by far the best that we have yet met with on the subject."—*Athenæum.*

Construction of Dynamos.

DYNAMO CONSTRUCTION: A Practical Handbook for the Use of Engineer Constructors and Electricians-in-Charge. Embracing Framework Building, Field Magnet and Armature Winding and Grouping, Compounding, &c. With Examples of leading English, American, and Continental Dynamos and Motors. By J. W. URQUHART, Author of "Electric Light," "Electric Light Fitting," &c. Second Edition, Revised and Enlarged. With 114 Illustrations. Crown 8vo, 7s. 6d. cloth. [*Just published.*

"Mr. Urquhart's book is the first one which deals with these matters in such a way that the engineering student can understand them. The book is very readable, and the author leads his readers up to difficult subjects by reasonably simple tests."—*Engineering Review.*

"The author deals with his subject in a style so popular as to make his volume a handbook of great practical value to engineer constructors and electricians in charge."—*Scotsman.*

"'Dynamo Construction' more than sustains the high character of the author's previous publications. It is sure to be widely read by the large and rapidly increasing number of practical electricians."—*Glasgow Herald.*

New Dictionary of Electricity.

THE STANDARD ELECTRICAL DICTIONARY. A Popular Dictionary of Words and Terms Used in the Practice of Electrical Engineering. Containing upwards of 3,000 Definitions. By T. O'CONNOR SLOANE, A.M., Ph.D., Author of "The Arithmetic of Electricity," &c. Crown 8vo, 630 pp., 350 Illustrations, 7s. 6d. cloth. [*Just published.*

"The work has many attractive features in it, and is beyond doubt, a well put together and useful publication. The amount of ground covered may be gathered from the fact that in the Index about 5,000 references will be found. The inclusion of such comparatively modern words as 'impedence,' 'reluctance,' &c., shows that the author has desired to be up to date, and indeed there are other indications of carefulness of compilation. The work is one which does the author great credit and it should prove of great value, especially to students."—*Electrical Review.*

"Very complete and contains a large amount of useful information."—*Industries.*

"An encyclopædia of electrical science in the compass of a dictionary. The information given is sound and clear. The book is well printed, well illustrated, and well up to date, and may be confidently recommended."—*Builder.*

"The volume is excellently printed and illustrated, and should form part of the library of every one who is connected with electrical matters."—*Hardware Trade Journal.*

Electric Lighting of Ships.

ELECTRIC SHIP-LIGHTING : A Handbook on the Practical Fitting and Running of Ship's Electrical Plant. For the Use of Shipowners and Builders, Marine Electricians, and Sea-going Engineers-in-Charge. By J. W. URQUHART, C.E. With 88 Illustrations. Crown 8vo, 7s. 6d. cloth.

"The subject of ship electric lighting is one of vast importance in these days, and Mr. Urquhart is to be highly complimented for placing such a valuable work at the service of the practical marine electrician."—*The Steamship.*

"Distinctly a book which of its kind stands almost alone, and for which there should be a demand."—*Electrical Review.*

Country House Electric Lighting.

ELECTRIC LIGHT FOR COUNTRY HOUSES : A Practical Handbook on the Erection and Running of Small Installations, with particulars of the Cost of Plant and Working. By J. H. KNIGHT. Crown 8vo, 1s. wrapper. [*Just published.*

Electric Lighting.

THE ELEMENTARY PRINCIPLES OF ELECTRIC LIGHTING. By ALAN A. CAMPBELL SWINTON, Associate I.E.E. Third Edition, Enlarged and Revised. With 16 Illustrations. Crown 8vo, 1s. 6d. cloth.

"Anyone who desires a short and thoroughly clear exposition of the elementary principles of electric-lighting cannot do better than read this little work."—*Bradford Observer.*

Dynamic Electricity.

THE ELEMENTS OF DYNAMIC ELECTRICITY AND MAGNETISM. By PHILIP ATKINSON, A.M., Ph.D., Author of "The Elements of Electric Lighting," &c. Cr. 8vo, with 120 Illustrations, 10s. 6d. cl.

Electric Motors, &c.

THE ELECTRIC TRANSFORMATION OF POWER and its Application by the Electric Motor, Including Electric Railway Construction. By P. ATKINSON, A.M., Ph.D., Author of "The Elements of Electric Lighting," &c. With 96 Illustrations. Crown 8vo, 7s. 6d. cloth.

Dynamo Construction.

HOW TO MAKE A DYNAMO : A Practical Treatise for Amateurs. Containing numerous Illustrations and Detailed Instructions for Constructing a Small Dynamo, to Produce the Electric Light. By ALFRED CROFTS. Fifth Edition, Revised and Enlarged. Crown 8vo, 2s. cloth.

"The instructions given in this unpretentious little book are sufficiently clear and explicit to enable any amateur mechanic possessed of average skill and the usual tools to be found in an amateur's workshop, to build a practical dynamo machine."—*Electrician.*

Text Book of Electricity.

THE STUDENT'S TEXT-BOOK OF ELECTRICITY. By HENRY M. NOAD, F.R.S. 630 pages, with 470 Illustrations. Cheaper Edition. Crown 8vo, 9s. cloth. [*Just published.*

Electricity.

A MANUAL OF ELECTRICITY : Including Galvanism, Magnetism, Dia-Magnetism, Electro-Dynamics. By HENRY M. NOAD, Ph D., F.R.S. Fourth Edition (1859). 8vo, £1 4s. cloth.

ARCHITECTURE, BUILDING, etc.

Building Construction.

PRACTICAL BUILDING CONSTRUCTION: A Handbook for Students Preparing for Examinations, and a Book of Reference for Persons Engaged in Building. By JOHN P. ALLEN, Surveyor, Lecturer on Building Construction at the Durham College of Science, Newcastle. Medium 8vo, 450 pages, with 1,000 Illustrations. 12s. 6d. cloth. [*Just published.*

"This volume is one of the most complete expositions of building construction we have seen. It contains all that is necessary to prepare students for the various examinations in building construction."—*Building News.*

"The author depends nearly as much on his diagrams as on his type. The pages suggest the hand of a man of experience in building operations—and the volume must be a blessing to many teachers as well as to students."—*The Architect.*

"The work is sure to prove a formidable rival to great and small competitors alike, and bids fair to take a permanent place as a favourite students' text book. The large number of illustrations deserve particular mention for the great merit they possess for purposes of reference, in exactly corresponding to convenient scales."—*Jour. Inst. Brit. Archts.*

Masonry.

PRACTICAL MASONRY: A Guide to the Art of Stone Cutting. Comprising the Construction, Setting-Out, and Working of Stairs, Circular Work, Arches, Niches, Domes, Pendentives, Vaults, Tracery Windows, &c. For the Use of Students, Masons and other Workmen. By WILLIAM R. PURCHASE, Building Inspector to the Town of Hove. Royal 8vo, 134 pages, including 50 Lithographic Plates (about 400 separate Diagrams), 7s. 6d. cloth. [*Just published.*

"The illustrations are well thought out and clear. The volume places within reach of the professional mason many useful data for solving the problems which present themselves day by day."—*Glasgow Herald.*

The New Builder's Price Book, 1896.

LOCKWOOD'S BUILDER'S PRICE BOOK FOR 1896. A Comprehensive Handbook of the Latest Prices and Data for Builders, Architects, Engineers, and Contractors. By FRANCIS T. W. MILLER. 800 closely-printed pages, crown 8vo, 4s. cloth.

"This book is a very useful one, and should find a place in every English office connected with the building and engineering professions."—*Industries.*

"An excellent book of reference."—*Architect.*

"In its new and revised form this Price Book is what a work of this kind should be—comprehensive, reliable, well arranged, legible, and well bound."—*British Architect.*

New London Building Act, 1894.

THE LONDON BUILDING ACT, 1894; with the By-Laws and Regulations of the London County Council, and Introduction, Notes, Cases and Index. By ALEX. J. DAVID, B.A., LL.M. of the Inner Temple, Barrister-at-Law. Crown 8vo, 3s. 6d. cloth. [*Just published.*

"To all architects and district surveyors and builders, Mr. David's manual will be welcome."—*Building News.*

"The volume will doubtless be eagerly consulted by the building fraternity."—*Illustrated Carpenter and Builder.*

Concrete.

CONCRETE: ITS NATURE AND USES. A Book for Architects, Builders, Contractors, and Clerks of Works. By GEORGE L. SUTCLIFFE, A.R.I.B.A. Crown 8vo, 7s. 6d. cloth. [*Just published.*

"The author treats a difficult subject in a lucid manner. The manual fills a long-felt gap. It is careful and exhaustive; equally useful as a student's guide and a architect's book of reference."—*Journal of Royal Institution of British Architects.*

"There is room for this new book, which will probably be for some time the standard work on the subject for a builder's purpose."—*Glasgow Herald.*

"A thoroughly useful and comprehensive work."—*British Architect.*

Mechanics for Architects.

THE MECHANICS OF ARCHITECTURE: A Treatise on Applied Mechanics, especially Adapted to the Use of Architects. By E. W. TARN, M.A., Author of "The Science of Building," &c. Second Edition, Enlarged. Illust. with 125 Diagrams. Cr. 8vo, 7s. 6d. cloth. [*Just published.*

"The book is a very useful and helpful manual of architectural mechanics, and really contains sufficient to enable a careful and painstaking student to grasp the principles bearing upon the majority of building problems. . . . Mr. Tarn has added, by this volume, to the debt of gratitude which is owing to him by architectural students for the many valuable works which he has produced for their use."—*The Builder.*

"The mechanics in the volume are really mechanics, and are harmoniously wrought in with the distinctive professional manner proper to the subject."—*The Schoolmaster.*

Designing Buildings.

THE DESIGN OF BUILDINGS: Being Elementary Notes on the Planning, Sanitation and Ornamentive Formation of Structures, based on Modern Practice. Illustrated with Nine Folding Plates. By W. WOODLEY, Assistant Master, Metropolitan Drawing Classes, &c. 8vo, 6s. cloth.

Sir Wm. Chambers's Treatise on Civil Architecture.

THE DECORATIVE PART OF CIVIL ARCHITECTURE. By Sir WILLIAM CHAMBERS, F.R.S. With Portrait, Illustrations, Notes, and an Examination of Grecian Architecture, by JOSEPH GWILT, F.S.A. Revised and Edited by W. H. LEEDS. 66 Plates, 4to, 21s. cloth.

Villa Architecture.

A HANDY BOOK OF VILLA ARCHITECTURE: Being a Series of Designs for Villa Residences in various Styles. With Outline Specifications and Estimates. By C. WICKES, Architect, Author of "The Spires and Towers of England," &c. 61 Plates, 4to, £1 11s. 6d. half-morocco.
"The whole of the designs bear evidence of their being the work of an artistic architect, and they will prove very valuable and suggestive."—*Building News.*

Text-Book for Architects.

THE ARCHITECT'S GUIDE: Being a Text-Book of Useful Information for Architects, Engineers, Surveyors, Contractors, Clerks of Works, &c. By F. ROGERS. Third Edition. Crown 8vo, 3s. 6d. cloth.
"As a text-book of useful information for architects, engineers, surveyors, &c., it would be hard to find a handier or more complete little volume."—*Standard.*

Linear Perspective.

ARCHITECTURAL PERSPECTIVE: The whole Course and Operations of the Draughtsman in Drawing a Large House in Linear Perspective. Illustrated by 43 Folding Plates. By F. O. FERGUSON. Second Edition, Enlarged. 8vo, 3s. 6d. boards. [*Just published.*
"It is the most intelligible of the treatises on this ill-treated subject that I have met with."—E. INGRESS BELL, Esq., in the *R.I.B.A. Journal.*

Architectural Drawing.

PRACTICAL RULES ON DRAWING, for the Operative Builder and Young Student in Architecture. By G. PYNE. 14 Plates, 4to, 7s. 6d., bds.

Vitruvius' Architecture.

THE ARCHITECTURE of MARCUS VITRUVIUS POLLIO. Translated by JOSEPH GWILT, F.S.A., F.R.A.S. New Edition, Revised by the Translator. With 23 Plates. Fcap. 8vo, 5s. cloth.

Designing, Measuring, and Valuing.

THE STUDENT'S GUIDE to the PRACTICE of MEASURING AND VALUING ARTIFICERS' WORK. Containing Directions for taking Dimensions, Abstracting the same, and bringing the Quantities into Bill, with Tables of Constants for Valuation of Labour, and for the Calculation of Areas and Solidities. Originally edited by EDWARD DOBSON, Architect. With Additions by E. WYNDHAM TARN, M.A. Sixth Edition. With 8 Plates and 63 Woodcuts. Crown 8vo, 7s. 6d. cloth.
"This edition will be found the most complete treatise on the principles of measuring and valuing artificers' work that has yet been published."—*Building News.*

Pocket Estimator and Technical Guide.

THE POCKET TECHNICAL GUIDE, MEASURER, AND ESTIMATOR FOR BUILDERS AND SURVEYORS. Containing Technical Directions for Measuring Work in all the Building Trades, Complete Specifications for Houses, Roads, and Drains, and an easy Method of Estimating the parts of a Building collectively. By A. C. BEATON. Seventh Edit. Waistcoat-pocket size, 1s. 6d. leather, gilt edges.
"No builder, architect, surveyor, or valuer should be without his 'Beaton.'"—*Building News.*

Donaldson on Specifications.

THE HANDBOOK OF SPECIFICATIONS; or, Practical Guide to the Architect, Engineer, Surveyor, and Builder, in drawing up Specifications and Contracts for Works and Constructions. Illustrated by Precedents of Buildings actually executed by eminent Architects and Engineers. By Professor T. L. DONALDSON, P.R.I.B.A., &c. New Edition. 8vo. with upwards of 1,000 pages of Text, and 33 Plates. £1 11s. 6d. cloth.
"Valuable as a record, and more valuable still as a book of precedents, . . . Suffice it to say that Donaldson's 'Handbook of Specifications' must be bought by all architects."—*Builder.*

Bartholomew and Rogers' Specifications.

SPECIFICATIONS FOR PRACTICAL ARCHITECTURE. A Guide to the Architect, Engineer, Surveyor, and Builder. With an Essay on the Structure and Science of Modern Buildings. Upon the Basis of the Work by ALFRED BARTHOLOMEW, thoroughly Revised, Corrected, and greatly added to by FREDERICK ROGERS, Architect. Third Edition, Revised, with Additions. With numerous Illustrations. Medium 8vo, 15s. cloth.

"The collection of specifications prepared by Mr. Rogers on the basis of Bartholomew's work is too well known to need any recommendation from us. It is one of the books with which every young architect must be equipped."—*Architect.*

House Building and Repairing.

THE HOUSE-OWNER'S ESTIMATOR; or, What will it Cost to Build, Alter, or Repair? A Price Book for Unprofessional People, as well as the Architectural Surveyor and Builder. By J. D. SIMON. Edited by F. T. W. MILLER, A.R.I.B.A. Fourth Edition. Crown 8vo, 3s. 6d. cloth.

"In two years it will repay its cost a hundred times over."—*Field.*

Construction.

THE SCIENCE OF BUILDING: An Elementary Treatise on the Principles of Construction. By E. WYNDHAM TARN, M.A., Architect. Third Edition, Revised and Enlarged. With 59 Engravings. Fcap. 8vo, 4s. cl.

"A very valuable book, which we strongly recommend to all students."—*Builder.*

Building; Civil and Ecclesiastical.

A BOOK ON BUILDING, Civil and Ecclesiastical, including Church Restoration; with the Theory of Domes and the Great Pyramid, &c. By Sir EDMUND BECKETT, Bart., LL.D., F.R.A.S. Fcap. 8vo, 5s. cloth.

"A book which is always amusing and nearly always instructive."—*Times.*

House Building.

DWELLING HOUSES, THE ERECTION OF. Illustrated by a Perspective View, Plans, Elevations and Sections of a Pair of Semi-Detached Villas, with the Specification, Quantities and Estimates. By S. H. BROOKS, Architect. Seventh Edition, thoroughly Revised. 12mo, 2s. 6d. cloth. [*Just published.*

Sanitary Houses, etc.

THE SANITARY ARRANGEMENT OF DWELLING-HOUSES: A Handbook for Householders and Owners of Houses. By A. J. WALLIS-TAYLER, A.M. Inst. C.E. With numerous Illustrations. Crown 8vo, 2s. 6d. cloth. [*Just published.*

"This book will be largely read; it will be of considerable service to the public. It is well arranged, easily read, and for the most part devoid of technical terms."—*Lancet.*

Ventilation of Buildings.

VENTILATION. A Text Book to the Practice of the Art of Ventilating Buildings. By W. P. BUCHAN, R.P. 12mo, 4s. cloth.

"Contains a great amount of useful practical information, as thoroughly interesting as it is technically reliable."—*British Architect.*

The Art of Plumbing.

PLUMBING. A Text Book to the Practice of the Art or Craft of the Plumber. By WILLIAM PATON BUCHAN, R.P. Sixth Edition. 4s. cloth.

"A text-book which may be safely put in the hands of every young plumber."—*Builder.*

Geometry for the Architect, Engineer, etc.

PRACTICAL GEOMETRY, for the Architect, Engineer, and Mechanic. Giving Rules for the Delineation and Application of various Geometrical Lines, Figures and Curves. By E. W. TARN, M.A., Architect. 8vo, 9s. cloth.

"No book with the same objects in view has ever been published in which the clearness of the rules laid down and the illustrative diagrams have been so satisfactory."—*Scotsman.*

The Science of Geometry.

THE GEOMETRY OF COMPASSES; or, Problems Resolved by the mere Description of Circles, and the use of Coloured Diagrams and Symbols. By OLIVER BYRNE. Coloured Plates. Crown 8vo, 3s. 6d. cloth.

CARPENTRY, TIMBER, etc.

Tredgold's Carpentry, Revised & Enlarged by Tarn.
THE ELEMENTARY PRINCIPLES OF CARPENTRY. A Treatise on the Pressure and Equilibrium of Timber Framing, the Resistance of Timber, and the Construction of Floors, Arches, Bridges, Roofs, Uniting Iron and Stone with Timber, &c. To which is added an Essay on the Nature and Properties of Timber, &c., with Descriptions of the kinds of Wood used in Building; also numerous Tables of the Scantlings of Timber for different purposes, the Specific Gravities of Materials, &c. By THOMAS TREDGOLD, C.E. With an Appendix of Specimens of Various Roofs of Iron and Stone, Illustrated. Seventh Edition, thoroughly revised and considerably enlarged by E. WYNDHAM TARN, M.A., Author of "The Science of Building," &c. With 61 Plates, Portrait of the Author, and several Woodcuts. In One large Vol., 4to, price £1 5s. cloth.
"Ought to be in every architect's and every builder's library."—*Builder*.
"A work whose monumental excellence must commend it wherever skilful carpentry is concerned. The author's principles are rather confirmed than impaired by time. The additional plates are of great intrinsic value."—*Building News*.

Carpentry.
CARPENTRY AND JOINERY. The Elementary Principles of Carpentry. Chiefly composed from the Standard Work of THOMAS TREDGOLD, C.E. With Additions, and a TREATISE ON JOINERY by E. W. TARN, M.A. Fifth Edition, Revised and Extended. 12mo, 3s. 6d. cloth.
⁎ ATLAS of Thirty-five Plates to accompany and illustrate the foregoing book. With Descriptive Letterpress. 4to, 6s. cloth.
"These two volumes form a complete treasury of carpentry and joinery, and should be in the hands of every carpenter and joiner in the empire."—*Iron*.

Woodworking Machinery.
WOODWORKING MACHINERY: Its Rise, Progress, and Construction. With Hints on the Management of Saw Mills and the Economical Conversion of Timber. Illustrated with Examples of Recent Designs by leading English, French, and American Engineers. By M. POWIS BALE, A.M.Inst.C.E., M.I.M.E. Second Edition, Revised, with large Additions. Large crown 8vo, 440 pp., 9s. cloth. [*Just published.*
"Mr. Bale is evidently an expert on the subject and he has collected so much information that the book is all-sufficient for builders and others engaged in the conversion of timber."—*Architect*.
"The most comprehensive compendium of wood-working machinery we have seen. The author is a thorough master of his subject."—*Building News*.

Saw Mills.
SAW MILLS: Their Arrangement and Management, and the Economical Conversion of Timber. (A Companion Volume to "Woodworking Machinery.") By M. POWIS BALE. Crown 8vo, 10s. 6d. cloth.
"The *administration* of a large sawing establishment is discussed, and the subject examined from a financial standpoint. Hence the size, shape, order, and disposition of saw-mills and the like are gone into in detail, and the course of the timber is traced from its reception to its delivery in its converted state. We could not desire a more complete or practical treatise."—*Builder*.

Nicholson's Carpentry.
THE CARPENTER'S NEW GUIDE; or, Book of Lines for Carpenters; comprising all the Elementary Principles essential for acquiring a knowledge of Carpentry. Founded on the late PETER NICHOLSON's Standard Work. New Edition, Revised by A. ASHPITEL, F.S.A. With Practical Rules on Drawing, by G. PYNE. With 74 Plates, 4to, £1 1s. cloth.

Circular Work.
CIRCULAR WORK IN CARPENTRY AND JOINERY: A Practical Treatise on Circular Work of Single and Double Curvature. By GEORGE COLLINGS. With Diagrams. Second Edit. 12mo, 2s. 6d. cloth limp.
"An excellent example of what a book of this kind should be. Cheap in price, clear in definition and practical in the examples selected."—*Builder*.

Handrailing.
HANDRAILING COMPLETE IN EIGHT LESSONS. On the Square-Cut System. By J. S. GOLDTHORP, Teacher of Geometry and Building Construction at the Halifax Mechanic's Institute. With Eight Plates and over 150 Practical Exercises. 4to, 3s. 6d. cloth.
"Likely to be of considerable value to joiners and others who take a pride in good work, we heartily commend it to teachers and students."—*Timber Trades Journal*.

Handrailing and Stairbuilding.

A PRACTICAL TREATISE ON HANDRAILING : Showing New and Simple Methods for Finding the Pitch of the Plank, Drawing the Moulds, Bevelling, Jointing-up, and Squaring the Wreath. By GEORGE COLLINGS. Second Edition, Revised and Enlarged, to which is added A TREATISE ON STAIRBUILDING. 12mo, 2s. 6d. cloth limp.

"Will be found of practical utility in the execution of this difficult branch of joinery."—*Builder.*
"Almost every difficult phase of this somewhat intricate branch of joinery is elucidated by the aid of plates and explanatory letterpress."—*Furniture Gazette.*

Timber Merchant's Companion.

THE TIMBER MERCHANT'S AND BUILDER'S COMPANION. Containing New and Copious Tables of the Reduced Weight and Measurement of Deals and Battens, of all sizes, from One to a Thousand Pieces, and the relative Price that each size bears per Lineal Foot to any given Price per Petersburg Standard Hundred; the Price per Cube Foot of Square Timber to any given Price per Load of 50 Feet; the proportionate Value of Deals and Battens by the Standard, to Square Timber by the Load of 50 Feet; the readiest mode of ascertaining the Price of Scantling per Lineal Foot of any size, to any given Figure per Cube Foot, &c. &c. By WILLIAM DOWSING. Fourth Edition, Revised and Corrected. Cr. 8vo, 3s. cl.

"Everything is as concise and clear as it can possibly be made. There can be no doubt that every timber merchant and builder ought to possess it."—*Hull Advertiser.*
"We are glad to see a fourth edition of these admirable tables, which for correctness and simplicity of arrangement leave nothing to be desired."—*Timber Trades Journal.*

Practical Timber Merchant.

THE PRACTICAL TIMBER MERCHANT. Being a Guide for the use of Building Contractors, Surveyors, Builders, &c., comprising useful Tables for all purposes connected with the Timber Trade, Marks of Wood, Essay on the Strength of Timber, Remarks on the Growth of Timber, &c. By W. RICHARDSON. Second Edition. Fcap. 8vo, 3s. 6d. cloth.

"This handy manual contains much valuable information for the use of timber merchants, builders, foresters, and all others connected with the growth, sale, and manufacture of timber."—*Journal of Forestry.*

Packing-Case Makers, Tables for.

PACKING-CASE TABLES; showing the number of Superficial Feet in Boxes or Packing-Cases, from six inches square and upwards. By W. RICHARDSON, Timber Broker. Third Edition. Oblong 4to, 3s. 6d. cl.

"Invaluable labour-saving tables."—*Ironmonger.*
"Will save much labour and calculation."—*Grocer.*

Superficial Measurement.

THE TRADESMAN'S GUIDE TO SUPERFICIAL MEASUREMENT. Tables calculated from 1 to 200 inches in length, by 1 to 108 inches in breadth. For the use of Architects, Surveyors, Engineers, Timber Merchants, Builders, &c. By JAMES HAWKINGS. Fourth Edition. Fcap., 3s. 6d. cloth.

"A useful collection of tables to facilitate rapid calculation of surfaces. The exact area of any surface of which the limits have been ascertained can be instantly determined. The book will be found of the greatest utility to all engaged in building operations."—*Scotsman.*
"These tables will be found of great assistance to all who require to make calculations in superficial measurement."—*English Mechanic.*

Forestry.

THE ELEMENTS OF FORESTRY. Designed to afford Information concerning the Planting and Care of Forest Trees for Ornament or Profit, with Suggestions upon the Creation and Care of Woodlands. By F. B. HOUGH. Large crown 8vo, 10s. cloth.

Timber Importer's Guide.

THE TIMBER IMPORTER'S, TIMBER MERCHANT'S, AND BUILDER'S STANDARD GUIDE. By RICHARD E. GRANDY. Comprising an Analysis of Deal Standards, Home and Foreign, with Comparative Values and Tabular Arrangements for fixing Net Landed Cost on Baltic and North American Deals, including all intermediate Expenses, Freight Insurance, &c. &c. Together with copious Information for the Retailer and Builder. Third Edition, Revised. 12mo, 2s. cloth limp.

"Everything it pretends to be built up gradually, it leads one from a forest to a treenail and throws in, as a makeweight, a host of material concerning bricks, columns, cisterns, &c."—*English Mechanic.*

DECORATIVE ARTS, etc.

Woods and Marbles (Imitation of).

SCHOOL OF PAINTING FOR THE IMITATION OF WOODS AND MARBLES, as Taught and Practised by A. R. VAN DER BURG and P. VAN DER BURG, Directors of the Rotterdam Painting Institution. Royal folio, 18¾ by 12¼ in., Illustrated with 24 full-size Coloured Plates; also 12 plain Plates, comprising 154 Figures. Second and Cheaper Edition. Price £1 11s. 6d.

List of Plates.

1. Various Tools required for Wood Painting—2, 3. Walnut: Preliminary Stages of Graining and Finished Specimen—4. Tools used for Marble Painting and Method of Manipulation—6. St. Remi Marble: Earlier Operations and Finished Specimen—7. Methods of Sketching different Grains, Knots, &c.—8, 9. Ash: Preliminary Stages and Finished Specimen—10. Methods of Sketching Marble Grains—11, 12. Breche Marble: Preliminary Stages of Working and Finished Specimen—13. Maple: Methods of Producing the different Grains—14, 15. Bird's-eye Maple: Preliminary Stages and Finished Specimen—16. Methods of Sketching the different Species of White Marble—17, 18. White Marble: Preliminary Stages of Process and Finished Specimen—19. Mahogany: Specimens of various Grains and Methods of Manipulation—20, 21. Mahogany: Earlier Stages and Finished Specimen—22, 23, 24. Sienna Marble: Varieties of Grain, Preliminary Stages and Finished Specimen—25, 26, 27. Juniper Wood: Methods of producing Grain, &c.; Preliminary Stages and Finished Specimen—28, 29, 30. Vert de Mer Marble: Varieties of Grain and Methods of Working Unfinished and Finished Specimens—31, 32, 33. Oak Varieties of Grain, Tools Employed, and Methods of Manipulation, Preliminary Stages and Finished Specimen—34, 35, 36. Waulsort Marble: Varieties of Grain, Unfinished and Finished Specimens.

"Those who desire to attain skill in the art of painting woods and marbles will find advantage in consulting this book. . . . Some of the Working Men's Clubs should give their young men the opportunity to study it."—*Builder.*

"A comprehensive guide to the art. The explanations of the processes, the manipulation and management of the colours, and the beautifully executed plates will not be the least valuable to the student who aims at making his work a faithful transcript of nature."—*Building News.*

House Decoration.

ELEMENTARY DECORATION. A Guide to the Simpler Forms of Everyday Art. Together with PRACTICAL HOUSE DECORATION. By JAMES W. FACEY. With numerous Illustrations. In One Vol., 5s. strongly half-bound.

House Painting, Graining, etc.

HOUSE PAINTING, GRAINING, MARBLING, AND SIGN WRITING, A Practical Manual of. By ELLIS A. DAVIDSON. Sixth Editior. With Coloured Plates and Wood Engravings. 12mo, 6s. cloth boards.

"A mass of information, of use to the amateur and of value to the practical man."—*English Mechanic.*

Decorators, Receipts for.

THE DECORATOR'S ASSISTANT: A Modern Guide to Decorative Artists and Amateurs, Painters, Writers, Gilders, &c. Containing upwards of 600 Receipts, Rules and Instructions; with a variety of Information for General Work connected with every Class of Interior and Exterior Decorations, &c. Sixth Edition. 152 pp., crown 8vo, 1s. in wrapper

"Full of receipts of value to decorators, painters, gilders, &c. The book contains the gist of larger treatises on colour and technical processes. It would be difficult to meet with a work so full of varied information on the painter's art."—*Building News.*

Moyr Smith on Interior Decoration.

ORNAMENTAL INTERIORS, ANCIENT AND MODERN. By J. MOYR SMITH. Super-royal 8vo, with 32 full-page Plates and numerous smaller Illustrations, handsomely bound in cloth, gilt top, price 18s.

"The book is well illustrated and handsomely got up, and contains some true criticism and a great many good examples of decorative treatment."—*The Builder.*

DECORATIVE ARTS, etc. 31

British and Foreign Marbles.

MARBLE DECORATION and the Terminology of British and Foreign Marbles. A Handbook for Students. By GEORGE H. BLAGROVE, Author of "Shoring and its Application," &c. With 28 Illustrations. Crown 8vo, 3s. 6d. cloth.

"This most useful and much wanted handbook should be in the hands of every architect and builder."—*Building World.*

"A carefully and usefully written treatise; the work is essentially practical."—*Scotsman.*

Marble Working, etc.

MARBLE AND MARBLE WORKERS: A Handbook for Architects, Artists, Masons, and Students. By ARTHUR LEE, Author of "A Visit to Carrara," "The Working of Marble," &c. Small crown 8vo, 2s. cloth.

"A really valuable addition to the technical literature of architects and masons."—*Building News.*

DELAMOTTE'S WORKS ON ILLUMINATION AND ALPHABETS.

A PRIMER OF THE ART OF ILLUMINATION, for the Use of Beginners: with a Rudimentary Treatise on the Art, Practical Directions for its Exercise, and Examples taken from Illuminated MSS., printed in Gold and Colours. By F. DELAMOTTE. New and Cheaper Edition. Small 4to, 6s. ornamental boards.

"The examples of ancient MSS. recommended to the student, which, with much good sense, the author chooses from collections accessible to all, are selected with judgment and knowledge, as well as taste."—*Athenæum.*

ORNAMENTAL ALPHABETS, Ancient and Mediæval, from the Eighth Century, with Numerals; including Gothic, Church-Text, large and small, German, Italian, Arabesque, Initials for Illumination, Monograms, Crosses, &c. &c., for the use of Architectural and Engineering Draughtsmen, Missal Painters, Masons, Decorative Painters, Lithographers, Engravers, Carvers, &c. &c. Collected and Engraved by F. DELAMOTTE, and printed in Colours. New and Cheaper Edition. Royal 8vo, oblong, 2s. 6d. ornamental boards.

"For those who insert enamelled sentences round gilded chalices, who blazon shop legends over shop-doors, who letter church walls with pithy sentences from the Decalogue, this book will be useful."—*Athenæum.*

EXAMPLES OF MODERN ALPHABETS, Plain and Ornamental; including German, Old English, Saxon, Italic, Perspective, Greek, Hebrew, Court Hand, Engrossing, Tuscan, Riband, Gothic, Rustic, and Arabesque; with several Original Designs, and an Analysis of the Roman and Old English Alphabets, large and small, and Numerals, for the use of Draughtsmen, Surveyors, Masons, Decorative Painters, Lithographers, Engravers, Carvers, &c. Collected and Engraved by F. DELAMOTTE, and printed in Colours. New and Cheaper Edition. Royal 8vo, oblong, 2s. 6d. ornamental boards.

"There is comprised in it every possible shape into which the letters of the alphabet and numerals can be formed, and the talent which has been expended in the conception of the various plain and ornamental letters is wonderful."—*Standard.*

MEDIÆVAL ALPHABETS AND INITIALS FOR ILLUMINATORS. By F. G. DELAMOTTE. Containing 21 Plates and Illuminated Title, printed in Gold and Colours. With an Introduction by J. WILLIS BROOKS. Fourth and Cheaper Edition. Small 4to, 4s. ornamental boards.

"A volume in which the letters of the alphabet come forth glorified in gilding and all the colours of the prism interwoven and intertwined and intermingled."—*Sun.*

THE EMBROIDERER'S BOOK OF DESIGN. Containing Initials, Emblems, Cyphers, Monograms, Ornamental Borders, Ecclesiastical Devices, Mediæval and Modern Alphabets, and National Emblems. Collected by F. DELAMOTTE, and printed in Colours. Oblong royal 8vo, 1s. 6d. ornamental wrapper.

"The book will be of great assistance to ladies and young children who are endowed with the art of plying the needle in this most ornamental and useful pretty work."—*East Anglian Times.*

Wood Carving.

INSTRUCTIONS IN WOOD-CARVING, for Amateurs; with Hints on Design. By A LADY. With Ten Plates. New and Cheaper Edition. Crown 8vo, 2s. in emblematic wrapper.

"The handicraft of the wood-carver, so well as a book can impart it, may be learnt from 'A Lady's' publication."—*Athenæum.*

NATURAL SCIENCE, etc.

The Heavens and their Origin.
THE VISIBLE UNIVERSE: Chapters on the Origin and Construction of the Heavens. By J. E. GORE, F.R.A.S. Illustrated by 6 Stellar Photographs and 12 Plates. 8vo, 16s. cloth.

"A valuable and lucid summary of recent astronomical theory, rendered more valuable and attractive by a series of stellar photographs and other illustrations."—*The Times.*
"In presenting a clear and concise account of the present state of our knowledge, Mr. Gore has made a valuable addition to the literature of the subject."—*Nature.*
"As interesting as a novel, and instructive withal; the text being made still more luminous by stellar photographs and other illustrations. . . . A most valuable book."—*Manchester Examiner.*
"One of the finest works on astronomical science that has recently appeared in our language.
Leeds Mercury.

The Constellations.
STAR GROUPS: A Student's Guide to the Constellations. By J. ELLARD GORE, F.R.A.S., M.R.I.A., &c., Author of "The Visible Universe," "The Scenery of the Heavens." With 30 Maps. Small 4to, 5s. cloth. silvered.

"A knowledge of the principal constellations visible in our latitudes may be easily acquired from the thirty maps and accompanying text contained in this work."—*Nature.*
"The volume contains thirty maps showing stars of the sixth magnitude—the usual naked-eye limit—and each is accompanied by a brief commentary, adapted to facilitate recognition and bring to notice objects of special interest. For the purpose of a preliminary survey of the 'midnight pomp' of the heavens, nothing could be better than a set of delineations averaging scarcely twenty square inches in area, and including nothing that cannot at once be identified."—*Saturday Review.*
"A very compact and handy guide to the constellations."—*Athenæum.*

Astronomical Terms.
AN ASTRONOMICAL GLOSSARY; or, Dictionary of Terms used in Astronomy. With Tables of Data and Lists of Remarkable and Interesting Celestial Objects. By J. ELLARD GORE, F.R.A.S., Author of "The Visible Universe," &c. Small crown 8vo, 2s. 6d. cloth.

"A very useful little work for beginners in astronomy, and not to be despised by more advanced students."—*The Times.*
"Astronomers of all kinds will be glad to have it for reference."—*Guardian.*

The Microscope.
THE MICROSCOPE: Its Construction and Management, including Technique, Photo-micrography, and the Past and Future of the Microscope. By Dr. HENRI VAN HEURCK. Re-Edited and Augmented from the Fourth French Edition, and Translated by WYNNE E. BAXTER, F.G.S. 400 pages, with upwards of 250 Woodcuts. Imp. 8vo, 18s. cloth.

"A translation of a well-known work, at once popular and comprehensive."—*Times.*
"The translation is as felicitious as it is accurate."—*Nature.*

The Microscope.
PHOTO-MICROGRAPHY. By Dr. H. VAN HEURCK. Extracted from the above Work. Royal 8vo, with Illustrations, 1s. sewed.

Astronomy.
ASTRONOMY. By the late Rev. ROBERT MAIN, F.R.S. Third Edition, Revised, by WM. T. LYNN, B.A., F.R.A.S., 12mo, 2s. cloth.

"A sound and simple treatise, and a capital book for beginners."—*Knowledge.*

Recent and Fossil Shells.
A MANUAL OF THE MOLLUSCA: Being a Treatise on Recent and Fossil Shells. By S. P. WOODWARD, A.L.S., F.G.S. With an Appendix on Recent and Fossil Conchological Discoveries, by RALPH TATE, A.L.S., F.G.S. With 23 Plates and upwards of 300 Woodcuts. Reprint of Fourth Edition, 1880. Crown 8vo, 7s. 6d. cloth.

"A most valuable storehouse of conchological and geological information."—*Science Gossip.*

Geology and Genesis.
THE TWIN RECORDS OF CREATION; or, Geology and Genesis: their Perfect Harmony and Wonderful Concord. By GEORGE W. VICTOR LE VAUX. Fcap. 8vo, 5s. cloth.

"A valuable contribution to the evidences of Revelation, and disposes very conclusively of the arguments of those who would set God's Works against God's Word. No real difficulty is shirked, and no sophistry is left unexposed."—*The Rock.*

Geology.
RUDIMENTARY TREATISE ON GEOLOGY, PHYSICAL AND HISTORICAL. With especial reference to the British series of Rocks. By R. TATE, F.G.S. With 250 Illustrations. 12mo, 5s. cloth boards.

DR. LARDNER'S COURSE OF NATURAL PHILOSOPHY.

HANDBOOK OF MECHANICS. Re-written and Enlarged by B. LOEWY, F.R.A.S. Post 8vo, 6s. cloth.

"Mr. Loewy has carefully revised the book, and brought it up to modern requirements."—*Nature*.

HANDBOOK OF HYDROSTATICS & PNEUMATICS. Enlarged by B. LOEWY, F.R.A.S. Post 8vo, 5s. cloth.

"For those 'who desire to attain an accurate knowledge of physical science without the profound methods of mathematical investigation,' this work is well adapted."—*Chemical News*.

HANDBOOK OF HEAT. Edited and almost entirely Re-written by BENJAMIN LOEWY, F.R.A.S., &c. Post 8vo, 6s. cloth.

"The style is always clear and precise, and conveys instruction without leaving any cloudiness, or lurking doubts behind."—*Engineering*.

HANDBOOK OF OPTICS. By Dr. LARDNER. Edited by T. O. HARDING, B.A. Post 8vo, 5s. cloth.

"Written by an able scientific writer and beautifully illustrated."—*Mechanic's Magazine*.

HANDBOOK OF ELECTRICITY AND MAGNETISM. By Dr. LARDNER. Edited by G. C. FOSTER, B.A. Post 8vo, 5s. cloth.

"The book could not have been entrusted to anyone better calculated to preserve the terse and lucid style of Lardner."—*Popular Science Review*.

HANDBOOK OF ASTRONOMY. By Dr. LARDNER. Fourth Edition by E. DUNKIN, F.R.A.S. Post 8vo, 9s. 6d. cloth.

"Probably no other book contains the same amount of information in so compendious and well arranged a form—certainly none at the price at which this is offered to the public."—*Athenæum*.

"We can do no other than pronounce this work a most valuable manual of astronomy, and we strongly recommend it to all who wish to acquire a general—but at the same time correct—acquaintance with this sublime science."—*Quarterly Journal of Science*.

DR. LARDNER'S MUSEUM OF SCIENCE AND ART.

THE MUSEUM OF SCIENCE AND ART. Edited by Dr. LARDNER. With upwards of 1,200 Engravings on Wood. In 6 Double Volumes, £1 1s. in a new and elegant cloth binding; or handsomely bound in half-morocco, 31s. 6d.

"A cheap and interesting publication, alike informing and attractive. The papers combine subjects of importance and great scientific knowledge, considerable inductive powers, and a popular style of treatment."—*Spectator*.

The 'Museum of Science and Art' is the most valuable contribution that has ever been made to the Scientific Instruction of every class of society."—Sir DAVID BREWSTER, in the *North British Review*.

*** *Separate books formed from the above, fully Illustrated, suitable for Workmen's Libraries, Science Classes, etc.*

Common Things Explained. 5s.	**Steam and its Uses.** 2s. cloth.
The Microscope. 2s. cloth.	**Popular Astronomy.** 4s. 6d. cloth.
Popular Geology. 2s. 6d. cloth.	**The Bee and White Ants.** 2s. cloth.
Popular Physics. 2s. 6d. cloth.	**The Electric Telegraph.** 1s.

Dr. Lardner's School Handbooks.

NATURAL PHILOSOPHY FOR SCHOOLS. Fcap. 8vo, 3s. 6d.

"A very convenient class-book for junior students in private schools.—*British Quarterly Review*.

ANIMAL PHYSIOLOGY FOR SCHOOLS. Fcap. 8vo, 3s. 6d.

"Clearly written, well arranged, and excellently illustrated."—*Gardener's Chronicle*.

THE ELECTRIC TELEGRAPH. By Dr. LARDNER. Revised by E. B. BRIGHT, F.R.A.S. Fcap. 8vo, 2s. 6d. cloth.

"One of the most readable books extant on the Electric Telegraph."—*English Mechanic*.

CHEMICAL MANUFACTURES, CHEMISTRY.

Refrigerating, etc.

REFRIGERATING AND ICE-MAKING MACHINERY: A Descriptive Treatise for the Use of Persons Employing Refrigerating and Ice-Making Installations, and others. By A. J. WALLIS-TAYLER, C.E. Assoc. Member Inst. C.E. With Illustrations. Crown 8vo, 7s. 6d. cloth.
[*Just published*

"Practical, explicit and profusely illustrated."—*Glasgow Herald.*

Chemistry for Engineers, etc.

ENGINEERING CHEMISTRY: A Practical Treatise for the Use of Analytical Chemists, Engineers, Iron Masters, Iron Founders, Students, and others. Comprising Methods of Analysis and Valuation of the Principal Materials used in Engineering Work, with numerous Analyses, Examples, and Suggestions. By H. JOSHUA PHILLIPS, F.I.C., F.C.S. formerly Analytical and Consulting Chemist to the Great Eastern Railway. Second Edition, Revised and Enlarged. Crown 8vo, 400 pp., with Illustrations, 10s. 6d. cloth.
[*Just published.*

"In this work the author has rendered no small service to a numerous body of practical men. . . . The analytical methods may be pronounced most satisfactory, being as accurate as the despatch required of engineering chemists permits."—*Chemical News.*

"The book will be very useful to those who require a handy and concise *resume* of approved methods of analysing and valuing metals, oils, fuels, &c. It is, in fact, a work for chemists, a guide to the routine of the engineering laboratory. . . . The book is full of good things. As a handbook of technical analysis, it is very welcome."—*Builder.*

"The analytical methods given are, as a whole, such as are likely to give rapid and trustworthy results in experienced hands. There is much excellent descriptive matter in the work, the chapter on 'Oils and Lubrication' being specially noticeable in this respect."—*Engineer.*

Manufacture of Explosives.

NITRO-EXPLOSIVES: A Practical Treatise concerning the Properties, Manufacture, and Analysis of Nitrated Substances; including the Fulminates, Smokeless Powders, and Celluloid. By P. GERALD SANFORD, F.I.C., F.C.S. With numerous Illustrations. Crown 8vo, 9s. cloth.
[*Just published.*

"Mr. Sanford goes steadily through the whole list of explosives commonly used. He names any given explosive, and tells us of what it is composed and how it is manufactured. The book is excellent throughout, and we heartily recommend it."—*The Engineer.*

Explosives and Dangerous Goods.

DANGEROUS GOODS: Their Sources and Properties, Modes of Storage, and Transport. With Notes and Comments on Accidents arising therefrom, together with the Government and Railway Classifications, Acts of Parliament, &c. A Guide for the use of Government and Railway Officials, Steamship Owners, Insurance Companies and Manufacturers and users of Explosives and Dangerous Goods. By H. JOSHUA PHILLIPS, F.I.C. F.C.S., Author of "Engineering Chemistry, &c." Crown 8vo, 350 pp., 9s. cloth.
[*Just published.*

Explosives.

A HANDBOOK ON MODERN EXPLOSIVES. Being a Practical Treatise on the Manufacture and Application of Dynamite, Gun-Cotton, Nitro-Glycerine, and other Explosive Compounds. Including the Manufacture of Collodion-Cotton. By M. EISSLER, Author of "The Metallurgy of Gold," &c. Crown 8vo, 10s. 6d. cloth.

"Useful not only to the miner, but also to officers of both services to whom blasting and the use of explosives generally may at any time become a necessary auxiliary."—*Nature.*

"A veritable mine of information on the subject of explosives employed for military, mining, and blasting purposes."—*Army and Navy Gazette.*

Alkali Trade, Manufacture of Sulphuric Acid, etc.

A MANUAL OF THE ALKALI TRADE, including the Manufacture of Sulphuric Acid, Sulphate of Soda, and Bleaching Powder. By JOHN LOMAS, Alkali Manufacturer, Newcastle-upon-Tyne and London. With 232 Illustrations and Working Drawings, and containing 390 pages of Text. Second Edition, with Additions. Super-royal 8vo, £1 10s. cloth.

"This book is written by a manufacturer for manufacturers. The working details of the most approved forms of apparatus are given, and these are accompanied by no less than 232 wood engravings, all of which may be used for the purposes of construction. Every step in the manufacture is very fully described in this manual, and each improvement explained."—*Athenæum.*

CHEMICAL MANUFACTURES, CHEMISTRY, etc. 35

The Blowpipe.
THE BLOWPIPE IN CHEMISTRY, MINERALOGY, AND GEOLOGY. Containing all known Methods of Anhydrous Analysis, many Working Examples, and Instructions for Making Apparatus. By Lieut.-Colonel W. A. Ross, R.A., F.G.S. With 120 Illustrations. Second Edition, Revised and Enlarged. Crown 8vo, 5s. cloth.

"The student who goes through the course of experimentation here laid down will gain a better insight into inorganic chemistry and mineralogy than if he had 'got up' any of the best text-books, and passed any number of examinations in their contents."—*Chemical News.*

Commercial Chemical Analysis.
THE COMMERCIAL HANDBOOK OF CHEMICAL ANALYSIS; or, Practical Instructions for the determination of the Intrinsic or Commercial Value of Substances used in Manufactures, in Trades, and in the Arts. By A. NORMANDY. New Edition, by H.M. NOAD, F.R.S. Crown 8vo, 12s. 6d. cloth.

"We strongly recommend this book to our readers as a guide, alike indispensable to the housewife as to the pharmaceutical practitioner."—*Medical Times.*

Dye-Wares and Colours.
THE MANUAL OF COLOURS AND DYE-WARES: Their Properties, Applications, Valuations, Impurities, and Sophistications. For the use of Dyers, Printers, Drysalters, Brokers, &c. By J. W. SLATER. Second Edition, Revised and greatly Enlarged. Crown 8vo, 7s. 6d. cloth.

"A complete encyclopædia of the *materia tinctoria*. The information given respecting each article is full and precise, and the methods of determining their value are given with clearness and are practical as well as valuable."—*Chemist and Druggist.*

Modern Brewing and Malting.
A HANDYBOOK FOR BREWERS: Being a Practical Guide to the Art of Brewing and Malting. Embracing the Conclusions of Modern Research which bear upon the Practice of Brewing. By HERBERT EDWARDS WRIGHT, M.A. Crown 8vo, 530 pp., 12s. 6d. cloth.

"May be consulted with advantage by the student who is preparing himself for examinational tests, while the scientific brewer will find in it a *resumé* of all the most important discoveries of modern times. The work is written throughout in a clear and concise manner, and the author takes great care to discriminate between vague theories and well-established facts."—*Brewers' Journal.*

"We have great pleasure in recommending this handybook, and have no hesitation in saying that it is one of the best—if not the best—which has yet been written on the subject of beer-brewing in this country, and it should have a place on the shelves of every brewer's library."—*The Brewer's Guardian.*

Analysis and Valuation of Fuels.
FUELS: SOLID, LIQUID, AND GASEOUS, Their Analysis and Valuation. For the Use of Chemists and Engineers. By H. J. PHILLIPS, F.C.S., formerly Analytical and Consulting Chemist to the Great Eastern Railway. Third Edition. Small crown 8vo, 2s. cloth.

"Ought to have its place in the laboratory of every metallurgical establishment, and wherever fuel is used on a large scale."—*Chemical News.*

"Cannot fail to be of wide interest, especially at the present time."—*Railway News.*

Pigments.
THE ARTIST'S MANUAL OF PIGMENTS. Showing their Composition, Conditions of Permanency, Non-Permanency, and Adulterations; Effects in Combination with Each Other and with Vehicles; and the most Reliable Tests of Purity Together with the Science and Art Department's Examination Questions on Painting. By H. C. STANDAGE. Second Edition. Crown 8vo, 2s. 6d. cloth.

"This work is indeed *multum-in-parvo*, and we can, with good conscience, recommend it to all who come in contact with pigments, whether as makers, dealers or users."—*Chemical Review.*

Gauging. Tables and Rules for Revenue Officers, Brewers, etc.
A POCKET BOOK OF MENSURATION AND GAUGING: Containing Tables, Rules and Memoranda for Revenue Officers, Brewers, Spirit Merchants, &c. By J. B. MANT (Inland Revenue). 18mo, 4s. leather.

"This handy and useful book is adapted to the requirements of the Inland Revenue Department, and will be a favourite book of reference."—*Civilian.*

"Should be in the hands of every practical brewer."—*Brewers' Journal.*

INDUSTRIAL ARTS, TRADES, AND MANUFACTURES.

Cotton Spinning.
COTTON MANUFACTURE: A Manual of Practical Instruction in the Processes of Opening, Carding, Combing, Drawing, Doubling and Spinning of Cotton, the Methods of Dyeing, &c. For the Use of Operatives, Overlookers and Manufacturers. By JOHN LISTER, Technical Instructor, Pendleton. 8vo, 7s. 6d. cloth. *Machinery.*
"This invaluable volume is a distinct advance in the literature of cotton manufacture."—
"It is thoroughly reliable, fulfilling nearly all the requirements desired."—*Glasgow Herald.*

Flour Manufacture, Milling, etc.
FLOUR MANUFACTURE: A Treatise on Milling Science and Practice. By Professor FRIEDRICH KICK. Translated from the Second Enlarged and Revised Edition with Supplement. By H. H. P. POWLES, A.-M.Inst.C.E. Nearly 400 pp. Illustrated with 28 Folding Plates, and 167 Woodcuts. Royal 8vo, 25s. cloth.
"This valuable work is, and will remain, the standard authority on the science of milling. . . The miller who has read and digested this work will have laid the foundation, so to speak, of a successful career; he will have acquired a number of general principles which he can proceed to apply. In this handsome volume we at last have the accepted text-book of modern milling in good, sound English, which has little, if any, trace of the German idiom."—*The Miller.*

Agglutinants.
CEMENTS, PASTES, GLUES AND GUMS: A Practical Guide to the Manufacture and Application of the various Agglutinants required in the Building, Metal-Working, Wood-Working and Leather-Working Trades, and for Workshop, Laboratory or Office Use. With upwards of 900 Recipes and Formulæ. By H. C. STANDAGE. Crown 8vo, 2s. cloth.
"We have pleasure in speaking favourably of this volume. So far as we have had experience, which is not inconsiderable, this manual is trustworthy."—*Athenæum.*
"As a revelation of what are considered trade secrets, this book will arouse an amount of curiosity among the large number of industries it touches."—*Daily Chronicle.*

Soap-making.
THE ART OF SOAP-MAKING: A Practical Handbook of the Manufacture of Hard and Soft Soaps, Toilet Soaps, etc. By ALEXANDER WATT, Fifth Edition, Revised, including Modern Candle-Making. Crown 8vo, 7s. 6d. cloth. [*Just published.*]
"The work will prove very useful, not merely to the technological student, but to the practical soap-boiler who wishes to understand the theory of his art."—*Chemical News.*
"A thoroughly practical treatise on an art which has almost no literature in our language. We congratulate the author on the success of his endeavour to fill a void in English technical literature."—*Nature.*

Paper Making.
PRACTICAL PAPER-MAKING: A Manual for Paper-makers and Owners and Managers of Paper-Mills. With Tables, Calculations, &c. By G. CLAPPERTON, Paper-maker. With Illustrations of Fibres from Micro-Photographs. Crown 8vo, 5s. cloth. [*Just published.*]
"The author caters for the requirements of responsible mill hands, apprentices, &c., whilst this manual will be found of great service to students of technology, as well as to veteran paper makers and mill owners. The illustrations form an excellent feature."—*Paper Trade Review.*
"We recommend everybody interested in the trade to get a copy of this thoroughly practical book."—*Paper Making.*

Paper Making.
THE ART OF PAPER MAKING: A Practical Handbook of the Manufacture of Paper from Rags, Esparto, Straw, and other Fibrous Materials, including the Manufacture of Pulp from Wood Fibre, with a Description of the Machinery and Appliances used. To which are added Details of Processes for Recovering Soda from Waste Liquors. By ALEXANDER WATT, Author of "The Art of Soap-Making" With Illusts. Crown 8vo, 7s. 6d. cloth.
"It may be regarded as the standard work on the subject. The book is full of valuable information. The 'Art of Paper-making,' is in every respect a model of a text-book, either for a technical class or for the private student."—*Paper and Printing Trades Journal.*

Leather Manufacture.
THE ART OF LEATHER MANUFACTURE. Being a Practical Handbook, in which the Operations of Tanning, Currying, and Leather Dressing are fully Described, and the Principles of Tanning Explained, and many Recent Processes Introduced; as also the Methods for the Estimation of Tannin, and a Description of the Arts of Glue Boiling, Gut Dressing, &c. By ALEXANDER WATT. Crown 8vo, 9s. cloth.
"A sound, comprehensive treatise on tanning and its accessories. It is an eminently valuable production, which redounds to the credit of both author and publishers."—*Chemical Review.*

Watch Adjusting.

THE WATCH ADJUSTER'S MANUAL: A Practical Guide for the Watch and Chronometer Adjuster in Making, Springing, Timing and Adjusting for Isochronism, Positions and Temperatures. By C. E. FRITTS. 370 pages, with Illustrations, 8vo, 16s. cloth. [*Just published*.

Horology.

A TREATISE ON MODERN HOROLOGY, *in Theory and Practice*. Translated from the French of CLAUDIUS SAUNIER, ex-Director of the School of Horology at Maçon, by JULIEN TRIPPLIN, F.R.A.S., Besançon Watch Manufacturer, and EDWARD RIGG, M.A., Assayer in the Royal Mint. With 78 Woodcuts and 22 Coloured Copper Plates. Second Edition. Super-royal 8vo, £2 2s. cloth; £2 10s. half-calf.

"There is no horological work in the English language at all to be compared to this production of M. Saunier's for clearness and completeness. It is alike good as a guide for the student and as a reference for the experienced horologist and skilled workman."—*Horological Journal.*

"The latest, the most complete, and the most reliable of those literary productions to which continental watchmakers are indebted for the mechanical superiority over their English brethren—in fact, the Book of Books, is M. Saunier's 'Treatise.'"—*Watchmaker, Jeweller and Silversmith.*

Watchmaking.

THE WATCHMAKER'S HANDBOOK. Intended as a Workshop Companion for those engaged in Watchmaking and the Allied Mechanical Arts. Translated from the French of CLAUDIUS SAUNIER, and considerably enlarged by JULIEN TRIPPLIN, F.R.A.S., Vice-President of the Horological Institute, and EDWARD RIGG, M.A., Assayer in the Royal Mint. With numerous Woodcuts and 14 Copper Plates. Third Edition. Crown 8vo, 9s. cloth.

"Each part is truly a treatise in itself. The arrangement is good and the language is clear and concise. It is an admirable guide for the young watchmaker."—*Engineering.*

"It is impossible to speak too highly of its excellence. It fulfils every requirement in a handbook intended for the use of a workman. Should be found in every workshop."—*Watch and Clockmaker.*

"This book contains an immense number of practical details bearing on the daily occupation of a watchmaker."—*Watchmaker and Metalworker* (Chicago).

Watches and Timekeepers.

A HISTORY OF WATCHES AND OTHER TIMEKEEPERS. By JAMES F. KENDAL, M.B.H.Inst. 1s. 6d. boards; or 2s. 6d. cloth gilt.

"Mr. Kendal's book, for its size, is the best which has yet appeared on this subject in the English language."—*Industries.*

"Open the book where you may, there is interesting matter in it concerning the ingenious devices of the ancient or modern horologer. The subject is treated in a liberal and entertaining spirit, as might be expected of a historian who is a master of the craft."—*Saturday Review.*

Electrolysis of Gold, Silver, Copper, etc.

ELECTRO-DEPOSITION: *A Practical Treatise on the Electrolysis of Gold, Silver, Copper, Nickel, and other Metals and Alloys*. With descriptions of Voltaic Batteries, Magneto and Dynamo-Electric Machines, Thermopiles, and of the Materials and Processes used in every Department of the Art, and several Chapters on Electro-Metallurgy. By ALEXANDER WATT, Author of "Electro-Metallurgy," &c. Third Edition, Revised. Crown 8vo, 9s. cloth.

"Eminently a book for the practical worker in electro-deposition. It contains practical descriptions of methods, processes and materials as actually pursued and used in the workshop."—*Engineer.*

Electro-Metallurgy.

ELECTRO-METALLURGY; *Practically Treated*. By ALEXANDER WATT, Author of "Electro-Deposition," &c. Tenth Edition, including the most recent Processes. 12mo, 4s. cloth boards.

"From this book both amateur and artisan may learn everything necessary for the successful prosecution of electroplating."—*Iron.*

Working in Gold.

THE JEWELLER'S ASSISTANT IN THE ART OF WORKING IN GOLD: A Practical Treatise for Masters and Workmen, Compiled from the Experience of Thirty Years' Workshop Practice. By GEORGE E. GEE, Author of "The Goldsmith's Handbook," &c. Cr. 8vo, 7s. 6d. cloth.

"This manual of technical education is apparently destined to be a valuable auxiliary to a handicraft which is certainly capable of great improvement."—*The Times.*

"Very useful in the workshop, as the knowledge is practical, having been acquired by long experience, and all the recipes and directions are guaranteed to be successful."—*Jeweller and Metalworker.*

Electroplating.

ELECTROPLATING: A Practical Handbook on the Deposition of Copper, Silver, Nickel, Gold, Aluminium, Brass, Platinum, &c. &c. With Descriptions of the Chemicals, Materials, Batteries, and Dynamo Machines used in the Art. By J. W. URQUHART, C.E. Third Edition. Cr. 8vo. 5s.
"An excellent work, giving the newest information."—*Horological Journal.*

Electrotyping.

ELECTROTYPING. The *Reproduction and Multiplication of Printing Surfaces and Works of Art by the Electro-deposition of Metals.* By J. W. URQUHART, C.E. Crown 8vo, 5s. cloth.
"The book is thoroughly practical. The reader is, therefore, conducted through the leading laws of electricity, then through the metals used by electrotypers, the apparatus, and the depositing processes, up to the final preparation of the work."—*Art Journal.*

Goldsmiths' Work.

THE GOLDSMITH'S HANDBOOK. By GEORGE E. GEE, Jeweller, &c. Third Edition, considerably Enlarged. 12mo, 3s. 6d. cl. bds.
"A good, sound educator, which will be accepted as an authority."—*Horological Journal.*

Silversmiths' Work.

THE SILVERSMITH'S HANDBOOK. By GEORGE E. GEE, Jeweller, &c. Second Edition, Revised. 12mo, 3s. 6d. cloth.
"The chief merit of the work is its practical character. . . The workers in the trade will speedily discover its merits when they sit down to study it."—*English Mechanic.*
** The above two works together, strongly half-bound, price 7s.

Sheet Metal Working.

SHEET METAL WORKER'S INSTRUCTOR: Comprising a Selection of Geometrical Problems and Practical Rules for Describing the Various Patterns Required by Zinc, Sheet-Iron, Copper, and Tin-Plate Workers. By REUBEN HENRY WARN, Practical Tin-Plate Worker. New Edition, Revised and greatly Enlarged by JOSEPH G. HORNER, A.M.I.M.E., Author of "Pattern Making," &c. Crown 8vo, 254 pages, with 430 Illustrations. 7s. 6d., cloth. [*Just published.*

Bread and Biscuit Baking.

THE BREAD AND BISCUIT BAKER'S AND SUGAR-BOILER'S ASSISTANT. Including a large variety of Modern Recipes. By ROBERT WELLS, Practical Baker. Crown 8vo, 2s. cloth.
"A large number of wrinkles for the ordinary cook, as well as the baker."—*Saturday Review.*

Confectionery for Hotels and Restaurants.

THE PASTRYCOOK AND CONFECTIONER'S GUIDE. For Hotels, Restaurants and the Trade in general, adapted also for Family Use. By ROBERT WELLS. Crown 8vo, 2s. cloth.
"We cannot speak too highly of this really excellent work. In these days of keen competition our readers cannot do better than purchase this book."—*Bakers' Times.*

Ornamental Confectionery.

ORNAMENTAL CONFECTIONERY: A Guide for Bakers, Confectioners and Pastrycooks; including a variety of Modern Recipes, and Remarks on Decorative and Coloured Work. With 129 Original Designs. By ROBERT WELLS. Crown 8vo, cloth gilt, 5s.
"A valuable work, practical, and should be in the hands of every baker and confectioner. The illustrative designs are alone worth treble the amount charged for the whole work."—*Bakers' Times.*

Flour Confectionery.

THE MODERN FLOUR CONFECTIONER. Wholesale and Retail. Containing a large Collection of Recipes for Cheap Cakes, Biscuits, &c. With Remarks on the Ingredients used in their Manufacture. By R. WELLS. Crown 8vo, 2s. cloth.

Laundry Work.

LAUNDRY MANAGEMENT. A Handbook for Use in Private and Public Laundries, Including Descriptive Accounts of Modern Machinery and Appliances for Laundry Work. Small crown 8vo, 2s. cloth.
"This book should certainly occupy an honoured place on the shelves of all housekeepers who wish to keep themselves *au courant* of the newest appliances and methods."—*The Queen.*

HANDYBOOKS FOR HANDICRAFTS.

By PAUL N. HASLUCK,

EDITOR OF "WORK" (NEW SERIES); AUTHOR OF "LATHEWORK," "MILLING MACHINES," &c.

Crown 8vo, 144 pages, cloth, price 1s. each.

☞ These HANDYBOOKS *have been written to supply information for* WORKMEN, STUDENTS, *and* AMATEURS *in the several Handicrafts, on the actual* PRACTICE *of the* WORKSHOP, *and are intended to convey in plain language* TECHNICAL KNOWLEDGE *of the several* CRAFTS. *In describing the processes employed, and the manipulation of material, workshop terms are used; workshop practice is fully explained; and the text is freely illustrated with drawings of modern tools, appliances, and processes.*

THE METAL TURNER'S HANDYBOOK. A Practical Manual for Workers at the Foot-Lathe. With over 100 Illustrations. Price 1s.
"The book will be of service alike to the amateur and the artisan turner. It displays thorough knowledge of the subject."—*Scotsman.*

THE WOOD TURNER'S HANDYBOOK. A Practical Manual for Workers at the Lathe. With over 100 Illustrations. Price 1s.
"We recommend the book to young turners and amateurs. A multitude of workmen have hitherto sought in vain for a manual of this special industry."—*Mechanical World.*

THE WATCH JOBBER'S HANDYBOOK. A Practical Manual on Cleaning, Repairing, and Adjusting. With upwards of 100 Illustrations. Price 1s.
"We strongly advise all young persons connected with the watch trade to acquire and study this inexpensive work."—*Clerkenwell Chronicle.*

THE PATTERN MAKER'S HANDYBOOK. A Practical Manual on the Construction of Patterns for Founders. With upwards of 100 Illustrations. Price 1s.
"A most valuable, if not indispensable, manual for the pattern maker."—*Knowledge.*

THE MECHANIC'S WORKSHOP HANDYBOOK. A Practical Manual on Mechanical Manipulation. Embracing Information on various Handicraft Processes, with Useful Notes and Miscellaneous Memoranda. Comprising about 200 Subjects. Price 1s.
"A very clever and useful book, which should be found in every workshop; and it should certainly find a place in all technical schools."—*Saturday Review.*

THE MODEL ENGINEER'S HANDYBOOK. A Practical Manual on the Construction of Model Steam Engines. With upwards of 100 Illustrations. Price 1s.
"Mr. Hasluck has produced a very good little book."—*Builder.*

THE CLOCK JOBBER'S HANDYBOOK. A Practical Manual on Cleaning, Repairing, and Adjusting. With upwards of 100 Illustrations. Price 1s.
"It is of inestimable service to those commencing the trade."—*Coventry Standard.*

THE CABINET WORKER'S HANDYBOOK: A Practical Manual on the Tools, Materials, Appliances, and Processes employed in Cabinet Work. With upwards of 100 Illustrations. Price 1s.
"Mr. Hasluck's thoroughgoing little Handybook is amongst the most practical guides we have seen for beginners in cabinet-work."—*Saturday Review.*

THE WOODWORKER'S HANDYBOOK OF MANUAL INSTRUCTION. Embracing Information on the Tools, Materials, Appliances and Processes employed in Woodworking. With 104 Illustrations. Price 1s.
[*Just published.*

THE METALWORKER'S HANDYBOOK. With upwards of 100 Illustrations. [*In preparation.*

*** OPINIONS OF THE PRESS.

"Written by a man who knows, not only how work ought to be done, but how to do it, and how to convey his knowledge to others."—*Engineering.*
"Mr. Hasluck writes admirably, and gives complete instructions."—*Engineer.*
"Mr. Hasluck combines the experience of a practical teacher with the manipulative skill and scientific knowledge of processes of the trained mechanician, and the manuals are marvels of what can be produced at a popular price."—*Schoolmaster.*
"Helpful to workmen of all ages and degrees of experience."—*Daily Chronicle.*
"Practical, sensible, and remarkably cheap."—*Journal of Education.*
"Concise, clear and practical."—*Saturday Review.*

COMMERCE, COUNTING-HOUSE WORK, TABLES, etc.

Commercial French.
A NEW BOOK OF COMMERCIAL FRENCH: Grammar—Vocabulary—Correspondence—Commercial Documents—Geography—Arithmetic—Lexicon. By P. CARROUÉ, Professor in the City High School J.—B. Say (Paris). Crown 8vo, 4s. 6d. cloth. [*Just published.*

Commercial Education.
LESSONS IN COMMERCE. By Professor R. GAMBARO, of the Royal High Commercial School at Genoa. Edited and Revised by JAMES GAULT, Professor of Commerce and Commercial Law in King's College, London. Second Edition, Revised. Crown 8vo, 3s. 6d. cloth. [*Just published.*

"The publishers of this work have rendered considerable service to the cause of commercial education by the opportune production of this volume. . . . The work is peculiarly acceptable to English readers and an admirable addition to existing class-books. In a phrase, we think the work attains its object in furnishing a brief account of those laws and customs of British trade with which the commercial man interested therein should be familiar."—*Chamber of Commerce Journal.*

"An invaluable guide in the hands of those who are preparing for a commercial career."—*Counting House.*

Foreign Commercial Correspondence.
THE FOREIGN COMMERCIAL CORRESPONDENT: Being Aids to Commercial Correspondence in Five Languages—English, French, German, Italian, and Spanish. By CONRAD E. BAKER. Second Edition. Crown 8vo, 3s. 6d. cloth.

"Whoever wishes to correspond in all the languages mentioned by Mr. Baker cannot do better than study this work, the materials of which are excellent and conveniently arranged. They consist not of entire specimen letters but—what are far more useful—short passages, sentences, or phrases expressing the same general idea in various forms."—*Athenæum.*

"A careful examination has convinced us that it is unusually complete, well arranged, and reliable. The book is a thoroughly good one."—*Schoolmaster.*

Accounts for Manufacturers.
FACTORY ACCOUNTS: Their Principles and Practice. A Handbook for Accountants and Manufacturers, with Appendices on the Nomenclature of Machine Details; the Income Tax Acts; the Rating of Factories; Fire and Boiler Insurance; the Factory and Workshop Acts, &c., including also a Glossary of Terms and a large number of Specimen Rulings. By EMILE GARCKE and J. M. FELLS. Fourth Edition, Revised and Enlarged. Demy 8vo, 250 pages, 6s. strongly bound.

"A very interesting description of the requirements of Factory Accounts. . . . the principle of assimilating the Factory Accounts to the general commercial books is one which we thoroughly agree with."—*Accountants' Journal.*

"Characterised by extreme thoroughness. There are few owners of factories who would not derive great benefit from the perusal of this most admirable work."—*Local Government Chronicle.*

Modern Metrical Units and Systems.
MODERN METROLOGY: A Manual of the Metrical Units and Systems of the Present Century. With an Appendix containing a proposed English System. By LOWIS D'A. JACKSON, A.M.Inst.C.E., Author of "Aid to Survey Practice," &c. Large crown 8vo, 12s. 6d. cloth.

"We recommend the work to all interested in the practical reform of our weights and measures."—*Nature.*

The Metric System and the British Standards.
A SERIES OF METRIC TABLES, in which the British Standard Measures and Weights are compared with those of the Metric System at present in Use on the Continent. By C. H. DOWLING, C.E. 8vo, 10s. 6d. strongly bound.

"Mr. Dowling's Tables are well put together as a ready-reckoner for the conversion of one system into the other."—*Athenæum.*

Iron Shipbuilders' and Merchants' Weight Tables.
IRON-PLATE WEIGHT TABLES: For Iron Shipbuilders, Engineers, and Iron Merchants. Containing the Calculated Weights of upwards of 150,000 different sizes of Iron Plates, from 1 foot by 6 in. by ¼ in. to 10 feet by 5 feet by 1 in. Worked out on the basis of 40 lbs. to the square foot of Iron of 1 inch in thickness. Carefully compiled and thoroughly Revised by H. BURLINSON and W. H. SIMPSON. Oblong 4to, 25s. half-bound.

"This work will be found of great utility. The authors have had much practical experience of what is wanting in making estimates; and the use of the book will save much time in making elaborate calculations."—*English Mechanic.*

Chadwick's Calculator for Numbers and Weights Combined.

THE NUMBER, WEIGHT, AND FRACTIONAL CALCULATOR. Containing upwards of 250,000 Separate Calculations, showing at a glance the value at 422 different rates, ranging from $\frac{1}{16}$th of a Penny to 20s. each, or per cwt., and £20 per ton, of any number of articles consecutively, from 1 to 470.—Any number of cwts., qrs., and lbs., from 1 cwt. to 470 cwts.—Any number of tons, cwts., qrs., and lbs., from 1 to 1,000 tons. By WILLIAM CHADWICK, Public Accountant. Third Edition, Revised and Improved. 8vo, 18s., strongly bound for Office wear and tear.

☞ *Is adapted for the use of Accountants and Auditors, Railway Companies, Canal Companies, Shippers, Shipping Agents, General Carriers, etc. Ironfounders, Brassfounders, Metal Merchants, Iron Manufacturers, Ironmongers, Engineers, Machinists, Boiler Makers, Millwrights, Roofing, Bridge and Girder Makers, Colliery Proprietors, etc. Timber Merchants, Builders, Contractors, Architects, Surveyors, Auctioneers, Valuers, Brokers, Mill Owners and Manufacturers, Mill Furnishers, Merchants, and General Wholesale Tradesmen. Also for the Apportionment of Mileage Charges for Railway Traffic.*

"It is as easy of reference for any answer or any number of answers as a dictionary, and the references are even more quickly made. For making up accounts or estimates the book must prove invaluable to all who have any considerable quantity of calculations involving price and measure in any combination to do."—*Engineer.*

Harben's Comprehensive Weight Calculator.

THE WEIGHT CALCULATOR. Being a Series of Tables upon a New and Comprehensive Plan, exhibiting at One Reference the exact Value of any Weight from 1 lb. to 15 tons, at 300 Progressive Rates, from 1d. to 168s. per cwt., and containing 186,000 Direct Answers, which, with their Combinations, consisting of a single addition (mostly to be performed at sight), will afford an aggregate of 10,266,000 Answers; the whole being calculated and designed to ensure correctness and promote despatch. By HENRY HARBEN, Accountant. Fifth Edition, carefully Corrected. Royal 8vo, £1 5s. strongly half-bound. [*Just published.*

"A practical and useful work of reference for men of business generally; it is the best of the kind we have seen."—*Ironmonger.*

"Of priceless value to business men. It is a necessary book in all mercantile offices."—*Sheffield Independent.*

Harben's Comprehensive Discount Guide.

THE DISCOUNT GUIDE. Comprising several Series of Tables for the use of Merchants, Manufacturers, Ironmongers, and others, by which may be ascertained the exact Profit arising from any mode of using Discounts, either in the Purchase or Sale of Goods, and the method of either Altering a Rate of Discount or Advancing a Price, so as to produce, by one operation, a sum that will realise any required profit after allowing one or more Discounts: to which are added Tables of Profit or Advance from 1¼ to 90 per cent., Tables of Discount from 1¼ to 98¾ per cent., and Tables of Commission, &c., from ⅛ to 10 per cent. By HENRY HARBEN, Accountant. New Edition, Revised and Corrected. Demy 8vo, 544 pp., £1 5s. half-bound.

"A book such as this can only be appreciated by business men, to whom the saving of time means saving of money. We have the high authority of Professor J. R. Young that the tables throughout the work are constructed upon strictly accurate principles. The work is a model of typographical clearness, and must prove of great value to merchants, manufacturers, and general traders."—*British Trade Journal.*

New Wages Calculator.

TABLES OF WAGES at 54, 52, 50 and 48 Hours per Week. Showing the Amounts of Wages from One-quarter-of-an-hour to Sixty-four hours in each case at Rates of Wages advancing by One Shilling from 4s. to 55s. per week. By THOS. GARBUTT, Accountant. Square crown 8vo, 6s. half-bound. [*Just published.*

Iron and Metal Trades' Calculator.

THE IRON AND METAL TRADES' COMPANION. For expeditiously ascertaining the Value of any Goods bought or sold by Weight, from 1s. per cwt. to 112s. per cwt., and from one farthing per pound to one shilling per pound. By THOMAS DOWNIE. 396 pp., 9s. leather.

"A most useful set of tables; nothing like them before existed."—*Building News.*
"Although specially adapted to the iron and metal trades, the tables will be found useful in every other business in which merchandise is bought and sold by weight."—*Railway News.*

"DIRECT CALCULATORS,"
By M. B. COTSWORTH, of Holgate, York.

QUICKEST AND MOST ACCURATE MEANS OF CALCULATION KNOWN.
ENSURE ACCURACY and SPEED WITH EASE, SAVE TIME and MONEY.

Accounts may be charged out or checked by these means in about one third he time required by ordinary methods of calculation. These unrivalled "Calculators" have very clear and original contrivances for instantly finding the exact answer, by its fixed position, without even sighting the top or side of the page. They are varied in arrangement to suit the special need of each particular trade.

All the leading firms now use Calculators, even where they employ experts.

N.B.—Indicator letters in brackets should be quoted.

"*RAILWAY & TRADERS' CALCULATOR*" **(R. & T.)** 10s. 6d. Including Scale of Charges for Small Parcels by Merchandise Trains. "Direct Calculator"—the only Calculator published giving exact charge for Cwts., Qrs. and Lbs., together. "Calculating Tables" for every 1d. rate to 100s. per ton. "Wages Calculator." "Percentage Rates." "Grain, Flour, Ale, &c., Weight Calculators."

"*DIRECT CALCULATOR* **(I R)**" including all the above except "Calculating Tables." 7s.

"*DIRECT CALCULATOR* **(A)**" by ½d., 2s. each opening, exact pence to 40s. per ton. 5s.

"*DIRECT CALCULATOR* **(B)**" by 1d., 4s. each opening, exact pence to 40s. per ton. 4s. 6d.

"*DIRECT CALCULATOR* **(C)**" by 1d. (with Cwts. and Qrs. to nearest farthing), to 40s. per ton. 4s. 6d.

"*DIRECT CALCULATOR* **(Ds)**" by 1d. gradations. (Single Tons to 50 Tons, then by fifties to 1,000 Tons, with Cwts. values below in exact pence payable, fractions of ½d. and upwards being counted as 1d. 6s. 6d.

"*DIRECT CALCULATOR* **(D)**" has from 1,000 to 10,000 Tons in addition to the (Ds) Calculator. 7s. 6d.

"*DIRECT CALCULATOR* **(Es)**" by 1d. gradations. (As (D) to 1,000 Tons, with Cwts. and Qrs. values shown separately to the nearest farthing). 5s. 6d.

"*DIRECT CALCULATOR* **(E)**" has from 1,000 to 10,000 Tons in addition to the (Es) Calculator. 6s. 6d.

"*DIRECT CALCULATOR* **(F)**" by 1d., 2s. each opening, exact pence to 40s. per ton. 4s. 6d.

"*DIRECT CALCULATOR* **(G)**" by 1d., 1s. each opening; 6 in. by 9 in. Nearest ¼d. Indexed (G I) 3s. 6d. 2s. 6d.

"*DIRECT CALCULATOR* **(H)**" by 1d., 1s. each opening; 6 in. by 9 in. To exact pence. Indexed (H I) 3s. 6d. 2s. 6d.

"*DIRECT CALCULATOR* **(K)**" Showing Values of Tons, Cwts. and Qrs. in even pence (fractions of 1d. as 1d.), for the Retail Coal Trade. 4s. 6d.

"*RAILWAY AND TIMBER TRADES MEASURER AND CALCULATOR* **(T)**" (as prepared for the Railway Companies). The only book published giving true content of unequal sided and round timber by eighths of an inch, quarter girth, Weights from Cubic Feet—Standards, Superficial Feet, and Stone to Weights—Running Feet from lengths of Deals—Standard Multipliers—Timber Measures—Customs Regulations, &c. 3s. 6d.

AGRICULTURE, FARMING, GARDENING, etc.

Dr. Fream's New Edition of "The Standard Treatise on Agriculture."

THE COMPLETE GRAZIER, and FARMER'S and CATTLE-BREEDER'S ASSISTANT: A Compendium of Husbandry. Originally Written by WILLIAM YOUATT. Thirteenth Edition, entirely Re-written, considerably Enlarged, and brought up to the Present Requirements of Agricultural Practice, by WILLIAM FREAM, LL.D., Steven Lecturer in the University of Edinburgh, Author of "The Elements of Agriculture," &c. Royal 8vo, 1,100 pp., with over 450 Illustrations. £1 11s. 6d. strongly and handsomely bound.

EXTRACT FROM PUBLISHERS' ADVERTISEMENT.

"A treatise that made its original appearance in the first decade of the century, and that enters upon its Thirteenth Edition before the century has run its course, has undoubtedly established its position as a work of permanent value. . . The phenomenal progress of the last dozen years in the Practice and Science of Farming has rendered it necessary, however, that the volume should be re-written, . . . and for this undertaking the publishers were fortunate enough to secure the services of Dr. FREAM, whose high attainments in all matters pertaining to agriculture have been so emphatically recognised by the highest professional and official authorities. In carrying out his editorial duties, Dr. FREAM has been favoured with valuable contributions by Prof. J. WORTLEY AXE, Mr. E. BROWN, Dr. BERNARD DYER, Mr. W. J. MALDEN, Mr. R. H. REW, Prof. SHELDON, Mr. J. SINCLAIR, Mr. SANDERS SPENCER, and others.

"As regards the illustrations of the work, no pains have been spared to make them as representative and characteristic as possible, so as to be practically useful to the Farmer and Grazier."

SUMMARY OF CONTENTS.

BOOK I. ON THE VARIETIES, BREEDING, REARING, FATTENING, AND MANAGEMENT OF CATTLE.
BOOK II. ON THE ECONOMY AND MANAGEMENT OF THE DAIRY.
BOOK III. ON THE BREEDING, REARING, AND MANAGEMENT OF HORSES.
BOOK IV. ON THE BREEDING, REARING, AND FATTENING OF SHEEP.
BOOK V. ON THE BREEDING, REARING, AND FATTENING OF SWINE.
BOOK VI. ON THE DISEASES OF LIVE STOCK.
BOOK VII. ON THE BREEDING, REARING, AND MANAGEMENT OF POULTRY.
BOOK VIII. ON FARM OFFICES AND IMPLEMENTS OF HUSBANDRY.
BOOK IX. ON THE CULTURE AND MANAGEMENT OF GRASS LANDS.
BOOK X. ON THE CULTIVATION AND APPLICATION OF GRASSES, PULSE, AND ROOTS.
BOOK XI. ON MANURES AND THEIR APPLICATION TO GRASS LAND & CROPS
BOOK XII. MONTHLY CALENDARS OF FARMWORK.

*** OPINIONS OF THE PRESS ON THE NEW EDITION.

"Dr. Fream is to be congratulated on the successful attempt he has made to give us a work which will at once become the standard classic of the farm practice of the country. We believe that it will be found that it has no compeer among the many works at present in existence. . . . The illustrations are admirable, while the frontispiece, which represents the well-known bull, New Year's Gift, bred by the Queen, is a work of art."—*The Times.*

"The book must be recognised as occupying the proud position of the most exhaustive work of reference in the English language on the subject with which it deals."—*Athenæum.*

"The most comprehensive guide to modern farm practice that exists in the English language to-day. . . . The book is one that ought to be on every farm and in the library of every landowner."—*Mark Lane Express.*

"In point of exhaustiveness and accuracy the work will certainly hold a pre-eminent and unique position among books dealing with scientific agricultural practice. It is, in fact, an agricultural library of itself."—*North British Agriculturist.*

"A compendium of authoritative and well-ordered knowledge on every conceivable branch of the work of the live stock farmer; probably without an equal in this or any other country."—*Yorkshire Post.*

British Farm Live Stock.

FARM LIVE STOCK OF GREAT BRITAIN. By ROBERT WALLACE, F.L.S., F.R.S.E., &c., Professor of Agriculture and Rural Economy in the University of Edinburgh. Third Edition, thoroughly Revised and considerably Enlarged. With over 120 Phototypes of Prize Stock. Demy 8vo, 384 pp., with 79 Plates and Maps, 12s. 6d. cloth.

"A really complete work on the history, breeds, and management of the farm stock of Great Britain, and one which is likely to find its way to the shelves of every country gentleman's library."—*The Times.*

"The latest edition of 'Farm Live Stock of Great Britain' is a production to be proud of, and its issue not the least of the services which its author has rendered to agricultural science.—*Scottish Farmer.*

"The book is very attractive . . . and we can scarcely imagine the existence of a farmer who would not like to have a copy of this beautiful work."—*Mark Lane Express.*

"A work which will long be regarded as a standard authority whenever a concise history and description of the breeds of live stock in the British Isles is required.'—*Bell's Weekly Messenger.*

Dairy Farming.

BRITISH DAIRYING. A Handy Volume on the Work of the Dairy-Farm. For the Use of Technical Instruction Classes, Students in Agricultural Colleges, and the Working Dairy-Farmer. By Prof. J. P. SHELDON, late Special Commissioner of the Canadian Government, Author of "Dairy Farming," &c. With numerous Illustrations. Crown 8vo, 2s. 6d. cloth.

"We confidently recommend it as a text-book on dairy farming."—*Agricultural Gazette.*
"Probably the best half-crown manual on dairy work that has yet been produced."—*North British Agriculturist.*
"It is the soundest little work we have yet seen on the subject."—*The Times.*

Dairy Manual.

MILK, CHEESE AND BUTTER: A Practical Handbook on their Properties and the Processes of their Production, including a Chapter on Cream and the Methods of its Separation from Milk. By JOHN OLIVER, late Principal of the Western Dairy Institute, Berkeley. With Coloured Plates and 200 Illusts. Crown 8vo, 7s. 6d. cloth. [*Just published.*

"An exhaustive and masterly production. It may be cordially recommended to all students and practitioners of dairy science."—*N.B. Agriculturist.*
"We strongly recommend this very comprehensive and carefully-written book to dairy-farmers and students of dairying. It is a distinct acquisition to the library of the agriculturist."—*Agricultural Gazette.*

Agricultural Facts and Figures.

NOTE-BOOK OF AGRICULTURAL FACTS AND FIGURES FOR FARMERS AND FARM STUDENTS. By PRIMROSE McCONNELL, B.Sc. Fifth Edition. Royal 32mo, roan, gilt edges, with band, 4s.

"Literally teems with information, and we can cordially recommend it to all connected with agriculture."—*North British Agriculturist.*

Small Farming.

SYSTEMATIC SMALL FARMING; or, The Lessons of my Farm. Being an Introduction to Modern Farm Practice for Small Farmers. By R. SCOTT BURN. With numerous Illustrations, crown 8vo, 6s. cloth.

"This is the completest book of its class we have seen, and one which every amateur farmer will read with pleasure and accept as a guide."—*Field.*

Modern Farming.

OUTLINES OF MODERN FARMING. By R. SCOTT BURN. Soils, Manures, and Crops—Farming and Farming Economy—Cattle, Sheep, and Horses — Management of Dairy, Pigs, and Poultry — Utilisation of Town-Sewage, Irrigation, &c. Sixth Edition. In One Vol., 1,250 pp., half-bound, profusely Illustrated, 12s.

"The aim of the author has been to make his work at once comprehensive and trustworthy and he has succeeded to a degree which entitles him to much credit."—*Morning Advertiser.*

Agricultural Engineering.

FARM ENGINEERING, THE COMPLETE TEXT-BOOK OF. Comprising Draining and Embanking; Irrigation and Water Supply; Farm Roads, Fences, and Gates; Farm Buildings; Barn Implements and Machines; Field Implements and Machines; Agricultural Surveying, &c. By Prof. JOHN SCOTT. 1,150 pages, half-bound, with over 600 Illustrations, 12s.

"Written with great care, as well as with knowledge and ability. The author has done his work well; we have found him a very trustworthy guide wherever we have tested his statements. The volume will be of great value to agricultural students."—*Mark Lane Express.*

Agricultural Text-Book.

THE FIELDS OF GREAT BRITAIN: A Text-Book of Agriculture, adapted to the Syllabus of the Science and Art Department. For Elementary and Advanced Students. By HUGH CLEMENTS (Board of Trade). Second Edition, Revised, with Additions. 18mo, 2s. 6d. cloth.

"A most comprehensive volume, giving a mass of information."—*Agricultural Economist.*
"It is a long time since we have seen a book which has pleased us more, or which contains such a vast and useful fund of knowledge."—*Educational Times.*

Tables for Farmers, etc.

TABLES, MEMORANDA, AND CALCULATED RESULTS for Farmers, Graziers, Agricultural Students, Surveyors, Land Agents, Auctioneers, etc. With a New System of Farm Book-keeping. By SIDNEY FRANCIS. Third Edition, Revised. 272 pp., waistcoat-pocket size, 1s. 6d. leather.

"Weighing less than 1 oz., and occupying no more space than a match box, it contains a mass of facts and calculations which has never before, in such handy form, been obtainable. Every operation on the farm is dealt with. The work may be taken as thoroughly accurate, the whole of the tables having been revised by Dr. Fream. We cordially recommend it."—*Bell's Weekly Messenger.*

AGRICULTURE, FARMING, GARDENING, etc. 45

Artificial Manures and Foods.
FERTILISERS AND FEEDING STUFFS: Their Properties and Uses. A Handbook for the Practical Farmer. By BERNARD DYER, D.Sc. (Lond.) With the Text of the Fertilisers and Feeding Stuffs Act of 1893, the Regulations and Forms of the Board of Agriculture and Notes on the Act by A. J. DAVID, B.A., LL.M., of the Inner Temple, Barrister-at-Law. Crown 8vo, 120 pages, 1s. cloth. [*Just published*.
"An excellent shillingsworth. Dr. Dyer has done farmers good service in placing at their disposal so much useful information in so intelligible a form."—*The Times*.

The Management of Bees.
BEES FOR PLEASURE AND PROFIT: A Guide to the Manipulation of Bees, the Production of Honey, and the General Management of the Apiary. By G. GORDON SAMSON. Crown 8vo, 1s. cloth.
"The intending bee-keeper will find exactly the kind of information required to enable him to make a successful start with his hives. The author is a thoroughly competent teacher, and his book may be commended."—*Morning Post*.

Farm and Estate Book-keeping.
BOOK-KEEPING FOR FARMERS & ESTATE OWNERS. A Practical Treatise, presenting, in Three Plans, a System adapted for all Classes of Farms. By JOHNSON M. WOODMAN, Chartered Accountant. Second Edition, Revised. Crown 8vo, 3s. 6d. cloth boards; or 2s. 6d. cloth limp.
"The volume is a capital study of a most important subject."—*Agricultural Gazette*.
"The young farmer, land agent, and surveyor will find Mr. Woodman's treatise more than repay its cost and study."—*Building News*.

Farm Account Book.
WOODMAN'S YEARLY FARM ACCOUNT BOOK. Giving a Weekly Labour Account and Diary, and showing the Income and Expenditure under each Department of Crops, Live Stock, Dairy, &c. &c. With Valuation, Profit and Loss Account, and Balance Sheet at the end of the Year. By JOHNSON M. WOODMAN, Chartered Accountant, Author of "Book-keeping for Farmers." Folio, 7s. 6d. half bound. [*culture*.
"Contains every requisite form for keeping farm accounts readily and accurately."—*Agri-*

Early Fruits, Flowers, and Vegetables.
THE FORCING GARDEN; or, How to Grow Early Fruits, Flowers, and Vegetables. With Plans and Estimates for Building Glass-houses, Pits, and Frames. By SAMUEL WOOD. Crown 8vo, 3s. 6d. cloth.
"A good book, and fairly fills a place that was in some degree vacant. The book is written with great care, and contains a great deal of valuable teaching."—*Gardeners' Magazine*.

Good Gardening.
A PLAIN GUIDE TO GOOD GARDENING; or, How to Grow Vegetables, Fruits, and Flowers. By S. WOOD. Fourth Edition, with considerable Additions, &c., and numerous Illustrations. Crown 8vo, 3s. 6d. cl.
"A very good book, and one to be highly recommended as a practical guide. The practical directions are excellent."—*Athenæum*.
"May be recommended to young gardeners, cottagers, and specially to amateurs, for the plain, simple, and trustworthy information it gives on common matters too often neglected."—*Gardeners' Chronicle*.

Gainful Gardening.
MULTUM-IN-PARVO GARDENING; or, How to make One Acre of Land produce £620 a-year by the Cultivation of Fruits and Vegetables; also, How to Grow Flowers in Three Glass Houses, so as to realise £176 per annum clear Profit. By SAMUEL WOOD, Author of "Good Gardening," &c. Fifth and Cheaper Edition, Revised, with Additions. Crown 8vo, 1s. sewed.
"We are bound to recommend it as not only suited to the case of the amateur and gentleman's gardener, but to the market grower."—*Gardeners' Magazine*.

Gardening for Ladies.
THE LADIES' MULTUM-IN-PARVO FLOWER GARDEN, and Amateurs' Complete Guide. With Illusts. By S. WOOD. Cr. 8vo, 3s. 6d. cl.

Receipts for Gardeners.
GARDEN RECEIPTS. Edited by CHARLES W. QUIN. 12mo, 1s. 6d. cloth limp.

Market Gardening.
MARKET AND KITCHEN GARDENING. By Contributors to "The Garden." Compiled by C. W. SHAW, late Editor of "Gardening Illustrated." 12mo 3s. 6d. cloth boards.

AUCTIONEERING, VALUING, LAND SURVEYING ESTATE AGENCY, etc.

Auctioneer's Assistant.

THE APPRAISER, AUCTIONEER, BROKER, HOUSE AND ESTATE AGENT AND VALUER'S POCKET ASSISTANT, for the Valuation for Purchase, Sale, or Renewal of Leases, Annuities and Reversions, and of property generally; with Prices for Inventories, &c. By JOHN WHEELER, Valuer, &c. Sixth Edition, Re-written and greatly extended by C. NORRIS, Surveyor, Valuer, &c. Royal 32mo, 5s. cloth.

"A neat and concise book of reference, containing an admirable and clearly-arranged list of prices for inventories, and a very practical guide to determine the value of furniture, &c."—*Standard.*
"Contains a large quantity of varied and useful information as to the valuation for purchase, sale, or renewal of leases, annuities and reversions, and of property generally, with prices for inventories, and a guide to determine the value of interior fittings and other effects."—*Builder.*

Auctioneering.

AUCTIONEERS: THEIR DUTIES AND LIABILITIES. A Manual of Instruction and Counsel for the Young Auctioneer. By ROBERT SQUIBBS, Auctioneer. Second Edition, Revised and partly Re-written. Demy 8vo, 12s. 6d. cloth.

*** OPINIONS OF THE PRESS.

"The standard text-book on the topics of which it treats."—*Athenæum.*
"The work is one of general excellent character, and gives much information in a compendious and satisfactory form."—*Builder.*
"May be recommended as giving a great deal of information on the law relating to auctioneers, in a very readable form."—*Law Journal.*
"Auctioneers may be congratulated on having so pleasing a writer to minister to their special needs."—*Solicitors' Journal.*
"Every auctioneer ought to possess a copy of this excellent work."—*Ironmonger.*
"Of great value to the profession. . . . We readily welcome this book from the fact that it treats the subject in a manner somewhat new to the profession."—*Estates Gazette.*

Inwood's Estate Tables.

TABLES FOR THE PURCHASING OF ESTATES, Freehold, Copyhold, or Leasehold; Annuities, Advowsons, etc., and for the Renewing of Leases held under Cathedral Churches, Colleges, or other Corporate bodies for Terms of Years certain, and for Lives: also for Valuing Reversionary Estates, Deferred Annuities, Next Presentations, &c.; together with SMART'S Five Tables of Compound Interest, and an Extension of the same to Lower and Intermediate Rates. By W. INWOOD. 24th Edition, with considerable Additions, and new and valuable Tables of Logarithms for the more Difficult Computations of the Interest of Money, Discount, Annuities, &c., by M. FEDOR THOMAN, of the Société Crédit Mobilier of Paris. Crown 8vo, 8s. cloth.

"Those interested in the purchase and sale of estates, and in the adjustment of compensation cases, as well as in transactions in annuities, life insurances, &c., will find the present edition of eminent service."—*Engineering.*
"'Inwood's Tables' still maintain a most enviable reputation. The new issue has been enriched by large additional contributions by M. Fedor Thoman, whose carefully arranged Tables cannot fail to be of the utmost utility."—*Mining Journal.*

Agricultural Valuer's Assistant.

THE AGRICULTURAL VALUER'S ASSISTANT. A Practical Handbook on the Valuation of Landed Estates; including Rules and Data for Measuring and Estimating the Contents, Weights, and Values of Agricultural Produce and Timber, and the Values of Feeding Stuffs, Manures, and Labour; with Forms of Tenant-Right-Valuations, Lists of Local Agricultural Customs, Scales of Compensation under the Agricultural Holdings Act, &c. &c. By TOM BRIGHT, Agricultural Surveyor. Second Edition, much Enlarged. Crown 8vo, 5s. cloth.

"Full of tables and examples in connection with the valuation of tenant-right, estates, labour, contents, and weights of timber, and farm produce of all kinds."—*Agricultural Gazette.*
"An eminently practical handbook, full of practical tables and data of undoubted interest and value to surveyors and auctioneers in preparing valuations of all kinds."—*Farmer.*

Plantations and Underwoods.

POLE PLANTATIONS AND UNDERWOODS: A Practical Handbook on Estimating the Cost of Forming, Renovating, Improving, and Grubbing Plantations and Underwoods, their Valuation for Purposes of Transfer, Rental, Sale, or Assessment. By TOM BRIGHT, Author of "The Agricultural Valuer's Assistant," &c. Crown 8vo, 3s. 6d. cloth.

"To valuers, foresters and agents it will be a welcome aid."—*North British Agriculturist.*
"Well calculated to assist the valuer in the discharge of his duties, and of undoubted interest and use both to surveyors and auctioneers in preparing valuations of all kinds."—*Kent Herald.*

AUCTIONEERING, VALUING, LAND SURVEYING, etc. 47

Hudson's Land Valuer's Pocket-Book.
THE LAND VALUER'S BEST ASSISTANT: Being Tables on a very much Improved Plan, for Calculating the Value of Estates. With Tables for reducing Scotch, Irish, and Provincial Customary Acres to Statute Measure, &c. By R. HUDSON, C.E. New Edition. Royal 32mo, 4s. leather.
"Of incalculable value to the country gentleman and professional man."—*Farmers' Journal.*

Ewart's Land Improver's Pocket-Book.
THE LAND IMPROVER'S POCKET-BOOK OF FORMULÆ, TABLES, and MEMORANDA *required in any Computation relating to the Permanent Improvement of Landed Property.* By JOHN EWART, Surveyor. Second Edition. Royal 32mo, 4s. leather.

Complete Agricultural Surveyor's Pocket-Book.
THE LAND VALUER'S AND LAND IMPROVER'S COMPLETE POCKET-BOOK. Being of the above Two Works bound together. Leather, with strap, 7s. 6d.

House Property.
HANDBOOK OF HOUSE PROPERTY. A Popular and Practical Guide to the Purchase, Mortgage, Tenancy, and Compulsory Sale of Houses and Land, including the Law of Dilapidations and Fixtures; with Examples of all kinds of Valuations, Useful Information on Building, and Suggestive Elucidations of Fine Art. By E. L. TARBUCK, Architect and Surveyor. Fifth Edition, Enlarged. 12mo, 5s. cloth.
"The advice is thoroughly practical."—*Law Journal.*
"For all who have dealings with house property, this is an indispensable guide."—*Decoration.*
"Carefully brought up to date, and much improved by the addition of a division on fine art. . . . A well-written and thoughtful work."—*Land Agent's Record.*

LAW AND MISCELLANEOUS.

Pocket-Book for Sanitary Officials.
THE HEALTH OFFICER'S POCKET-BOOK: A Guide to Sanitary Practice and Law. For Medical Officers of Health, Sanitary Inspectors, Members of Sanitary Authorities, &c. By EDWARD F. WILLOUGHBY, M.D. (Lond.), &c., Author of "Hygiene and Public Health." Fcap. 8vo, 7s. 6d. cloth, red edges, rounded corners. [*Just published.*
"A mine of condensed information of a pertinent and useful kind on the various subjects of which it treats. The matter seems to have been carefully compiled and arranged for facility of reference, and it is well illustrated by diagrams and woodcuts. The different subjects are succinctly but fully and scientifically dealt with."—*The Lancet.*
"An excellent publication, dealing with the scientific, technical and legal matters connected with the duties of medical officers of health and sanitary inspectors. The work is replete with information."—*Local Government Journal.*

Journalism.
MODERN JOURNALISM. A Handbook of Instruction and Counsel for the Young Journalist. By JOHN B. MACKIE, Fellow of the Institute of Journalists. Crown 8vo, 2s. cloth. [*Just published.*
"This invaluable guide to journalism is a work which all aspirants to a journalistic career will read with advantage."—*Journalist.*

Private Bill Legislation and Provisional Orders.
HANDBOOK FOR THE USE OF SOLICITORS AND ENGINEERS Engaged in Promoting Private Acts of Parliament and Provisional Orders, for the Authorization of Railways, Tramways, Gas and Water Works, &c. By L. LIVINGSTON MACASSEY, of the Middle Temple, Barrister-at-Law, M.Inst.C.E. 8vo, 25s. cloth.

Law of Patents.
PATENTS FOR INVENTIONS, AND HOW TO PROCURE THEM. Compiled for the Use of Inventors, Patentees and others. By G. G. M. HARDINGHAM, Assoc.Mem.Inst.C.E., &c. Demy 8vo, 1s. 6d. cloth.

Labour Disputes.
CONCILIATION AND ARBITRATION IN LABOUR DISPUTES; A Historical Sketch and Brief Statement of the Present Position of the Question at Home and Abroad. By J. S. JEANS, Author of "England's Supremacy," &c. Crown 8vo, 200 pp., 2s. 6d. cloth. [*Just published.*
"Mr. Jeans is well qualified to write on this subject, both by his previous books and by his practical experience as an arbitrator."—*The Times.*

A Complete Epitome of the Laws of this Country.

EVERY MAN'S OWN LAWYER: A Handy-Book of the Principles of Law and Equity. With A CONCISE DICTIONARY OF LEGAL TERMS. By A Barrister. Thirty-third Edition, carefully Revised, and including New Acts of Parliament of 1895. Comprising the *Summary Jurisdiction (Married Women) Act*, 1895 (giving to Magistrates largely increased powers for the Protection of ill-used Wives), as well as new enactments comprised in the *Factory and Workshop Act*, 1895; *Law of Distress Amendment Act*, 1895; *Corrupt and Illegal Practices Act*, 1895; *Local Government Act*, 1894 (establishing District and Parish Councils); *Finance Act*, 1894 (imposing the New Death Duties); *Prevention of Cruelty to Children Act*, 1894; *Married Women's Property Act*, 1893; *Betting and Loans (Infants) Act*, 1892; with many other Acts of recent years. Crown 8vo, 750 pp., price 6s. 8d. (saved at every consultation!) strongly bound in cloth.

[*Just published.*]

*** The Book will be found to comprise (amongst other matter)—

The Rights and Wrongs of Individuals—Landlord and Tenant—Vendors and Purchasers—Leases and Mortgages—Principal and Agent—Partnership and Companies—Masters, Servants, and Workmen—Contracts and Agreements—Borrowers, Lenders, and Sureties—Sale and Purchase of Goods—Cheques, Bills, and Notes—Bills of Sale—Bankruptcy—Railway and Shipping Law—Life, Fire, and Marine Insurance—Accident and Fidelity Insurance—Criminal Law—Parliamentary Elections—County Councils—District Councils—Parish Councils—Municipal Corporations—Libel and Slander—Public Health and Nuisances—Copyright, Patents, Trade Marks—Husband and Wife—Divorce—Infancy—Custody of Children—Trustees and Executors—Clergy, Churchwardens, etc.—Game Laws and Sporting—Innkeepers—Horses and Dogs—Taxes and Death Duties—Forms of Agreements, Wills, Codicils, Notices, etc.

☞ *The object of this work is to enable those who consult it to help themselves to the law; and thereby to dispense, as far as possible, with professional assistance and advice. There are many wrongs and grievances which persons submit to from time to time through not knowing how or where to apply for redress; and many persons have as great a dread of a lawyer's office as of a lion's den. With this book at hand it is believed that many a SIX-AND-EIGHTPENCE may be saved; many a wrong redressed; many a right reclaimed; many a law suit avoided; and many an evil abated. The work has established itself as the standard legal adviser of all classes, and has also made a reputation for itself as a useful book of reference for lawyers residing at a distance from law libraries, who are glad to have at hand a work embodying recent decisions and enactments.*

*** Opinions of the Press.

"The amount of information squeezed into this volume is wonderful."—*Law Journal* (Feb. 8, 1890).

"A complete code of English Law, written in plain language, which all can understand. Should be in the hands of every business man, and all who wish to abolish lawyers' bills."—*Weekly Times.*

"A complete digest of the most useful facts which constitute English law."—*Globe.*

"Admirably done, admirably arranged, and admirably cheap."—*Leeds Mercury.*

"A concise, cheap and complete epitome of the English law. So plainly written that he who runs may read, and he who reads may understand."—*Figaro.*

"The 'Concise Dictionary' adds considerably to its value."—*Westminster Gazette.*

"A complete epitome of the law; thoroughly intelligible to non-professional readers."—*Bell's Life.*

Legal Guide for Pawnbrokers.

THE LAW OF LOANS AND PLEDGES. With Statutes and a Digest of Cases. By H. C. Folkard, Esq., Barrister-at-Law. Fcap. 8vo, 3s. 6d. cloth.

The Law of Contracts.

LABOUR CONTRACTS: A Popular Handbook on the Law of Contracts for Works and Services. By D. Gibbons. Fourth Edition, with Appendix of Statutes by T. F. Uttley, Solicitor. Fcap. 8vo, 3s. 6d. cloth.

The Factory Acts.

SUMMARY OF THE FACTORY AND WORKSHOP ACTS (1878–1891). For the Use of Manufacturers and Managers. By Emile Garcke and J. M. Fells. (Reprinted from "Factory Accounts.") Crown 8vo, 6d. sewed.

OGDEN, SMALE AND CO. LIMITED, PRINTERS, GREAT SAFFRON HILL, E.C.

www.ingramcontent.com/pod-product-compliance
Lightning Source LLC
Chambersburg PA
CBHW032044230426
43672CB00009B/1468